THE STORY OF ÆNEAS

T0382364

THE
STORY OF ÆNEAS

Virgil's *Æneid*
Translated into English Verse

BY

HENRY S. SALT

*Formerly Scholar of King's College, Cambridge
and Assistant Master at Eton*

CAMBRIDGE
AT THE UNIVERSITY PRESS
MCMXXVIII

CAMBRIDGE
UNIVERSITY PRESS

University Printing House, Cambridge CB2 8BS, United Kingdom

Published in the United States of America by Cambridge University Press, New York

Cambridge University Press is part of the University of Cambridge.

It furthers the University's mission by disseminating knowledge in the pursuit of education, learning and research at the highest international levels of excellence.

www.cambridge.org
Information on this title: www.cambridge.org/9781107637306

First published 1928
First paperback edition 2014

A catalogue record for this publication is available from the British Library

ISBN 978-1-107-63730-6 Paperback

To

MY FRIEND

G. BERNARD SHAW

PREFACE

I

The *Æneid* of Virgil falls naturally into two parts, the first six books corresponding in general outline with Homer's *Odyssey*, and the last six with the *Iliad*; but whereas in Homer the wanderings of Ulysses form a sequel to the battle-scenes of the *Iliad*, in Virgil the order is reversed, and the first half of the story is devoted to the trials and adventures which befall Æneas in his long voyage to Italy, the remainder to the war which he wages against the Italian tribes.

Virgil's Æneas, the legendary Trojan hero whom it pleased the Romans to claim as their ancestor, is a man who is divided at heart between two contending influences—on the one hand, his heaven-ordained mission, to convey his country's fallen gods to a new home in Italy; and on the other, his personal desires, his craving for renewed rest and happiness after the tragedy of Troy. In this struggle Dido stands as the type of the individual love that is in conflict with a national destiny; and, as such, her presence is strongly felt throughout the earlier books, while it wholly dominates the tense drama of the fourth, and is not finally lost to sight until the well-known passage in the sixth, where Æneas takes his last farewell of her in Hades. Thenceforth the personal impulse, always the weaker, is merged wholly in the national.

The imperial interest of the story was much heightened by making Carthage—the great rival city which, though destroyed for over a century before the *Æneid* was written, still figured largely in Roman imagination—the meeting-place between Æneas and the Phœnician queen. That the tale was mythical did not at all lessen its effect, for so was the whole tradition on which the *Æneid* was founded.

The three books of the *Æneid* which, if we may trust the story, Virgil himself read to Augustus Cæsar as his masterpieces, were the second, describing the fall of Troy;

the fourth, the death of Dido; and the sixth, the descent into Hades. If it is in the sixth book that he reaches his highest level as poet, it must be owned that, as a work of art, the fourth is the most flawless; whether for its dramatic interest, or for the deep tragedy of its close, it will stand for all time as one of the greatest romances ever written on the theme of ill-fated love.

The second half of the *Æneid*, taken separately, is perhaps inferior to what precedes it, both in sustained human interest and in majesty of verse; but there are many splendid passages scattered throughout; and in the twelfth book (the death of Turnus) the poet attains a height which is nowhere surpassed. To conclude a work of art is always more difficult than to begin it; but here the *Æneid* is beyond criticism, for nothing could be finer than the manner in which the poem culminates in that great duel which decides the fortunes of a race. Some readers will think that the real hero of the latter books of the *Æneid*, as Dido is the heroine of the earlier ones, is the brave and single-hearted Turnus, who goes unawed to the death to which he sees himself doomed by the Fates.

There is nothing archaic in Virgil's treatment of his story; for, in spite of the introduction of supernatural agencies, the gods, as depicted in the poem, are quite anthropomorphous in character. Virgil, no less than Lucretius, though he lived and died nearly two thousand years ago, was essentially modern in spirit. His true and broad humanity, notwith-standing the references to a few savage customs of warfare or sacrifice, makes itself indirectly felt in many passages; and the number of his lines that have become proverbial and lasting possessions of mankind testifies to his deep hold on our affections. Perhaps the very reason why we sometimes question and resent the doings of his Æneas is that we are inclined to judge his heroes by the most advanced ethical standards; and it is the less amiable characteristics of the "man with a mission" that Æneas displays in some of the chief crises, notably in his betrayal and desertion of Dido.

It is doubtless Virgil's human qualities, in conjunction

with the transcendent charm of his style, that have caused him to be loved, as few writers have been, by many generations of readers, and still make us feel towards him as to no other old-world writer. He is a great poet not only of nature, but of the human heart. His medieval reputation was that of a mystic and necromancer; but he is as modern as Milton in his handling of ancient themes. Of all English writers, in fact, Milton is nearest akin to him; and what greater praise can be given to either?

It is, perhaps, only to those readers who are in some measure sympathetic that a lover of Virgil can convey his feelings about the Master; only a Virgilian can fully understand a Virgilian; for there is a sort of freemasonry in the cult which separates it from all the world beside. The tendency that has for many years existed in the schools, to depreciate Virgil as "less original" than Homer and than some other writers of antiquity, troubles the Virgilian no whit; to him the author of the *Æneid* is the greatest of the Classics, not only as a supreme craftsman in verse, but because he is a psychologist and a modern—as human as Euripides, and a consummate artist as well.

As a stylist, Virgil has no rival among his Latin fellow-countrymen, and but few in any language. It may be held that the Greek *Iliad* and *Odyssey* are greater epics than the *Æneid*, as being more primitive, more massive, and in a sense more original; but though it is true that in the construction of his story Virgil imitated Homer, the imitation was of a sort which, in the hands of a great artist, brings to the task an equal genius and originality of its own. In subtlety of mind, and in varied melody and rhythm, the Greek bard cannot be compared with the Latin, whose stately and sententious lines, rich in thought and still richer in the haunting beauty of their music, are indeed one of the greatest achievements of literature. And, after all, it is *achievement*, not "originality," that is the final test in art; it is by the actual beauty of its work, not by the novelty of the scheme on which it is constructed, that a masterpiece must be appraised.

For example, Virgil's treatment of the theme of death, in
his pictures of the fabulous Hades, which as a poet he accepted
for the purposes of his story, inevitably invites comparison
not only with those passages in the *De Rerum Natura* of
Lucretius in which a rationalistic explanation is given of the
popular beliefs concerning the dead, but with the Homeric
original; and the Virgilian poem, steeped as it is in a profound
sense of mystery and darkness, quite transcends the much less
impressive description given in the *Odyssey*.

II

But it is of the difficulty, the impossibility perhaps, of
translating Virgil into English verse that I must here speak.
The Latin hexameter being longer, by at least two syllables,
than that which is its natural equivalent in English—the
ten-syllabled iambic verse, in which the main characteristic
of the Latin line, its grave measured harmony, can be most
nearly reproduced—it follows that a translator must often
have recourse to a larger number of lines or to a stricter
compression of words. Efforts have been made to avoid this
alternative by employing a long English line, such as the
hexameter itself, or even a fourteen-syllabled verse; but it
can hardly be said that the results have been encouraging.

For first, in regard to the hexameter, owing to organic
differences between the two languages, this metre, which in
Latin has a native dignity and charm, is apt in English to
become a tedious jog-trot, irritating to a sensitive ear; so
that, as a vehicle for translating Virgil, the very form in
which he himself wrote is about the least appropriate that
could be chosen.

Nor is the fourteen-syllabled verse any more successful;
for though William Morris' rendering of the *Æneid* is the
work of a poet, it fails to convey any impression of the
Virgilian spirit or style; its long jerky lines do not in the
least reflect the sustained roll of the hexameter. Such a metre
may be well adapted for a Norse legend; but the genius of
Virgil refuses to be domiciled in it.

But if a longer verse than the decasyllabic does not in practice commend itself, still less does a shorter one—as, for example, that which Professor Conington used in his spirited and sympathetic translation of the *Æneid*, the metre of Scott's *Lay of the Last Minstrel*. All lovers of Virgil are indebted to Conington for the insight with which he caught the meaning of the Latin poet; but the rapid short-paced movement of the Scottish Border minstrelsy is a strange form, indeed, for reproducing the long, slow, rhythmic swing of the Virgilian lines. It raises a smile to find Conington saying of this metre: "I certainly do not pretend that it is the one true equivalent of the Virgilian hexameter."

We come back, then, to the decasyllabic, as the English metre which, in spite of its lack of length, best corresponds with the Latin hexameter; and here it may be asked, Did not so great a poet as Dryden translate the *Æneid*? He did; but the "heroic" couplet, made famous by Dryden and Pope, is vitiated as a medium of translation by its cramped structure and monotony of rhyme. The unbroken sequence of the hexameter can rarely be portrayed in such a form; a few Virgilian passages lend themselves to it; but in the great majority the unfitness of the medium must defeat the skill even of a real poet. It is doubtless this fact which, in Dryden's translation, accounts for the rarity of that "mighty line" which elsewhere in his poems is so frequent and so glorious.

Is rhyme, then, to be condemned and discarded? "I will venture to assert," said Cowper, "that a just translation of any ancient poem in rhyme is impossible. No human ingenuity can be equal to the task of closing every couplet with sounds homotonous, expressing at the same time the full sense, and only the full sense, of the original." In like manner other writers have inveighed against the trammels of "regularly recurring sounds"; and Mr Frederic Harrison complained that "rhyme embarrasses the writer and often irritates the reader."

But here it has to be noted that Cowper's objection, if valid, is obviously valid not against rhyme in itself, but against the rhymed heroic couplet; and so, with later critics, it is not the rhyme-sounds but their "regular recurrence" against which the complaint holds good. This point, a very important one, seems to have been overlooked in Mr Frederic Harrison's conclusion that "a verse translation of the *Æneid* must be in the stately involuted blank verse of *Paradise Lost* and of *The Excursion*—i.e. iambic metre of ten syllables, without rhyme, without archaisms, without cryptic novelties."[1]

Before going farther, we have to face the fact that the adoption of blank verse is itself subject to one serious practical disadvantage. Be it granted that verse such as that of Milton would be the nearest approach in English to the Latin of Virgil. But who is going to compose it? Only great poets can write attractive blank verse; and as no translation of the *Æneid* which is devoid of attractiveness can merit to be called a translation, it is clear that in the absence of a Milton (and Miltons, unfortunately, are not less rare than Virgils) blank verse, however ideal in theory, must in practice fail, like other forms that have been mentioned.

This was long ago recognized by Dr Johnson, when he remarked, in his Life of Milton, that "he that thinks himself capable of astonishing, may write blank verse; but those that only hope to please must condescend to rhyme." Conington, too, spoke truth when he wrote in the Preface to his Virgil: "Blank verse, really deserving the name, I believe to be impossible, except to one or two eminent writers in a generation."

But there is a manner of rhyme—and here I come to the main point of my contention—which is not liable to the strictures justly passed on the cramped heroic couplet or on any regularly composed stanza—viz. an irregular sequence of lines such as that of Milton's *Lycidas*. Herein a double advantage is secured for a translator; a much greater ease

[1] *English Review*, May, 1915. But in some correspondence which I had with him three years later he practically withdrew his objection to rhyme. Speaking of my version of *Georgic IV*, 464–527 (Orpheus and Eurydice), he wrote: "I think it is astonishingly successful. It seems to knock the bottom out of my canon of Virgilian translation."

and freedom in the choice of rhyme-sounds, and the possi-
bility, as in blank verse, of adapting the length and fashion
of the English sentence to those of the Latin—that is, of
reproducing to some extent, and this is a matter of high
importance, the graduated structure of those Virgilian periods
which are built up with elaborate care, each successive verse,
and each *cæsura* or pause in a verse, contributing to the final
effect.

Be it noted, too, that under this arrangement it is not
necessary that every single line should rhyme with some
other; on the contrary, a blank verse may be left, now and
then, with no offence to the ear of the reader, and at times
with the positive advantage of preventing an accumulation
of rhyme-sounds which might cloy. I have also in a few
cases used the couplet-form, and I think with good results;
viz. where a version had to be given of some solemn or
formal utterance, such as an oracle, a prophecy, or the
asseveration made by either party to a truce.[1] In such
passages, where the Latin original is usually simpler and less
involved than is Virgil's wont, the objections to the rhymed
couplet disappear, and its introduction lends variety to the
poem.

It has been said that Virgil "ought to be translated more
or less lineally as well as literally."[2] There are certainly
passages where it is even more necessary that the version
should be lineal than literal; for example, in dealing with
those terse, gnomic utterances, full of wisdom as of beauty,
which have in many cases become proverbial, it is better to
drop some of the words than to impair the conciseness of
the line. On the other hand, there are verses of which it is
impossible to give a lineal rendering without missing an
essential part of their effect; and in such cases it seems the
lesser evil to use more words in the English than to fail to
convey the finer shades of the Latin. A translator will refuse

[1] E.g. on pp. 125, 152, 281, 282.
[2] Sir C. Bowen in the Preface to his *Virgil in English Verse*.

to be bound by any rigid rule in these matters; for though literalness is a great virtue, it must not be made into a fetish.[1]

Indeed, the strictly literal may at times be even misleading, so marked are the differences of idiom between the two languages; and Virgil's frequent use of patronymics, of distinctive epithets (such as *pius*), and of historical or mythological allusions—familiar to Roman readers, but needing explanation in English—would of itself preclude a literal translation in verse. In prose it is otherwise; for the first object of a prose rendering of a poem must be to give the letter of the text; whereas a poetical version, however great its difficulties and imperfections, does at least aim at a more intimate and personal interpretation. A translator of Virgil in verse *may* succeed in giving what no prose can ever give—a glimpse, however distant, of the poet's manner and mood.

I would not, however, be misunderstood as in any way disparaging the value of literalness; it is, in fact, much easier to keep near to the sense of the original when, as in the form which I have adopted, one is free from the shackles of couplet or stanza, and the rhyme can fall early or late as may be desired. Indeed, there are many passages which I think could hardly be rendered more closely in blank verse than as I have presented them.

If any apology be needed for this latest essay in the fields of Virgilian translation, I would plead that as final success, if ever to be obtained, must be founded upon many previous failures, it cannot be wholly unprofitable to make a new adventure along a less trodden path. What I have criticized in my predecessors is not their workmanship but their medium; what I view with satisfaction in my own attempt is rather the medium than the work.[2]

---

[1] Thus Dryden, in the Dedication to his *Æneid*, avows his determination, if necessary, to "pursue the elegance and forsake the brevity."

[2] I have incorporated with these remarks the substance of the Introduction to my translation of the fourth book of the *Æneid*, separately published in 1926. That Preface was itself partly reprinted from an article which originally appeared in the *Fortnightly Review*, February, 1923.

Among the questions that face a translator of Virgil is that of how to deal with the "hemistichs," or half-lines, of which there are about fifty in the *Æneid*. A study of these, in relation to the passages where they occur, makes it difficult to maintain the old theory that they are mere gaps ("short-comings" is Conington's word for them) in an unfinished poem, which the author intended to fill up at a later date; for some of them are as full of significance and beauty as the half-lines in *Lycidas*, and the rest seem designed to add to the general effect by breaking the monotony of the hexameters. I have therefore tried to reproduce them, when possible, in the passages where their purpose is evident. I have to thank Mr Hugh Macnaghten, Vice-Provost of Eton, for drawing my attention to this point, and to the error of regarding the *Æneid* as in any sense an imperfect work.

I am also indebted for friendly encouragement and helpful suggestions to several other well-known scholars, among whom are Sir Herbert Warren, Master of Magdalen College, Oxford; Professor Gilbert Murray; Dr J. W. Mackail; and my old schoolfellow, Sir George Greenwood.

H. S. S.

THE ÆNEID

BOOK I

ARGUMENT

THE poem opens at the point where Æneas, already in the seventh
year of his wanderings since the fall of Troy, has sailed from
Sicily, where he had been entertained by king Acestes. Owing to the
vindictive wrath of Juno, whose hatred of Troy plays a great part
throughout the Æneid, the fleet is shipwrecked, and the Trojans are
cast on the Libyan shore. Thence, by the help of his mother, Venus,
Æneas makes his way to the court of queen Dido, at Carthage, and
is hospitably welcomed by her. At the banquet which follows, Dido,
by the design of Venus, conceives a fatal love for her guest.

Of arms, and of that Trojan chief I sing,
Who first, fate-exiled, to Italia came—
To shores that echo still Lavinia's name—
Long time o'er land and waters wandering,
And wronged of heaven through Juno's fell design;
Much, too, in wars he suffered for his claim
To found a city, build his gods a home
In Latium. Lo! from him our Latin line,
Our Alban sires, our lofty walls of Rome.
   I pray thee, Muse, the primal causes tell;
For what affront to her high godhead given,
Stung by what slight, the mighty queen of heaven
Drove man of peerless piety to bear
Long train of sorrows, task on task to dare:
In hearts celestial can such passions dwell?
   An ancient town there was, of Tyrian race,
Carthage, confronting Tiber's mouths afar,
Rich, prosperous, schooled in sternest arts of war;

So blest, men said, with Juno's special grace,
Her Samos less she loved: her arms here stood,
Her chariot; yea, that this her cherished land
Should reign triumphant o'er a world subdued,
Ev'n then, would fate permit, she strove, she planned.
But this she heard, that folk of Trojan blood
Sometime that Tyrian fortress should o'erthrow,
Sires of a conquering race, in battle bold,
Her Libya's bane to be: 'twas fated so.
This fearing, nor forgetful how of old
'Gainst Troy, for her dear Argos, war she waged;
For in her heart still rankled unassuaged
Deep-sunk resentment of an earlier ill—
Her beauty by false Paris turned to scorn;
Her foemen honoured, when the Trojan boy,
Jove's minion, Ganymede, was heavenward borne—
Enkindled by such wrongs, she spared not still
To chase the storm-tossed remnant saved from Troy,
That 'scaped the Greeks and dread Achilles' spear,
Far from their long-sought goal. Wide seas around,
Fate-driven they wandered homeless, year on year:
Such toil it was the Roman race to found.

   Scarce was Sicilia fading from their eyes,
As glad they sailed, and clove the foamy brine,
When Juno, nursing still her wound malign,
Thus mused: "Must my firm will admit defeat,
And fear to bar this Trojan from his prize,
Since fate, forsooth, says nay? Feared Pallas aught,
When in her wrath she burned the Argive fleet,
And 'neath the sea sunk many a guiltless head,
For that one crime infatuate Ajax wrought?
Herself Jove's lightning from the clouds she sped,
And smote the ships, and roused the wind-swept main;
And him, forth-breathing fire from stricken breast,
She caught aloft on wings of hurricane,
And nailed on rifted rock sharp-pinnacled.
But I, who pace heaven's courts the stateliest,

Jove's spouse and sister both, contend in vain
For years with one weak tribe! What mortal, more,
Will bring his votive gifts to Juno's fane,
Or her once dreaded deity adore?"
   Such burning thoughts she pondered in her mind;
Then sought that storm-land, big with many a blast,
Æolia. There king Æolus holds sway
O'er blaring tempest and rebellious wind
And tames their wrath, and curbs them to obey.
Loud groans the mountain, as, in bondage fast,
They fight for freedom. He, on lofty mound,
Sits sceptred, and subdues their frantic force;
Else earth and sea and sky they would confound
And sweep before them in tumultuous course.
Wherefore the almighty Father did ordain
A deep and darksome cavern for their bound,
And o'er them piled the massy mountain high,
And that stern ruler set in sovranty,
Well skilled to tighten or relax the rein.
To him spake Juno then, with suppliant cry:
   "Friend, since this power thou hast from heaven's high lord,
The seas to lull, or lash to fury wild,
Lo! to the Italian strand a race abhorred
Sails with its vanquished gods, from Troy exiled.
Spur thou thy winds to whelm them in the wave,
Or drive them scattered o'er the ocean deep!
If this thou wilt—twice seven fair nymphs I have,
Of wondrous charm; the fairest shall be thine,
For aid to Juno given, thy wedded bride:
So shall she dwell forever at thy side,
And make thee father of a noble line."
   Quoth Æolus: "Thy task it is, great queen,
To frame thy purpose; mine to work thy will.
To thee I owe this kingdom, and such trust
As Jove vouchsafes me; on thine aid I lean,
When at celestial feasts my place I fill,
God of the storm-cloud and tempestuous gust."

He spake, and straight his javelin turned, and thrust
Through hollow mountain-side. In riotous train
Forth rushed the winds, and blustering o'er the land
Swooped down, and stirred the bottoms of the main.
In one array, East, South, and strong South-West,
They race, and roll vast billows to the strand.
Follow the shouts of men, the cordage creaks,
And sudden clouds the firmament invest
With darkness; o'er the sea broods pitchy night.
Then loud the thunder rolls; with fiery streaks
The pole is rent; and all things threaten death.
Chill runs Æneas' blood with dire affright,
As, groaning, thus to heaven he witnesseth,
With hand up-raised: "Thrice blest, who fell in fight,
'Neath Troy's high walls, before their parents' eyes!
Why chanced it not to me to yield my breath
To thine armed hand, great Diomede, foeman brave,
And fall in combat on that Trojan plain,
Where, by Achilles' spear, bold Hector lies,
Where tall Sarpedon, where, 'neath Simois' wave,
Roll many a shield and helm of warriors slain?"
 Ev'n as he cries, the North, in shrieking squall,
Buffets his sail, and heavenward lifts the deep.
The barque, with shattered oars, and prow swung round,
Lies broadside to the waves; and high o'er all
Tumbles the broken sea in mountainous heap.
Some hang on wave-tops poised; some, from the verge,
Through yawning gulfs revealed, see solid ground,
Where whirlpools rage with mingling sand and surge.
Three keels the South has dashed on hidden rocks,
"Altars" by name, that stand in deep mid-sea,
Huge reef that sailors dread; on quicksands, three
The strong East flings, and there, in comrades' view,
'Mid circling shoal with sandy barrier locks.
One, with Orontes and his Lycians true,
Before the chieftain's eyes, a breaker vast
Swamps from astern; the pilot, headlong cast,

Falls from his ship, and thrice the raging tide
Whirls her around, by eddying depths devoured.
Then saw they, floating on the waters wide,
Men, armour, planks, and Trojan wealth adrift,
The good ship of Ilioneus o'erpowered;
Of brave Achates, of Aletes old—
So fierce the tempest—all, from deck to hold,
Drinking the perilous flood through chink and rift.
　　Anon, this tumult in his deep demesne—
The calm of his still waters swayed and stirred
By lawless gusts let loose—grave Neptune heard,
And o'er the surface raised his head serene:
Then, when the Trojans' scattered ships were seen
(Themselves by seas and lowering skies oppressed),
Plain was the work of Juno's guileful spleen;
East wind and South he called, and thus addressed:
　　"How now, ye saucy spirits of the air!
Have ye such boldness ye would flout my will?
Is't thus to mingle heaven and earth ye dare,
And watery mass of billows to up-raise?
Whom I—but first yon breakers must I still:
Henceforth who does such deeds more dearly pays.
Quick! fly, and to your King this message bear.
Not his the lordship of the mighty main;
My hands the trident hold. To him alone
Belong those savage rocks wherein ye dwell:
There lies his palace proud, his citadel;
The dungeon of the winds—be that his throne."
　　Sooner than said, he lulled the surging sea,
Dispelled the thick-massed clouds, brought back the sun;
Nor slow were Triton and Cymothoë
To lend their strength the rock-bound ships to free;
Himself, with trident, deigned to lift each keel,
Till through the hindering shoals a way was won;
Then light he rode the brine on buoyant wheel.
Thus oft, in concourse vast, if discord rise,
And anger stir the passions of the crowd,

Stones, firebrands fly—such arms as wrath supplies;
But when they see some man of strength, endowed
With righteous heart, and known for noble deeds,
Silent they stand and rapt attention keep;
He with wise counsel guides, and soothes their ire:
So sank all ocean's turmoil, when the Sire
Gazed out 'neath opening skies, and drove his steeds
On smooth majestic course along the deep.

Craving to cast them on the nearest land,
The Libyan shores the weary Trojans seek.
A tranquil cove there was, a winding bay,
Guarded by isle that off the seaboard lay,
Where wave on wave that travelled to the strand
Broke soft, and gently lapped each branching creek.
On either side a stern precipitous peak
Rose skyward; 'neath their sheltering height the sea
Stretched calm and still, o'erhung by canopy
Of rustling woods that cast a solemn shade;
And in the cliff's sheer front a cavern lone
Gave cool recess, where pure spring-waters played,
And natural seats were carved in solid stone:
Haunt of the nymphs. Here tempest-shaken ship
Nor cable needs nor steadfast anchor's grip.
Such port he gained with galleys seven, no more,
Mustered from all that fleet; then, famishing
For earth's embrace his Trojans leapt ashore,
Their spray-drenched bodies on the sand to fling;
And there, from heart of flint, Achates first
Struck fiery spark, 'mid withered leaves, and nursed
The growing flame, and with dry fuel fed:
Then from aboard they bring their wheat, besprent
With bitter brine, and many an implement
For Ceres' use; and strive, discomfited,
With stone to grind, with fire to roast the grain.

Meanwhile Æneas scales the rocks, to gain
A prospect wide, if thence he may espy
Antheus, with Phrygian galleys tempest-tost,

Or Capys, or Caicus' ensign high.
No ship he sees, but wandering by the coast
Three stags, with goodly herds that range behind,
And, grazing, far adown the valley wind.
Instant he stopped, and grasped the ready bow
With arrows that his squire Achates bore;
And first he brought those antlered leaders low,
Then drove the herd fear-stricken through the brake;
Nor paused, till seven stout stags for booty lay,
To match his seven brave ships upon the shore:
Soon of their flesh partition did he make,
And bade his comrades that good wine partake
Which lord Acestes gave in bounteous store,
When from Sicilian isle they went their way:
Then thus, to cheer their fainting hearts, he spake:
  "Comrades, with grief acquainted from of old!
Worse evils have ye suffered; doubt not, these
Shall have their end from heaven. Ye, who could brave
Fierce Scylla's echoing rocks, the Cyclops' cave,
Cast off such wan misgivings, and be bold.
Years hence, maybe, these memories too shall please.
Through all our strange mishaps, though hope seem vain,
We journey still towards Latium's coast, where fate
Points us a blissful home beyond the seas;
There shall our Trojan kingdom rise again:
Endure, then, and those happier times await."
  So saying, a smile he feigned, and hid the care
That racked him, buried deep within his breast.
Forthwith they gird them for the coming feast;
They flay the carcase, and the flesh, laid bare,
Cut small, and fix still quivering on the spit;
Or place the caldrons o'er the flames new-lit;
Then, on the sward reposed, a heartened throng,
Of venison and old vintage take their fill.
Their hunger thus appeased, in converse long
Of those lost shipmates sad discourse they hold,
Wavering 'twixt hope and fear—if breathe they still,

Or, dying, hear no more their comrades' call.
The while, Æneas scarce his grief controlled,
That death should thus brave Amycus befall,
Brave Gyas, and Cloanthus, warrior bold.
    'Twas then great Jove, down looking from the skies,
O'er sail-swept seas, and outspread continent,
And tribes of men, on heaven's high summit stood,
And fixed his gaze where Libya's kingdom lies.
To him, on such deep thoughts and cares intent,
Thus spake fair Venus; pensive was her mood,
And tears were welling in her lustrous eyes:
    "Monarch of gods and men! Thou mightiest,
Who hold'st the dreaded levin in thine hand!
How hath Æneas thy stern will transgressed?
My Trojans how? that yon sore-stricken band,
Who fain would seek in Italy their home,
Must find the wide world closed against their quest?
Thou, sure, didst promise that an age should come,
When from old Teucer's renovated line
Romans should rise, a race majestical,
Destined the sea and land to dominate:
So saidst thou. What hath changed thy firm design?
Such was my solace for Troy's piteous fall—
Grief recompensed by gladness, fate by fate—
Yet still like fortunes on their footsteps wait:
How long, almighty Sire, must they endure?
Antenor, 'scaped from sword of Grecian foe,
Had power to pass the Illyrian gulf secure
To far Liburnian realms, beyond the source
Of swift Timavus, where with sea-like force
Through channels nine those roaring rapids flow
And flood the pastures in torrential course.
His city there, Patavium, did he build,
Trojan, there hung his Trojan arms at rest,
And now in peace he sleeps, his days fulfilled.
But we, of thine own blood, whom thou, our Sire,
Didst beckon to a mansion 'mid the Blest,

Roam shipwrecked, from Italia's shores debarred,
Betrayed to glut one Being's quenchless ire:
Is this our crown? this, piety's reward?"
    Gently he smiled, the Sire of gods and men,
With grave and gracious countenance, as when
He smooths the storm-cloud from the tranquil sky;
Then kissed his daughter's lips, and made reply:
"Fear not, sweet goddess! Still for thee and thine
The fates abide unshaken. Thou shalt see
Thy city, and thy promised empery;
Æneas still the heights of heaven shall scale
Great-hearted: naught hath changed my firm design.
This know—for, since such cares thy soul oppress,
More distant destinies will I unveil—
Long must he war, to tame the lawlessness
Of tribes Italian and fair peace ordain,
Till summer suns have thrice beheld him reign,
And winter thrice hath left his foemen cowed.
Ascanius next, that now Iulus hight,
Full thirty years shall wield the sceptre proud,
And from Lavinium's walls transfer his might
To Alba Longa's strong embattled towers.
There, centuries three, shall rest the royal powers
In hands of Hector's kinsmen; till to Mars
The priestess Ilia lusty twins shall bring,
And Romulus, the dauntless fosterling
Of brinded wolf, shall lord it o'er the state,
And build a city for the god of wars,
And from his name the name of Rome create.
To Rome is given an empire without end,
Marred by no niggard term of time or space:
Yea, Juno too, who now with jealous hate
Plagues sea and sky, implacable, shall mend
Her vengeful purpose, and with me befriend
Earth's destined lords, the freeborn Roman race.
Thus have I willed it. Ay, the day decreed
Comes with the circling years, when Priam's seed

Proud Argos and Mycenæ's strength shall tame:
Then from thy Trojan blood shall Cæsar rise—
Julius, of great Iulus distant son—
Girt with such power, such plenitude of fame,
As naught can bound but ocean and the skies.
Him, decked with trophies from far Orient won,
Thou'lt welcome to his place in heaven; and then
He, too, a god, shall hear the prayers of men.
So strife shall cease, and in that milder age
Hoar Faith and Vesta pure the world shall win,
While Remus governs with Quirinus sage;
Then shall the nations close War's frowning gate
With iron bolts tight-drawn: red Wrath within,
Seated on blood-stained arms infuriate,
And bound in brazen bonds, shall wildly rage."

He spake, and high command to Carthage sent,
By Maia's son, those woe-worn folk to greet
With hospitable care and succour meet;
Lest Dido, wotting naught of fate's intent,
Might thrust them from her realm. He downward glides
On oarlike wings, and lights on Libya's strand.
Forthwith, his message given, at Jove's behest
No thought of wrong in Punic heart abides;
Nor doubts their queen to greet the Trojan band
With friendly solace and benignant breast.

Long mused Æneas ere the night was passed;
Then this resolved: when earliest dawn should rise,
Forth must he fare that region strange to scan;
On what secluded foreland was he cast,
By what wild race 'twas peopled, beast or man;
This would he learn, and so his friends apprise.
His fleet in wooded creek he harboured fast,
'Mid hanging cliff and frowning forest pent;
Then with Achates, and none else, he went,
Grasping two lances barbed with ample blade.
And lo! there met him in the midmost wood
His goddess mother, seen as Spartan maid—

Thus featured, thus attired, thus armed she stood—
Or like that Thracian queen who spurs her team
To flight ev'n swifter than swift Hebrus' stream.
An huntress, from her shoulder had she slung
The handy bow, as wonted; to the breeze
Her tresses flowed in freedom; bare her knees,
And from a loop her sinuous vestment hung:
Then "Ho!" she cried, "good comrades, have ye seen
One of my quivered sisters wandering nigh,
In spotted lynx-skin clad, or pressing keen
On tracks of foaming boar with eager cry?"
So Venus spake, and this her son's reply:
    "Naught of thy sisterhood to me is known,
Fair maid—how shall I name thee? for thy face
Not earthly seems, nor mortal is thy tone.
O, sure, a goddess, this vouchsafe, I pray:
Art Phœbus' sister, or a nymph by race?
Whate'er thou art, be gracious, and allay
Our cares, and learn us through what region lone,
In what remotest clime we blindly stray;
For here nor path we know, nor humankind,
Lost voyagers, by winds and waves up-thrown:
So shall thine altar many a tribute find."
    Then Venus: "Nay, such honour claim not I.
We Tyrian maidens go thus habited,
With bow, and bind the purple buskin high.
'Tis Carthage ye approach, a Tyrian state,
Round which the tameless tribes of Libya range.
Here Dido rules. From native Tyre she fled
Her brother's hatred: dark her wrongs, and strange
Her story; but the sum I will relate.
Rich was the lord Sychæus whom she wed,
And love he lacked not from his hapless bride,
Betrothed a virgin by her royal sire,
Her first espousals. But the throne of Tyre
Her brother held, Pygmalion, deeply dyed
In impious guilt all mortal men above.

Then discord fierce arose. He, crazed with thirst
For gold, and reckless of his sister's love,
Her husband stabbed at holy altar-side,
Ta'en unawares; and long that crime accurst
He hid, and mocked her grief with lying tale.
But lo! in sleep a wondrous thing befell:
The phantom form of her unburied spouse
Uplifted to her sight his visage pale,
And sparing not that altar's guilt to tell,
And how the murderer's steel had pierced his heart,
Laid bare the ghastly secret of their house.
Then from her native shores he bade her part,
And for her help revealed his treasures old,
Long-hidden hoards of silver and of gold.
Thus scared, she tarried not, but planned by stealth
Swift flight, with friends who held in hate or dread
That ruthless tyrant. Ships that lay ashore
They loaded deep with gold; and thus the wealth
Pygmalion fain had grasped, to sea they bore;
Boldly the deed they wrought, by woman led.
To yonder coast where now, in youthful pride,
New-rising walls and Carthage towers thou'lt see,
Those exiles journeyed; there they brought them ground—
Not less than bull-hide's girth could compass round—
Named Byrsa from that bargain of the hide:
So runs the tale. But, prithee, who be ye?
Whence sail ye, sirs, and whither?" Sore he sighed,
And deep the tones that from his bosom burst:
   "Goddess, were I to tell thee from the first,
And thou hadst leisure all our toils to hear,
Ere half were said, swart eventide were near.
From ancient Troy—maybe thou'st heard Troy's name—
We roamed the trackless waters of the world,
Then by chance tempest on this shore were hurled.
Thou seest Æneas, known to pious fame,
Who bears his household gods across the brine,
From foemen snatched. In Italy we claim

A fatherland, an ancestry divine.
With ships twice ten the Phrygian deep I dared,
Impelled by fate, by goddess mother led;
Now, wrecked by wind and wave, scarce seven are spared.
Myself obscure, despised, these wilds I tread,
Earth's outcast." Thus his wrongs, dispirited,
He mourned, but ere his sorrowing tale was closed
These gracious words of cheer she interposed:
　"Whoe'er thou art, in Jove's celestial court
Methinks not unbefriended hast thou been,
Whose steps to yonder Tyrian town have strayed.
Then doubt not! Seek the palace of the queen.
This know: ev'n now thy ships are safe in port,
Rescued thy comrades all, the whirlwind stayed:
Else vainly schooled in auguries was I.
For see! twelve swans in joyous band disport,
Whom late an eagle, swooping from the sky,
Drove scattered; now in ordered line they light,
Or round their mates alit are wheeling nigh!
As with loud clang of wings those birds unite,
And gleeful cries, encircling heaven with speed,
Ev'n so thy crews, debarked, their fellows hail,
Or harbour-mouth approach with swelling sail:
Doubt not; but follow where yon track shall lead."
　She spake, and, as she turned, a roseate hue
Shone from her shoulders; and she wafted sweet
Immortal fragrance from ambrosial hair;
Down flowed her regal vesture to her feet;
Her port proclaimed the goddess. Then he knew
His mother's fading form, and breathed a prayer:
"Thou, too, unkind thou art, in phantasies
Thus ever to illude and mock thy son!
Why meet we not in living union,
Where hand clasps hand, and voice to voice replies?"
Chiding he spoke; then on toward Carthage hies.
But she hath power divine their steps to shroud
In vaporous mantle of close-folding cloud,

That none may watch or touch them as they go,
Nor stay their coming, nor the cause inquire:
Herself to Paphos soars, her mansion proud,
Where hundred altars with rich incense glow,
And fresh-culled wreaths with perfume sweet suspire.

So, where the footpath points, they take their way,
And soon a high o'erhanging crest they win,
Whence they behold fair Carthage, face to face.
Wondrous its bulk, where late but hamlet lay;
Wondrous its gates, its streets, its busy din.
Eager the Tyrians toil: here walls they trace,
Or hoist huge stones to high embattled rock;
Or mark the bounds of some choice dwelling-place;
Or laws enact and sacred Senate choose;
Or delve a harbour deep; or build the base
Of lofty stage, and carve from marble block
Tall pillars which shall stand its prop and pride.
So, through the flowery meads, in fair springtide,
Do bees in sunshine toil; what time they tend
Their full-grown young; or liquid honey store,
And with such nectar pure the cells distend;
Anon with aid returning comrades meet,
Or chase the drones, those sluggards, from the door:
So thrives the work, and thymy scent is sweet.

"Ah, happy ye, whose walls ev'n now arise!"
Thus mused Æneas, as he gazed, intent,
At soaring pinnacle and battlement,
And wrapped in magic cloud from mortal eyes,
Unseen of all, through crowded concourse went.

Full in that city's midst, a leafy grove
Gave copious shade. 'Twas there the Punic band,
When shoreward first their wave-worn vessels drove,
A noble horse's head had dug from ground,
Portending—such the sign of Juno's love—
The power and plenty of a sovran land.
There, for great Juno's praise, would Dido found
(Her godhead's holiest haunt) a pompous fane,

Whereto rose brazen steps; the beams with brass
Glistered; with brass the groaning gates were bound.
In that proud temple, by strange chance, it was,
Æneas first had respite from his pain,
And dared to lift his heart from grief to joy;
For as the queen he waited, and his fill
Gazed on the splendours of the lofty dome—
The wealth, the miracles of craftsman's skill—
His eyes beheld the battlefields of Troy,
And wars far-famed beyond the ocean foam:
There Atreus' sons, there Priam stood, and lo!
The great Achilles, feared of friend and foe.
Weeping he stood: "What utmost shores of earth,
Where tale of Troy's sore travail hath not come?
'Tis Priam! Here, ev'n here, men honour worth;
Tears fall, and hearts are touched by mortal woe.
No danger is, where fame thus tells our deeds."
So on that painted scene his fancy feeds,
And many a time he sighs and weeps withal;
For this he marks, how round Troy's ancient wall
The battle raged, and here the Trojans pressed
The Greeks in flight, and there themselves they fled,
While hard behind them flamed Achilles' crest.
Anigh, slain Rhesus' snowy tents were seen,
Betrayed in that first sleep which entry gave
To ruthless Diomede, who captive led
His fiery steeds, ere yet Troy's pastures green
They tasted, or had drunk of Xanthus' wave.
Here Troïlus—for what could boyhood brave,
Matched 'gainst the great Achilles' strength, avail?—
Fall'n backward, as to empty car he clings,
Yet grasps the reins; on earth his tresses trail;
Scored is the dust by his loose-hanging spear.
And there is seen the sacred peplus, brought
By Trojan matrons to stern Pallas' fane;
In woful suppliant garb they draw anear,
Then hair they rend and bosoms beat in vain:

She, with averted eyes, relenteth naught.
Thrice round the walls of Troy had Hector slain
Been dragged by fierce Achilles, and with gold
For ransom his pale corse ev'n now was bought.
Deep groans Æneas as his eyes behold
The spoils, the chariot, the dear comrade dead,
And Priam, helpless sire, with hands outspread.
Himself he sees in combat on that field,
With Grecian chieftains, in the armies' van:
There swarthy Memnon's Ethiopian clan;
There charge wild Amazons, with crescent shield,
By dauntless queen, Penthesilea, led;
Bare-breasted, with broad belt of gold below,
She rushes in hot haste upon the foe,
Nor shuns fierce shock of battle, maid 'gainst man.
    While still upon that wondrous sight he gazed,
And stood, as one entranced, in thought profound,
Queen Dido walked in beauty to the fane,
Majestic, by her courtiers compassed round.
So, on Eurotas' bank, or Cynthus' side,
Diana leads the dance, and in her train
Cluster her Oreads; she, in quivered pride,
Towers o'er her comrades all, with stately pace;
While silent joys Latona's bosom thrill.
Ev'n such was Dido; so, with blithesome grace,
She passed, her royal duties to fulfil:
'Neath vaulted dome, anigh the goddess' gate,
High-throned, and ringed with gleaming swords, she sate;
There laws she dealt, and justice, and assigned
Fit task to each, that none should suffer wrong.
When lo! he sees advance 'mid clamorous throng
Antheus, Sergestus, and beside them, all
His shipwrecked Trojan followers, whom the wind
Had scattered to strange shores with blustering squall.
Amazed he stood 'twixt joy and fear, nor less
Achates marvelled. Much they yearned to press
Their comrades' hands, but doubt was in their mind:

Cloud-covered still they watched from their retreat,
To learn how fared their friends, where lay their fleet;
Nor knew them sent as envoys, in distress,
The royal grace and clemency to find.
  So to her throne they came, and, audience given,
Grey-haired Ilioneus thus calmly spoke:
"Queen, who hast built these walls by Jove's command,
And tamed unruly tribes with righteous yoke,
Trojans are we, o'er stormy waters driven,
Who crave thy pity. Shall the cruel brand
Be flung on our wrecked ships? Nay, vex not more
A guileless race, but mark our woful state!
No thought is ours your Libyan homes to spoil,
Or drive the captured booty to the shore:
Too weak we are such wrong to meditate.
A land there is, the Greeks Hesperia name,
Ancient, renowned in battle, rich of soil;
Erst by Œnotrians held; a later age
Italia called it, from their chieftain's fame.
Thither our course was set:
When, risen in sudden storm, Orion's rage
Dashed us on hidden shoals before the blast,
Through surf and rock-bound channels blindly borne,
Scattered—we few upon your borders cast.
What race of men are these, in what wild land,
The laws of hospitality forget,
Draw sword, and drive the stranger from their strand?
Bethink ye, though all mortal claims ye scorn,
High heaven shall still regard the wrong, the right!
Æneas led us; ne'er was chief more true,
In duty faithful, fearless heart in fight:
If still he breathes, and gazes on the sun,
Nor lies in darksome grave, ne'er shalt thou rue
Aught that in gracious aid thine hand hath done.
Nor lacks Sicilia towns, and pastures fair,
Where rules Acestes, prince of Trojan blood.
Grant us to haul our scattered ships ashore,

New planks to fit, to trim each broken oar;
So, if kind fate our chief, our comrades, spare,
Gladly for shores Italian will we part;
But if that saving faith to which we cling
Be lost, and he, the leader of our heart,
Beneath yon Libyan waves lie weltering,
And ev'n the hope of young Iulus fail,
Still to Sicilian waters would we sail,
There bide, and own Acestes for our king."
With that he ceased, his followers murmuring
In hush'd assent.
Then Dido thus replied, with looks down bent:
   "Nay, fear not, Trojans: cast your cares aside;
Albeit mine empire's early needs compel
A jealous watch to keep o'er frontiers wide.
Who hath not heard of Troy, nor knoweth well
Æneas' fame, and what brave feats befell,
When that great conflict lit the fires of war?
Not so obtuse of heart we Tyrians are,
Nor so remote from heaven's glad sunshine dwell.
Seek, if ye will, Saturnian shores renowned;
Or to Sicilian king your fealty lend;
Our help, our wealth, shall speed ye on your way.
Or if in this my kingdom ye would stay,
Yours is our city: haul your ships aground:
Trojan or Tyrian—all shall find me friend.
I would the selfsame storm had hither blown
Your lord Æneas! Trusty scouts we'll send,
Wide search to make through Libya's utmost bound,
If haply in wild woods he wanders lone."
   Cheered by her words, those chieftains longed to burst
The cloud that hid them. Thus Achates first:
   "Say, goddess-born, what deem'st thou we should do?
Saved are our comrades: one alone hath died,
Who sank 'neath whelming billows in our view:
Ev'n as thy Mother spake, doth all betide."
Scarce uttered, when that screen of vapour fled,

Disparting, and was lost in azure skies:
Revealed Æneas stood, in stainless light,
Godlike in face and form; o'er hair and head
The radiant gleam of youth had Venus shed,
And lit a joyous lustre in his eyes:
As when some craftsman's hand pure ivory dyes
With richer hues; or Parian marble white,
Or silver is enchased in gleaming gold:
So shone the hero sudden on their sight
As thus unto the queen he spake: "Behold,
I whom ye seek am here—the Trojan chief,
Æneas, rescued from the Libyan foam!
O thou in whom alone Troy's nameless grief
Hath found compassion! from whose gentle hand
We outcasts, 'scaped from Grecian sword, who roam
All friendless, comfortless, o'er sea and land,
Win welcome to thy kingdom and thy home!
To give thee worthy thanks for thy sweet grace,
Dido, no power have I, nor all the race
Of Troy, now scattered far in lone exile:
But may the gods, if kindness they revere,
And justice, and the heart that knows no guile,
Requite thee richly! From what blissful sphere
Cam'st thou, fair daughter of what parents blest?
While streams still seaward run, while shadows rest
On hollows of the hills, while stars shine pure,
So long, where'er I wander, shall endure
Thy memory, prized and honoured, in my breast."
    So saying, with hand outstretched the hand he pressed
Of those true friends, Ilioneus to right,
To left Sergestus; then in turn the rest,
Brave Gyas, and Cloanthus, fearless knight.
    Amazed at sight of that heroic mien,
Such greatness in such grief, thus spake the queen:
"What perils, goddess-born, thy course pursue,
That thus thy ships are flung on savage shore!
Art thou that warrior son whom Venus bore

To lord Anchises by swift Simois' tide?
It minds me now that, seeking kingdoms new,
To Sidon city banished Teucer came,
Guest of my sire—my sire ev'n then had thrown
O'er conquered Cyprus his dominion wide.
Thenceforth Troy's fall, and thine illustrious name,
And Grecian kings, to me full well were known:
Ay, Teucer's self would vaunt his foeman's fame,
And from old Trojan stock far lineage claim.
Come, then; I bid ye to my palace turn!
Me, too, like fortune to this land hath brought,
Storm-tossed by much calamity, and taught,
Mourning myself, to succour them that mourn."
So to her royal porch their way they wend
Where she proclaims a feast with rites divine,
Nor fails for those wrecked mariners to send
Large stores of viands—many a goodly steer,
Fat lambs with ewes in flock, and bristly swine;
And Bacchus' kindly gifts, the generous wine,
Man's heart to cheer.
Within the palace, all is holiday;
There, in the stately banquet-hall, they lay
Rich rugs of purple plush; the tables groan
With gold and silver plate, engraved whereon
Are scenes of olden days, the long array
Of valorous deeds bequeathed from sire to son.
  Æneas, by a father's fondness spurred,
Straight to the ships in haste Achates sent,
Of fortune's change to bear Ascanius word,
And thence to Carthage lead the princely boy;
On young Ascanius all his thought was bent;
Gifts, too, preserved from wreck of burning Troy,
He bade him bring; a mantle richly wrought,
With solid gold emblazoned; and a veil
Purfled with margin of acanthus pale,
Of Argive Helen once the ornament;
The which from far Mycenæ she had brought,

What time she fled, on lawless love intent:
Nor goodlier gift from mother's hand might be.
A sceptre, likewise, that had decked the hand
Of Priam's daughter, fair Ilione;
Her necklace, strung with pearls; her coronet
With twofold cirque of gold and gems inset.
So sped Achates on his lord's command.

This Venus sees, and hastens to devise
New arts, new wiles, to compass her desire:
That Cupid, masked in young Ascanius' guise,
Shall greet the queen with treacherous gifts that burn,
And plant within her heart his quenchless fire.
Much fears she what that Tyrian tribe may dare,
Perfidious, double-tongued: then Juno's ire
Galls her; at fall of night her doubts return;
Wherefore to light-winged Love she breathes her prayer:
    "Son, in whose power I trust, my champion strong;
Son, whom Jove's awful bolts no whit dismay,
To thee I come, thy godhead's help to pray!
How Juno's bitter spite hath hindered long
Thy brother's course, storm-tossed from land to land,
This know'st thou, and hast shared my sorrows oft:
Him now Phœnician Dido's speeches soft
Enthral, in Juno's realms a shipwrecked guest;
Much fear I from such kindness what shall spring;
No time is this for Juno's hate to rest.
Wherefore I needs must tarry not, but fling
My toils about the queen, and gird her round
With amorous flame, that so her passionate will
Yield to no alien power, but hold her still
By changeless love to my Æneas bound.
How this thou mayst accomplish, learn of me.
Anon the prince, fond object of my care,
By summons of his sire, in courtesy
Rich gifts to Dido's Tyrian town will bear,
Saved from Troy's ruins and the stormy sea.
Him, lulled in slumber deep, I will detain

In some secluded temple, where I reign
In high Cythera or Idalian dell,
Unweeting of our wiles, hid far from sight.
Do thou his image take, for one short night,
And, boy thyself, his boyish features feign;
So when, 'mid sumptuous feast, and wine's sweet spell,
The queen shall clasp thee to her glowing heart,
And kisses sweet and soft embraces deign,
Thy secret fiery pang thou shalt impart."
    Then Love obeys his mother's voice, and throws
His wings aside, and foots it, blithe and gay,
In young Ascanius' semblance as he goes.
She o'er the prince entrancing slumber strows,
And, fondling in her bosom, far away
Bears him aloft to cool Idalian bowers,
Where banks of marjoram sweet in soft repose
Enfold him, propped on beds of fragrant flowers.
    So Cupid, tripping by Achates' side,
Bore those brave gifts to Dido's palace-gate:
She, when he came, had ta'en her place of pride,
'Neath gorgeous canopy on throne of state;
And there, an honoured guest, the Trojan king
On cushioned couch among his chieftains sate.
Then water for their hands the servants bring,
And napkins white with tufted fringe close-shorn,
And Ceres' gifts in dainty baskets borne:
Full fifty damsels wait in ordered line,
Whose charge it is to serve the feast, and light
On hearths of household gods the flame divine;
An hundred more the loaded board adorn—
An hundred pages, of like comeliness—
With viands rich and gleaming flagons bright.
Next, at the banquet bidden to recline,
The Tyrian lords through festive portals press;
In wonderment Æneas' gifts they view—
Mantle, and broidered veil of saffron hue—
And that fair child with glowing cheeks; nor guess

A god it is that speaks so false, so true.
But most the queen, foredoomed to love's sore stress,
Gazes unsated still, with heart afire,
And dotes on those rare gifts, that beauteous boy.
He, loosed from long embrace of seeming sire,
Whose breast he thrills with all a parent's joy,
On Dido turns his wiles. With fond desire
She greets him, eyes and breast with frenzy fraught,
Then folds him in her arms, suspecting naught
How great a god is plotting for her ill:
Poor Dido! Mindful of his mother's will,
He strives her husband's memory to remove,
And with a living passion to refill
Her placid thoughts and heart unused to love.

When flags the banquet, mighty bowls of wine
Are set before them, wreathed with flowery crown;
Surges the din of talk through spacious hall;
From gilded ceiling lighted lamps hang down,
And o'er the vanquished darkness torches shine.
Then doth the queen for brimming tankard call,
By Belus and his kinsmen used of old,
With sparkling gems embossed and massy gold;
Signal for silence on the feast to fall:
"Great Jove, since thou presidest, as folk say,
O'er hospitable rites, let this fair day
Bring joy to Tyrian host, to Trojan guest,
And in men's memories live forever blest!
May Bacchus, god of gladness, lend his cheer,
And Juno's gracious presence brood anear!
And ye, my faithful Tyrians, as is meet,
With frank and friendly hearts this union greet!"

She spake; and straight the due libation made,
Then gently to her lips the cup conveyed,
And next to Bitias passed it, nor refrained
From words of playful challenge; he, full lief,
In deep carouse the foaming beaker drained:
So went the flagon round from chief to chief.

Now to resounding harp the minstrel sings,
Long-haired Iopas, whom old Atlas taught:
Great themes are his; the pale moon's wanderings;
The sun's long travail; whence to birth were brought
The tribes of beasts and men; the primal springs
Of fire, of water; with what wondrous light
Arcturus, and the rainy Hyades,
And that great northern Wain, can burn so bright;
Then how the winter sun, by changeless laws,
So hastes to plunge his orb beneath the seas;
And what dark power retards the slow-foot night.
This sings he; and the Tyrians shout applause,
Nor less the listening Trojans praise the song.

Thus in long converse passed the night; and long
Ill-fated Dido drank of love's sweet pain:
For oft to ask of Priam was she fain,
Of Hector oft; then how Aurora's son
In heaven-wrought armour trod the Trojan plain;
Then of those fiery steeds by Diomede won;
Then of the great Achilles' peerless power.
"Come, guest," she cried, "and tell the tragic tale
Of Grecian treachery from its earliest hour;
Thy country's fated fall, thine exile drear,
Ere this the seventh summer brought thee here,
Condemned far lands to roam, far seas to sail."

BOOK II

ARGUMENT

A^T Dido's request, Æneas relates at the banquet the story of the fall of Troy—the stratagem of the wooden Horse, the craft by which Sinon induced the Trojans to draw the monster within their walls, the capture of the city, and the tragic scenes, including the death of Priam, of which the speaker had been a witness. The book ends with an account of the escape of Æneas to Mount Ida, accompanied by his father Anchises and his son Iulus (or Ascanius), but with the loss of his wife Creusa.

Silent, with looks intent, they waited all;
Then from his lofty couch Æneas spoke:

    Sorrow past words, O queen, thou bid'st recall:
Troy's glorious realm—its lamentable fall—
What piteous scenes I saw, what deeds mine hand
Had mighty part in. Who, with tearless eye,
Could tell the tale of such calamity?
Nay, ev'n Achilles' Myrmidons might weep,
Or war-worn soldier of Ulysses' band!
And now the dewy night adown the sky
Wanes fast, and setting stars bid mortals sleep;
Yet, if thou hast such longing, and wouldst hear
Brief record of Troy's last, most dolorous, day—
Though from these memories shrinks my soul in fear,
The task I will assay.
    Baffled by fate, and smitten still in fight,
The Grecian leaders, as the years fast fled,
Built high—so Pallas lent her skill divine—
A Horse of mountainous bulk; with planks of pine
Its ribs they wove; then, feigning homeward flight,
And votive offering reared, such rumour spread:
But in the dim depths of that secret den

Picked warriors they disposed, with dark design,
And filled its hollow womb with arméd men.
    In sight lay Tenedos, to fame once known,
Rich, prosperous isle, when Priam yet was king,
Now naught but treacherous bay and roadstead bare:
Shipped hither, and close concealed on foreland lone,
We deemed them toward Mycenæ voyaging;
So Troy, unfettered from its long despair,
Oped wide its gates, and forth its glad folk went
Where lay our foemen's camping-ground revealed:
Here had the dread Achilles pitched his tent;
Here ships were moored; here stretched the oft-fought field.
Some gazed on that huge Horse in wonderment,
Minerva's deadly boon. Thymœtes first
Its frame within the ramparts bade them bring,
From treachery, or perchance Troy neared its doom;
But Capys, with the wiser minds, was fain
Such Grecian craft in deepest sea to fling—
To burn with fire such perilous gift accurst—
Or stab its sides and probe their secret gloom:
Thus was the people's fancy torn in twain.
    Foremost, companioned by an eager train,
Laocoön from the castle runs distraught,
And cries, "What frenzy sets your hearts aflame?
Think ye the foe is fled—put faith in aught
Bestowed by Greeks? Is this Ulysses' fame?
Behind yon planks our hidden foes are penned;
Or 'gainst our city's walls such engine rear,
To spy o'er roofs and on our homes descend;
Trust not! With some deep guile the thing is fraught:
Ev'n when 'tis gifts they proffer, Greeks I fear."
    So saying, with mighty strength he hurled his spear:
Deep through the monster's jointed side it drave;
Then quivering stood; while, resonant from the blow,
Rumbled and groaned the hollows of the cave:
And if the harsh fates had not willed it so,
That our infatuate hearts should guide us ill,

Spurred by his warnings, we had hewn our way
To that dark lair—and Troy had stood to-day,
And Priam's tall towers were soaring skyward still!
    Anon, a youth, his hands behind him bound,
Is haled before the presence of the king
By Dardan shepherds loudly clamouring.
A stranger, he had flung him at their feet
With this intent—Troy's counsels to confound:
Dauntless, prepared, howe'er it might befall,
To work his wiles, or certain death to meet.
Eager for news, the Trojans gather round,
Each vying at their captive taunts to fling:
Mark thou what deadly plots the Greeks devise;
One crime shall speak for all.
For when he stood unarmed before our eyes,
And ranged about him saw the Phrygian band,
"Alas, what seas can shield me now, what shore?"
He cried: "Doth aught remain to crown my woes?
The Greeks have cast me forth; my Trojan foes
A savage vengeance with my blood demand."
Whereat, in altered mood, nor wrathful more,
We bade him learn us from what stock he sprung,
How thus our camp he dared, what message bore.
Then soon his fears were calmed, and loosed his tongue,
"All will I tell thee, king, whate'er my fate,
All truth; nor my Greek blood will I deny:
This first. Though Sinon's lot be desolate,
Yet Fortune's malice shall not make him lie.
Thou'st heard, perchance, of martyred Palamede,
That high-born knight of glorious renown,
Who dared against a wrongful war to plead;
Wherefore by judgment false he met his doom—
Guiltless, by hateful perjury borne down—
And now, too late, they mourn him in the tomb.
His kinsman I, the son of lowly sire,
In earliest youth was sent to join his train;
And while he flourished in his royal right,

The counsellor of kings, I, too, his squire,
My share of fame and honour might attain:
But when, by false Ulysses' jealous spite,
(Too true the tale,) a wrongful death he died,
Then shame and sorrow did my life o'ercloud,
And on my comrade's fall I brooded lone:
Not silent; for I rashly spake, and vowed
That if perchance occasion should betide,
When home to native Argos I had gone,
I would seek vengeance: thus was fierce hate bred.
Thenceforth my life was tainted; day by day
His charges scared me, now dark hints he spread,
Now sought him armed associates of his guile;
Nor ceased, until, by Calchas seconded—
But why this tale of woe do I retell?
Ye know me Greek—what boots it to delay?
If in your thoughts all Greeks alike are vile,
Take vengeance now: 'twould please Ulysses well;
For this the Atridæ goodly price would pay."

Eager, we bade him all the plot unfold;
So witless were we of Greek treachery:
Then, feigning fear, his lying tale he told:
"Oft yearned the Greeks, in weary warfare spent,
To quit the strand of Troy and homeward flee:
Would they had done so! But the waves ran high,
And wild winds broke their purpose ere they went;
Most, when they saw yon Horse full-fashioned stand,
The din of tempest thundered through the sky.
Then, in suspense, Eurypylus we sent,
To learn at Phœbus' shrine the god's command;
And back he bore this dolorous reply:
With blood of virgin slain the winds ye prayed,
When first to Trojan shore your voyage was made:
With blood your homeward passage must ye seek,
And give in sacrifice the life of Greek.

"Now when this résponse reached the people's ear,
Awestruck they marvelled, as their blood ran chill,

To whom that dreadful destiny drew near:
Then did Ulysses, with vociferous zeal,
Drag Calchas forth, and bid him straight reveal
The hidden purport of the heavenly will.
So was that crafty plot made plain to all;
Silent they guessed what deadly deed should be.
For twice five days the seer was dumb, and vowed
By word of his no living wight should fall:
Then, moved by his confederate's clamour loud,
Silence he broke, and laid the doom on me.

  "All gave assent, and what they viewed with dread,
Each for himself, on one poor wretch they cast:
And now the day had dawned, with hideous rite—
The salted grain, the garlands for my head—
Be this confessed, I broke my bonds, and fled,
And in the sedgy swamp lay hid the night,
Until, maybe, their ships should brave the blast.
Now hope is none to see my native shore,
Or children dear, or face of much-loved sire;
My foes will glut their vengeance for my flight
On those poor souls, and pains of death require.
Nay, by the gods above us, I implore—
By Truth's own guardian powers, by whatsoe'er
Of faith unsullied to mankind is left—
Pity a heart, of human aid bereft,
That merits not such grievous woes to bear."

  His life we grant, nor meed of pity spare;
Then Priam's self in friendly speech bids loose
His fetters, and the stranger thus doth hail:
  "Reck not of Greeks henceforth, whoe'er thou art.
Ours shalt thou be, and this in truth impart:
Why built they yon huge Horse? Who planned its use,
Their gods to worship, or their foes assail?"

  Then he, in native faithlessness arrayed,
Cried, with unshackled hand uplifted high:
  "Ye everlasting stars, be witness now!
By your inviolable sanctity—

By those curst altars that I 'scaped, the blade,
The fatal fillets on the victim's brow—
No wrong I do, breaking my clansmen's oath,
No wrong their hated plots unravelling,
Nor ban of law upon my lips is laid;
Let Troy, by me preserved, preserve its troth,
If true my tale, if guerdon great I bring!
 "Sole hope of Greeks, their boldness rested all
On help of Pallas: but when impious deed
Was wrought by hand of reckless Diomede,
And him, Ulysses, that arch-criminal,
Who dragged her sacred image from its shrine
On Troy's embattled hill, its guardians slew,
And with red hands her maiden chaplets soiled:—
Thenceforth our ebbing hopes receded; foiled
Our strength was; and estranged her grace divine.
Nor dubious were the tokens of her ire;
For scarce the statue in our camp was set,
When from her upraised eyes flashed baleful fire,
Indignant, and the limbs were moist with sweat;
And thrice from earth—as still our wonder grew—
She rose in wrath, with brandished spear and shield.
Then Calchas bade them launch their ships in flight,
Since Troy to Grecian onset ne'er would yield,
Till back at Argos they had sought anew,
Ev'n as when first they sailed, her friendly might.
Wherefore to far Mycenæ have they sped,
Their gods to fetch, and forces for the fight;
And, doubt not, thence they will return ere long,
Unlooked for: Calchas thus the signs hath read.
Counselled by him, to purge them of their guilt
For Pallas' plundered shrine, yon Horse they built,
Raised high its bulk, of timber stout and strong,
Lest haply through Troy's gates it should be led,
An holy thing, and guard thy folk from wrong:
For if your hand by sacrilegious blow,
To Pallas' gift should offer violence,

On Priam's realm, he vowed, will vengeance fall
(Ye gods, on his own head direct such fate!);
But if 'tis lodged within the city's wall,
Her power o'er vanquished Greece will Asia throw,
And the like doom our children's children wait."
   Thus his insidious speech, his tears untrue,
Our credence won, and that bold race o'ercame
Which Diomede nor Achilles' self could tame,
Nor years of war, nor thousand ships, subdue.
But soon, to fright our heedless hearts the more,
A sudden monstrous portent met our view.
It chanced Laocoön, priest of Neptune's shrine,
A victim choice was offering by the shore,
When lo! from Tenedos, o'er the tranquil brine—
I shudder to recall it—side by side,
Incumbent on the bosom of the main,
Two snakes, of girth enormous, glided near.
The high-uplifted heads o'ertop the tide
With menace of their blood-red crests; the rear
Winds far along the deep in sinuous train;
The salt spray seethes around. As land they gain,
Their bloodshot eyes are bright with wicked fire,
And flickering tongues from hissing jaws make play:
We flee in terror. Straight, in fixed array,
Laocoön they beset; but first they clasp
His children twain, each gripped in strangling spire,
With fangs close fastened on their hapless prey:
Then, when he lifts his hand, armed aid to bring,
They clutch him in their giant coils, and fling
Twice round his waist, his neck, their scaly grasp,
And high above him tower with breast and head.
Desperate, to loose those deadly knots he tries,
Drenched with foul venom o'er his fillets shed,
The while resound to heaven his anguished cries;
As when a maddened ox, sore stricken and maimed,
Loud bellowing from some altar-side has fled,
And shaken from his neck the axe ill-aimed.

Then to our citadel the serpents glide,
Seeking the temple of their goddess fierce,
And 'neath her feet and orbéd buckler hide;
While all who saw were thrilled with sudden fear;
He paid, 'twas said, just penance for his sin,
Whose hand that sacred effigy dared pierce,
And 'gainst its structure hurl unhallowed spear:
Now must they draw the Horse her courts within,
Her maiden grace to win.
So through the ramparts a broad breach we clear,
And to that task the people gird them all.
Its feet with rollers shod, its neck fast bound
With cords, the fatal engine scales the wall,
Big with destruction. Boys and girls around
Sing hymns, and on the rope glad hands are laid:
It enters, gliding on its path, and lowers
High o'er the city with such menace crowned.
O Troy, blest home of gods! O far-famed towers!
Four times, i' the very gates, its course was stayed;
Four times the clang of arms gave hollow sound:
Yet on we pressed, infatuate, undismayed,
And to our sacred height that monster drew.
Ev'n then Cassandra's lips spake warning true,
Though ne'er to her wise words was credence given:
'Twas Troy's last day; and we regardless, blind,
The gods' abodes with festal boughs entwined!
And now, with circling skies, night's shadows fall,
And wrap in widespread darkness earth and heaven,
And lurking Greeks: the Trojans, by their wall,
Lie silent, weary limbs in sleep reclined.
   Meantime, befriended by the still moonbeam,
From that near isle had sailed the Argive host
Seeking our well-known strand; and high the gleam
Of signal-fire from royal poop they wave.
Then Sinon, shielded by fate's perfidy,
Fails not to loose those warriors from their post
In that dark lair imprisoned; they, set free,

Leap forth full gladly from their wooden cave:
Thessander, Sthenelus, and our foe accurst,
Ulysses, and Machaon 'mid the first,
Down-gliding by the lowered rope; and there
Are Acamas and Thoas, dauntless pair,
With Neoptolemus, from Achilles sprung,
Proud Menelaus, and the craftsman wise,
Epëus, who that ambush did devise.
Ill fares our city, sunk in sleep and wine;
Slain are its guards, its trusty gates wide-flung:
Then in they rush, and all their bands combine.
    'Twas that calm hour when the sad heart of man
Is lulled with heavenly boon of slumber sweet:
Lo, in my dreams came Hector, weeping, wan;
His limbs disfigured still with dust and blood,
As when his corse to chariot-wheels was tied,
And cruel thongs had pierced his swollen feet.
How changed from him, our Hector, as he stood,
Decked with Achilles' spoils, in fearless pride,
Or hurled his flaming brands on Grecian fleet!
Unkempt his beard, his locks befouled with gore;
And still those wounds were on him, which he bore
When 'neath his native walls he fought and died.
Meseemed I first accosted him, and cried
In sorrow-laden accents, weeping sore:
    "O hope of Troy, our never-failing star!
What doom hath hid thee from our sight so long,
Beloved Hector? From what region far
Com'st thou, so fondly waited? Ah, the pain
Borne by thy folk, the many comrades slain,
Since our tired eyes beheld thee! But what wrong
Hath marred thy features that these wounds I see?"
Such idle plaint and quest naught heeded he,
But cried, as from his heart deep groans he gave:
    "Fly, goddess-born, from where these death-fires glow;
Ev'n now our walls are mastered by the foe,
And high-throned Troy is sinking to her grave.

Thou canst no more for country or for king.
If mortal hand our lofty towers could save,
This hand had saved them. Now must Troy confide
To thee each household god, each holy thing:
These take for partners in thy wandering;
With these go seek that city of fair fame
Which thou shalt build them far o'er ocean tide."
Therewith the chaplets from the shrine he brought,
And holy Vesta's never-dying flame.

Now from the city rose one mingled wail.
Ev'n where my father's dwelling lay remote,
By trees protected, clearer and more clear
The clash of arms upon our senses smote.
From broken sleep aroused, the roof I scale,
And watchful stand, intent with listening ear;
So, when on cornfield, fanned by southern gale,
Fire rages, or some mountain flood pours fast
O'er fruitful crops and oxen-laboured lands,
With wreck of forests—on high cliff, aghast,
Dazed by the sudden sound, the shepherd stands.
Soon is all doubt dispelled, our eyes must own
That craft has triumphed. See, as flames mount higher,
The mansion of Deiphobus o'erthrown;
Ucalegon, our neighbour, is a-fire:
The broad Sigean wave reflects the glare;
Then rise the shouts of men, the trumpets' blare.
Wildly I arm, yet, armed, lack clear intent.
To muster men—to rally toward the height—
So rush my thoughts, on rage and vengeance bent,
And sweet it seems to perish in such fight.

Lo, Panthus, priest of Phœbus, Othrys' son,
'Scaped from the foemen's arrows, to our gate,
With infant grandchild wandering desperate,
Bears in his arms his exiled deities.
"How fare we, Panthus? May the heights be won?"
Scarce said, when he, with groan of grief, replies:
"'Tis come—the end—the inevitable hour;

Troy was, and is not; we are Troy's no more:
Gone is the glory of the Dardan power,
Transferred by wrath of Jove to Argive shore.
The Greeks they lord it o'er the burning town,
And midmost, high installed, the Horse sends down
Its arméd warriors: Sinon spreads the flame,
Exultant. At our gaping gates they stand—
The mighty host that from Mycenæ came—
Or gird with ring of steel each narrow way:
Stern gleam the spear-point and the keen-edged brand,
Naked, foreboding death: o'erpowered, unmanned,
Our guards resist not in that blind affray."
    Stung by his words—since the gods willed it thus—
I rushed to arms at the fierce Fury's call,
Where the dread din of battle echoed wide.
With me were Rhipeus, and bold Epytus,
Who sought my presence with the moon as guide;
Came Dymas too, and Hypanis withal,
Both loyal comrades, cleaving to my side;
And young Corœbus, who, with heart on fire
For mad love of Cassandra, had made speed
To fight for Phrygia and the king, her sire,
Yet to the warnings of prophetic bride,
Luckless, had paid no heed.
    There stood they, banded fearless for the fight,
And thus I spake: "Strong hearts, though strong in vain,
If, certes, in such leader ye delight
Who from no desperate venture would abstain,
Ye see what fortune waits us! Forth they go,
Our gods, in exile from their shrines laid low,
Who were the prop and stay of Priam's reign;
Burnt walls to succour, shall the worst be braved?
Then die we will, flung headlong on the foe:
Safest are they who hope not to be saved."
    Thus were their minds to fury spurred, and bold
As ravening wolves that range some misty wold,
When pitiless hunger goads them, and at home

Starved cubs with bloodless jaws would fain be fed,
We dare the foemen's darts, and blindly roam
The city's midst to certain death, while Night
Flits round us with her shadowy plumes outspread.
Alas, what words men speak, what tears men shed,
Could equal that night's deeds of blood and pain?
Now sinks in dust Troy's ancient empery:
And there, by house, and street, and holy fane,
Lie strewn the dumb stark bodies of the dead;
Nor Troy alone war's penance suffereth;
The vanquished oft their dauntless heart regain,
Oft falls the conquering Greek: naught else we see
But grief, and fear, and ghastly scenes of death.

Then did Androgeus first, with Grecian band,
Our unfamiliar troop as comrades meet,
Deceived, and thus with friendly chidings greet:
"Now haste ye, sirs! Why thus in idlesse stand,
While others sack and burn Troy's towers so high?
Do ye but now wend hither from the fleet?"
Therewith—when, much misdoubting the reply,
His evil case, 'mid foemen fall'n, he knew—
Dumbfounded, step and speech he quick withdrew;
As one who, walking by rough woodland path,
Treads on a snake unseen, and shrinks at view
Of dusky swollen neck upreared in wrath:
Thus 'gan Androgeus to retreat in fear;
But on we rushed, and circling them around,
Ta'en unawares, and trapped on foreign ground,
Dispersed and slew them; so did fortune cheer
Our first assault. Then, "Onward let us press,"
Corœbus cried rejoicing, "where Success
Hath pointed us a path with glory crowned:
How if their Grecian shields and garb we wear?
Or craft, or courage—all in war is fair:
Our foes themselves shall arm us." At the word
He dons Androgeus' pluméd helm and shield,
And braces at his thigh the Argive sword;

So Rhipeus, and so Dymas; all our band,
None loth, the newly taken trophies wield.
Then, mingled with the Greeks, far o'er the field,
In alien garb, 'neath alien gods, we went:
Full many a fight we waged with darkling hand;
Full many a foeman to his doom was sent:
Some to the ships escaped and sheltering shore;
Some scaled the Horse in craven wilderment,
And in the same dark cavern hid once more.

   Yet naught can prosper save by will divine!
We saw Cassandra, daughter of Troy's king,
Dragged with dishevelled locks from Pallas' shrine,
Lifting to heaven in vain her burning eyes—
Her eyes, for chains her hands were fettering;
Whereat so fierce Corœbus' wrath did rise,
Into their midst he rushed distractedly,
Hard followed by our troop in order close;
Anon our friends, from roof of temple high,
Misled by borrowed plumes of Grecian helm,
With fratricidal darts our ranks o'erwhelm,
While, jealous for their captive maid, our foes
From all around us rally to the fray—
Grim Ajax, and the great Atridæ twain,
With mighty host of Grecian chivalry:
As when, in storm, opposing winds contend—
Wild West, and boisterous South—and onward sweep
The strong East's lusty steeds, the woods to rend,
While Nereus' trident smites the surging main
To foam, and stirs the bottoms of the deep.
They, too, from cover of the darkness creep,
Whom we had driven in rout through diverse ways,
And mark us by our lying shield and spear,
And doubtful speech that alien tone bewrays.
Soon numbers whelm us. First, Corœbus dies,
The temple of the warrior goddess near;
Next Rhipeus, in all Troy the justest heart,
Most resolute the true and right to prize;

Yet thus the great gods willed it! Comrade's dart
Slew Hypanis and Dymas: Panthus fell,
Whom not his faithfulness unchangeable,
Nor ev'n Apollo's sacred fillet saved.
Ashes of Troy, and death-fires of my land!
Be witness—in that final hour, I braved
All strokes of war, all perils; and had fate
Decreed my death, I earned it with this hand.
But soon our troop was parted; at my side
Went Iphitus and Pelias—one with weight
Of bygone years encumbered; one the brand
Of dread Ulysses had sore wounded: straight
To Priam's palace did the clamour guide.
    Here raved the fight, as though all war elsewhere
Had ceased, nor death throughout Troy's bounds were known;
So sturdily the Greek assault is thrown
'Neath close-locked bucklers 'gainst the castle wall;
Then, ladders laid, they strive to scale the stair,
In strong left-hand their guardian shields upheld,
The while, with right, they grasp the bulwarks tall.
Unawed, the Trojans from the roof have felled
Turrets and tiles, wherewith, when lost is all,
Ev'n in the hour of death, to stay the foe.
By some, great gilded beams, that decked of old
Their fathers' stately mansions, are down-rolled;
Some with drawn rapiers guard the gates below
In dense array. We rush, with strength renewed,
To succour royal house and comrades bold,
And fire the vanquished with fresh fortitude.
    A secret way there was, a postern blind,
Gave access through the palace of the king;
Where oft, ere Troy's proud pomp had yet declined,
Andromache was wont to pass unknown,
And to his grandsire's arms her infant bring.
Thus crept I to the crest of that high roof
Where Trojan spears were impotently thrown:
A turret there rose steeply to the sky;

Whence, gazing down o'er Troy's expanse, the eye
Saw Grecian ships and camp that lay aloof.
With iron bars we forced its joints to yield,
Till, wrenched and wrested from its lofty base,
We thrust it to the verge: sudden it reeled,
Then on the ranks of Greece crashed down apace:
Yet still their onset falters not nor fails,
Still storm of stones and darts the wall assails.

Full in the gateway's front, proud Pyrrhus led
The charge, his brazen armour gleaming bright,
Like venomous snake, on baleful herbage fed,
That lurks, till winter's season be o'erpast,
And hides his bloated coils below the ground;
Then, gay in youth, his wintry garments shed,
Uprears his sleek folds to the warm sunlight,
With threat of triple tongue that flickers fast.
With him great Periphas, and that squire renowned,
Automedon, Achilles' charioteer;
And all his Scyrian men-at-arms draw near,
And on the palace roof their firebrands cast.
Foremost himself, with wielded axe, he bore
The portal down, and burst the brazen door
From off its hinge; till lo! through solid wood
Was riven a yawning gap with naught to screen:
Then seen were Priam's royal chambers; seen
His stately halls where dwelt the kings of yore;
And arméd guards that on the threshold stood.

Within is muffled sound of sobs and sighs;
And loud laments through hollow galleries ring,
And wail of women smites the starry skies;
Fond mothers roam the courts in passionate woe,
And, trembling, to the doors with kisses cling.
But Pyrrhus, dauntless sire's undaunted son,
Nor bolts nor guards can hinder; 'neath his blow
The battered gate lies prone upon the ground:
Force fails not, and the foeman's way is won:
Then soon, the sentries slain, the hall they fill.

Less furious flows the flood, when earthen mound
Has yielded to the raging water's will,
And swift it surges, billowing o'er the plain,
Swamping the flocks and folds. Myself, I saw
Pyrrhus red-handed, and the Atridæ twain;
Saw Hecuba, with all her weeping train
Of wedded daughters; and that sight of awe,
Old Priam's blood his own pure hearths defile.
Those chambers, gorgeous with barbaric gold,
Those hopes of royal issue nursed awhile,
Are fall'n: what flames have spared, the foemen hold.
   Perchance thou'lt ask me what was Priam's end.
Soon as he sees his city lost, his walls
Dismantled, and the foe within his gate,
Vainly—for what can age-worn warrior do?—
His armour, long disused, he dons anew
On trembling shoulders; for his old sword calls,
And courting death, goes forth to meet his fate.
   Within the palace, 'neath the open heaven,
An ancient bay-tree leaning o'er the shrine,
Shielded the household gods with gentle shade:
Here huddling, like scared doves by tempest driven,
The queen and all her daughters sat and prayed;
Clasping in grief those images divine;
But when she saw her aged spouse arrayed
In warrior's garb, "What madness urges thee,
Husband," she cried, "in this extremity,
To arm thee thus? or whither wouldst thou wend?
Not now such aid, such championship, we need,
Ev'n if my glorious Hector's self were nigh.
Then rest thee, where this altar shall defend,
Or die beside me." Softly did she plead,
And drew him back to share her sanctuary.
   But lo! escaped from Pyrrhus' ruthless hand,
Polites, Priam's son, the carnage flies,
Down empty corridors and galleries,
Deep wounded, by pursuer close beset;

And now, ev'n now, he feels the impending brand;
Then in his parents' view he falls and dies,
And with his life-blood spilt the ground is wet.
Then Priam, albeit environed by death's snare,
Forbore not burning words of wrath and pain:
"For this thy crime," he cried, "this deed abhorred,
May heaven, if aught for such foul wrongs it care,
Repay thee to the full thy just reward,
Since thus, before mine eyes, my son thou'st slain,
And cursed a father's presence with such sight!
Not so did he, whom thou dost falsely feign
Thy sire, Achilles, use me with despite,
Nor grudged me Hector's body for the grave,
But nobly reverenced his suppliant's right,
And safe return to mine own country gave."

So saying the sire his weakly javelin flung,
Hurtless, by sounding brass repelled; and there,
Caught in the targe's boss, it idly hung:
But Pyrrhus: "Go thou, then; such tidings bear,
And tell my father what this hand hath done—
The dastard deeds of a degenerate son:—
Now die!" He spake; and where that altar stood
He dragged him, stumbling in his slain son's blood,
And wound his left hand in his hoary hair,
And with the right his gleaming falchion drew,
Then plunged it, to the hilt, deep in his side.
Thus did great Priam die, a king no more,
But seeing his Troy o'erthrown, his towers in dust—
He who had governed with imperial pride
His Asian kingdoms. Outcast on the shore,
His headless trunk, a nameless corse, was thrust.

Then first great horror compassed me around.
Aghast I stand, as anxious thoughts upspring
Of mine own father, agéd as the king
Whose life was ebbing from that cruel wound;
And sad Creusa, of all aid bereft;
And plundered home, and young Iulus' fate.

I glanced to see what friendly force was left;
Gone were my comrades; all had leapt to ground,
Or in the flames had flung them desperate:
None else survived: when lo! by Vesta's gate,
In silence lurking at that shrine of peace,
Was Helen, shown me by the glare of fire,
As round I roamed and turned my gaze on all.
'Twas she—the scourge, alike of Troy and Greece—
Who, dreading Trojan anger at Troy's fall,
And Grecian vengeance, and her husband's ire,
Had crouched beside that holy fane unseen.
Then burned my heart, for thought of true blood spilt,
To take fierce vengeance on her traitorous guilt:
"What! shall this wretch go scatheless from our house,
To Sparta borne triumphant, as a queen,
And proud Mycenæ, there to see once more—
With captive Trojan maidens in her train—
Her native land, her sire, her sons, her spouse,
While Troy lies burnt, its monarch foully slain,
And all our ravaged coast still steams with gore?
Nay! for altho' nor honour nor fair fame
By wreaking wrath on woman can I win,
Yet to have quenched in death that thing of shame,
Exacting vengeance meet, were praise enow;
Nor will it bring me aught but joy, I trow,
To glut my soul in righteous anger's flame,
And gratify the ashes of my kin."
  In wrath I spake, to frantic deed addressed:
When lo! revealed, as ne'er before, to sight,
And shining with pure radiance through the night,
My Mother stood—a goddess manifest—
Stately and fair as seen among the Blest,
And stayed my steps, and laid her hand on mine,
With gracious speech from roseate lips divine:
  "Son, is thy grief so great that naught can heal
This madness? Hath thy love for me quite gone?
Wilt thou not first thine agéd sire reseek?

Wilt not bethink thee of Creusa's weal,
And young Ascanius, by marauding Greek
Ev'n now begirt, and through mine aid alone
Saved from the thirsty sword, the flame's embrace?
'Tis not the Spartan woman's hated face,
Nor guilty Paris, that hath worked this woe;
The gods, the gods it is, whose wrath hath bowed
Tall Troy, and laid her glorious empire low.
Look! I will lift from off thine eyes the cloud
That dims thy mortal sight. Have faith and trust,
Nor fear thy Mother's bidding to obey.
Here, where thou seest but sundered piles, and stone
From stone o'erturned, and surging smoke and dust,
'Tis Neptune's trident hath this realm o'erthrown,
Till ev'n its firm foundations shake and sway;
There, by the Scæan gate, see Juno wield
Stern arms, and call her followers to the fray;
There, on the heights, sits Pallas, wrathful maid,
Fulgent with luminous cloud and Gorgon shield;
Yea, Jove himself doth give the Greeks his aid,
And stirs the gods to succour Troy no more.
Then haste thee, son, this weary strife to end;
For still my presence shall thy steps befriend,
And set thee safe beside thy father's door."
She spake, and vanished in that murky shade,
Wherein I saw dim forms and faces blend,
Dread powers 'gainst Troy arrayed.
   Then did all Troy, methought, in flame subside,
Uprooted utterly from base to cope:
As when some ancient ash, on mountain slope,
'Gainst which sharp axes, blow on blow, are plied
By sturdy woodmen, o'er the steep verge bent
Trembles with quivering foliage and bowed head,
Till, by prolonged assault subdued and spent,
With one last groan it falls in ruin wide.
The roof I quitted, and with god for guide
Homeward through foes and fires unhindered sped;

While harmless fell the darts, the flames down died.
   But when I reached the threshold of my sire,
And sought him first, him foremost, in desire
To bear him thence to mountain solitude,
He vowed, since Troy was dead, he too would die,
Nor live an exile: "'Tis for you, whose blood
Age hath not dulled, nor sapped your hardihood;
For you it is to fly.
For me, if heaven had willed me longer life,
It would have spared my home. Too much of strife
Have I beheld, outliving thus my land
Made captive in my sight by fraud and force.
Cry hail, then; leave me, as they leave a corse:
Myself will seek for death; the foeman's hand,
Striking in mercy, give the boon I crave;
'Twill reck me little that I lack a grave.
Too long, unblest, to worthless life I cling,
Since Jove, of gods and men the sire and king,
Hath smote me with the breath of fiery brand."
   He spoke, and changed not, his firm will unbent;
While we, in sorrow, gathering to his side,
With all our household, prayed him to relent,
Nor thus to ruin all, and add his weight
To quicken the fast-sinking scale of fate:
Naught moved him; where he stood, he would abide.
Then back to arms I turned, on death intent,
Since hope in counsel, or in chance, was none:
"Didst think that sire might thus be left by son?
Ah, that such thought in parent's heart could be!
If heaven ordain that Troy must perish quite,
And thou'rt resolved to doom thyself and thine
To die with Troy—that road to death is free!
Soon will arrive old Priam's murderer—he
Who slays the son within the father's sight,
And with the father's blood pollutes the shrine.
For *this* didst snatch me from that warfare wild
Sweet Mother—that the foeman I should see

Here, on our very hearth, and wife and child
And father sprinkled each with other's blood?
To arms, my mates! 'Tis our last day doth call.
Back to the Greeks, then! Be the fight renewed:
We few to-day not unavenged will fall."

Then, sword in hand, with trusty shield anew
To left arm buckled, forth to fight I fare;
But lo! Creusa, clinging round my feet,
Holds up the child Iulus to my view:
"If die thou wilt, we twain thy death would share;
But if thou still hast hope in arms, 'twere meet
This unprotected home had first thy care:
What fate shall else thy sire, thy son, befall,
And me, whom once thy consort thou didst call?"
So crying, she filled the house with sobs and sighs:
When lo! there chanced a sudden, wondrous thing;
Ev'n 'twixt his parents' hands, and 'fore their eyes,
It seemed above Iulus' head uprist
A point of shimmering light, wherefrom did spring
A clear, innocuous flame which gently kissed
His soft young hair, and round his temples played.
Then we, o'ercome with foolish fear, had striven
To quench the mystic flame with water pure;
But glad Anchises raised his orbs to heaven,
And thus, with suppliant palms uplifted, prayed:
"Almighty Jove, if by men's prayers thou'rt swayed,
Hear us, this once; then be thy blessing given—
If true our hearts—and make this omen sure!"

Scarce said, when sudden crash of thunder pealed
Loud on our left, and streamed athwart the gloom
A star, with copious trail of light revealed.
High o'er the topmost roofs we watched it glide,
And in far Ida's woods its splendour hide,
While sheeny rays its lengthening track illume,
And all around was left a sulphurous fume.
Then rose my sire, his sorrow turned to joy,
And blessed the gods for that fair star, and cried:

"Now linger we no more. Our footsteps guide,
Gods of my sires; my house, my grandson shield!
Yours was that omen: in your hands be Troy.
Son, I will share thy flight: to heaven I yield."
  Ev'n as he spake, still louder grew the blare
Of flames, and nearer surged the fiery tide.
"Come, then, my father! Let these shoulders bear
Thy weight; nor, sooth, shall I be tasked thereby.
Whate'er our lot, one peril will we share,
One safety: young Iulus at my side
Shall journey, and Creusa follow nigh.
And ye, my henchmen, to this word give ear.
Without the city, on a mound, ye know
That lonely shrine of Ceres, and anear
A cypress, held in reverence from of old:
To that one spot by diverse ways we go.
Father, thy hand shall our Penates hold;
Myself, but late returned from war's array,
Must touch them not, till, where pure waters flow,
Blood's taint be washed away."
  So saying, across my shoulders' breadth I cast
The skin of tawny lion wide outspread,
And to my burden stooped: my child I led,
Pacing beside me—hand in hand locked fast—
With steps unequal; then Creusa came.
Through many a dark and shadowy way we sped;
And I who, late, such reckless courage wore,
Not all the ranks of Greece my heart could tame,
Now started at each breath, each sound, that passed,
Trembling for him I led, for him I bore.
  The gates well-nigh attained, I deemed our flight
Was ended; when the sudden sound we hear
Of tramping feet; and peering through the night
My sire exclaims, "Fly, son; the foe is near!
Their gleaming shields I see, their armour bright."
Then, in my sore distress, some evil sprite
So mazed me that, while devious paths I crossed,

From more familiar roads compelled to turn,
All unbeknown was my Creusa lost;
Stopped she, or strayed aside, or sat outworn,
I know not, but I saw her ne'er again,
Nor marked her absence, nor had chance to learn,
Till on the mound, by Ceres' sacred fane,
Of our united band was missed but one,
From friends, from child, from mourning husband fled.
What charges wild 'gainst gods and men I brought,
For that most cruel blow of all that fell!
To comrades I commend my sire and son,
And household gods, in that secluded dell;
Back to the town myself the path I trace,
In shining arms, resolved to shrink from naught,
But search all Troy once more, all perils face.

First that dim portal 'neath the walls I seek,
Wherethrough we issued, and dark roadways tread,
Scanning each step anew with anxious care:
The very silence fills my soul with dread,
Then to our home, if haply, haply, there
Her feet had borne her, I return: the Greek
Had ravaged all, and held the guarded door.
And soon the hungry fire our roof o'erflows,
Fanned by the wind, and high its billows roar.
Then back to Priam's palace-gates once more:
And there, by Juno's sacred porticoes,
Dread guardians, Phœnix and Ulysses, stand,
Watching the spoil, where all Troy's wealth untold,
Snatched from the flaming temples desolate,
Altars, rich raiment, cups of solid gold,
Lie heaped; and round them, boys, a captive band,
With trembling women, wait.
This, too, I dared; where stretched the darkness wide,
Lifting my voice amid those desolate ways,
Again and yet again, her name I cried:
Still was I wandering frantic on my quest,
When lo! a mournful phantom met my gaze,

Her very ghost, but statelier and more tall:
Aghast I stood, nor found I words at all,
Till thus she spake, and soothed my sad unrest:
   "Why dost thou nurse this foolish grief for me?
Dear heart, 'twas willed in heaven these things should be;
On that strange journey wouldst thou take thy spouse?
This may not be, nor Jove, our lord, allows.
Long is thy voyage, vast the leagues of foam,
Yet to that distant western land thou'lt come,
Whose fertile fields are lapped by Tiber's tide;
There wait thee rich domain and royal bride.
Go, then; for loved Creusa weep no more:
I shall not see the hated Grecian shore,
Slave to the wife of some proud Myrmidon—
I, Trojan born, who wedded Venus' son—
But here with gracious Cybele I dwell.
Love thou the child I bore thee, and farewell!"
   Much would I fain have said, yet could but weep;
As, speaking thus, she vanished in thin air:
Thrice in my arms to fold her I assayed;
Thrice did the phantom form my clasp evade,
Like fickle wind or fleeting shape of sleep.
So back, as night was waning, I repair.
   There found I goodly throng of comrades new,
Matrons and men, in wondrous number met
For exile's lot, a sorrow-stricken crew.
From all around they came, prepared to go,
Brave, generous hearts, where'er my sails were set.
And now o'er Ida's crest we saw the fire
Of dawning day; and still the watchful foe
Our gateways guarded, nor of help was aught.
Then, for the end had come, I raised my sire
High on my shoulders, and the mountains sought.

BOOK III

ARGUMENT

ÆNEAS, continuing his story, describes his wanderings by sea. He is warned by an oracle to seek the ancient motherland of the Trojan race, which is at first interpreted as referring to Crete; but after a disastrous attempt to settle there, he learns that the land of his quest is Italia, the home of his ancestor Dardanus. After an adventure with the Harpies, he comes to Epirus, where he finds a Trojan colony, ruled by Helenus and Andromache, and obtains instructions about his further voyage. Thence he passes to Sicily; and after escaping the perils of Scylla and Charybdis, and the monstrous Cyclops, he skirts the coast to Drepanum, where his father dies and is buried. This concludes the story, which has brought him to the point where the first book began.

When that proud Asian kingdom, and the race
By Priam ruled, was ruthlessly o'erthrown
In downfall undeserved, by will of heaven,
And Troy lay prostrated from cope to base
In smoking ruins—then to regions lone
We fled for shelter, by dark auguries driven.
Hard by Antandros' walls, 'neath Ida's shade,
A fleet we built, and secret muster made
Doubtful what refuge by the fates was given.
Scarce summer smiled, ere sire Anchises bade
Unfurl our sails adventurous and be gone.
Weeping I watched the shores and harbours fade,
Once Troy's; then passed, an exile, o'er the seas,
With comrades, child, and guardian deities.

A spacious land we reached, of martial fame,
By Thracians tilled, where erst Lycurgus reigned,
Bound by old ties to Troy, ere fortune waned,
And kindred gods. There built I, on the shore,
New walls, and named the people with my name;
But fate had smiled not when that place I sought.

To Venus, and the gods, it chanced I bore
Due gifts, their blessing on my deeds to pray,
And at Jove's shrine a goodly victim slew:
Anigh me was a mound, whereon there grew
Cornels and myrtle shafts in dense array;
But when I strove to pluck their stems away,
The verdant foliage o'er the shrine to spread,
A grim and wondrous prodigy I saw:
For from the first root I would fain up-draw
By force, black blood-drops trickled down, and dyed
The crimsoned soil. Then, smit with chilly dread,
I shuddered, and my heart stood still with awe.
Again to pluck a stubborn stalk I tried,
The hidden cause of that strange sight to learn;
Again there flowed the same dark sanguine tide.
Much marvelling, to the Nymphs in prayer I turn,
And Mars, of that wild race the lord and friend,
If thus the portent may be sanctified,
And grievous omen lightened of its fear;
But when a third time to the task I bend,
Straining with knees hard pressed upon the ground—
Dare tongue describe it?—from the hollow mound
A dismal groan, a piteous voice, I hear:
   "Why woundest thou my bleeding flesh? Refrain
From wronging thus a sufferer's tomb, nor stain
Thy pure and pious hands with human gore!
Trojan am I; no stranger. From my heart,
Not senseless wooden stock, those blood-drops start:
Flee, then; for Avarice haunts this guilty shore.
'Tis Polydorus speaks. Here fell I, slain
'Neath murderous spears that thus have strewn me o'er,
An iron crop, with many a pointed dart."
Aghast I stood, in mute bewilderment;
Bristled my hair with dread, tied was my tongue.
This Polydore, his son, had Priam sent—
Mistrustful of Troy's power to struggle long,
And seeing his realm beleaguered by the foe—

A precious charge to Thracian monarch's hands;
And with him ample mass of treasure went:
But he, when fortune frowned on Troy laid low,
Courting the haughty Greek's victorious bands,
In lawless fury slew the prince, and then
Pillaged that wealth. Unhallowed lust of gold,
To what detested deeds, what crimes untold,
Canst not constrain the hearts of mortal men!

My fears allayed, these signs and portents grave
To chiefs in council met, my sire the first,
I straight discover, and their judgment crave.
One mind have all—to quit that shore accurst,
Scene of perfidious guilt, and dare the wave.
So funeral rites we pay, heap high the mound,
And to his troubled ghost sad altars build,
Decked with sepulchral wreaths and cypress gloom:
Dishevelled stand the Trojan matrons round;
Warm frothing milk we bring, and tankards filled
With sacrificial blood; then in the tomb
Bid rest his soul, and speak the last adieu.
Soon, when the faithless waves are lulled to sleep,
And winds soft-whispering lure us to the deep,
Launching our keels afresh, the beach we crowd;
So forth we sail, till lands are lost to view.

A sacred isle there is, in deep mid-sea,
To Neptune, and the Nereids' mother, dear;
The which, by cape and foreland drifting free,
Apollo—for his cherished home was here—
To Gyarus and to Myconus bound fast,
Unmoved, undaunted by what winds might be.
Hither we sail: here wearied, anchor cast
In restful port; then reverently greet
The walls where lord Apollo dwells enshrined:
And here, his brow with sacred laurel twined,
King Anius, priest and monarch both, we meet,
To sire Anchises in old friendship known;
So hand clasps hand, and welcome cheer we find.

4-2

Then, by that hoary pile of ancient stone,
The godhead's grace and guidance I entreat:
   "God of our country! grant us, sore distressed,
A home assured, a lasting fatherland,
And save this second Troy, this war-worn band,
Poor remnant that hath 'scaped Achilles' ire!
Where is our guide, our goal, our place of rest?
A sign vouchsafe us, and our hearts inspire!"
   Scarce said, when sudden tempest seemed to shake
The sacred court, the bay-tree; round us reeled
The mountain-ridges, and with hollow din
Trembled the tripod from the shrine revealed;
Then prone to earth we sank, as, far within,
That awful voice did solemn résponse make:
   "Long-suffering race of Dardanus, this know:
Back to the fertile bosom must ye go
Of ancient motherland that gave ye birth:
Be this your quest—to find your primal home.
There Trojan blood shall lord it o'er the earth,
Sons of your sons, and children yet to come."
   Thus Phœbus; and his words our comrades thrill
With joy exceeding great; no hearts but yearn
To guess where lies that far, ancestral shore,
Whereto he bade our wandering feet return.
Then spake Anchises, as he pondered still
The dim memorials of the men of yore:
   "Hear, chieftains, what high hopes I bid ye share!
In seagirt Crete, Jove's sacred island, stands
Mount Ida: there the cradle of our race;
An hundred cities, fruitful realms, are there:
Thence, if tradition's lore I rightly trace,
Came ancient Teucer to Rhœtean lands,
In quest of new domain. Not yet upsoared
Troy's towers; in lowly vale men's dwelling was.
Thence our great Mother, Cybele, adored
With mystic cymbals and the clash of brass,
Or silent rites, on Ida's wooded lawn,

Her car by team of harnessed lions drawn.
Come, sail we thither, at the gods' command,
When we have wooed the favour of the wind:
Not distant is the goal; so Jove be kind,
On the third morn we touch the Cretan strand."
    He spake, and at the shrines made offerings due;
To Neptune, to Apollo's grace, a steer—
To the dark storm-wind's power, a black-fleeced ewe—
To Zephyr fair, a spotless victim bled.
And now winged Rumour whispers in our ear,
From native kingdom disinherited,
The lord of Crete, Idomeneus, has fled;
And there, no ruler left, no foeman near,
Deserted lands new colonists await.
The Delian port we quit, and ride the seas,
Past Naxos' hills, to Bacchus dedicate;
Past green Donysa; past white Paros' stone,
And all the host of clustered Cyclades,
Whose countless islets stud the straitened tide.
Then shouts of sailors rise in vying tone,
Mate cheering mate to seek their sires' abode;
Astern a soft breeze wafts us on our road,
Till to that age-worn coast of Crete we glide.
    Eager I planned the longed-for city, called
By the glad name of Pergamus, and bade
Rise cherished homestead, and strong fortress walled;
Anon our wave-worn keels were high up-hauled;
Then, on new lands and marriage-ties intent,
Our youths were busied; and ev'n now I made
Laws for their ruling; when from tainted sky,
A sudden mortal malady was sent,
That sapped our strength; a season pestilent
To trees and fields: men died despairingly,
Or dragged their aching limbs; by Sirius burned,
Nor withered crops, nor parching herb, could live.
Once more Anchises bade our prows be turned
To Delos' isle and Phœbus' friendly fane:

What end to our long travail would he give?
What respite from our toil? What goal ordain?
　'Twas night; all earth was bound in slumber's spell.
Lo! as I slept, there rose before mine eyes
Troy's guardian gods—those sacred effigies,
Which from the burning city I had brought:
There stood they, in broad radiance visible,
Where through embrasures deep the moonlight fell;
Then gravely they bespake, and thus, methought,
In soothing words their solemn tale did tell:
　"That résponse which from Phœbus thou hadst heard,
If thou hadst sought it at his Delian shrine,
Here, to thy gates, we bring—his holy word.
We, outcast gods, who followed in thy train,
We, thy companions o'er the heaving main,
Shall yet exalt to heaven thy children's line,
And grant them empire. Great their glory; great
The city thou shalt build them. Shun no toil
Of exile; for thou still must sail the brine:
Not here the shores apportioned thee by fate.
A land there is, the Greeks Hesperia name;
Ancient, renowned in battle, rich of soil;
Erst by Œnotrians tilled; its folk more late
Italia called it, from their chieftain's fame.
There lies our destined mansion. Thence, of yore,
Sprung Dardanus, from whom Troy's kingdom came.
Rise, then, and to thine aged sire repeat
These sure and joyful tidings. Bid him claim
A western realm, the far Hesperian shore;
For Jove concedes thee not the fields of Crete."
　Awed by that vision and dread voice divine
(No sleep it was, wherein I seemed aware
Of the gods' very features, of their hair
With fillets wreathed, their looks that shunned not mine),
I felt the cold sweat down my body run;
Then, leaping from my couch, with suppliant hands,
Up-raised my voice to heaven, and poured in prayer

Libation on the hearth; which service done,
I warned Anchises of the fates' commands:
Seen was Troy's mixed descent from parents twain,
Himself misled 'twixt tales of ancient lands.

"Son, by Troy's troubled destinies beset,
None but Cassandra these events foretold;
For now I mind me, how she spake, of old,
Of those far-distant realms that wait us yet,
And oft Hesperia, oft Italia, named.
But who could deem that Troy would touch the West?
Who trust Cassandra, prophetess defamed?
Come, let us bow to Phœbus' high behest,
And seek his guidance on this wiser way."

He spake; and straight his bidding we obey.
Few folk we leave behind us; then again
Our haven quit, and sail the mighty main.

The deep we reached, where land was none to view;
Around, above, lay naught but sea and sky:
Then black the storm-cloud hovered o'er my head,
And waves were ruffled as the darkness grew.
Wild winds the surging waters buffeted,
And tossed us to and fro distractedly:
Fair day to night was turned; in clouds the heaven
Was veiled; with flash on flash the welkin riven.
Flung from our course, we wandered far in dread,
Nor Palinure himself knew day from night,
But owned his memory foiled, his bearings lost.
Three days—if days they were, bereft of light—
Three starless nights, that stormy sea we roam,
Till the fourth morn reveals a far dim coast,
With mountains risen to view and curling smoke;
Then sails are lowered, and soon, with sweeping stroke,
Our oarsmen lash the steely sea to foam.

Saved from the deep to those strange shores I drew,
Isles stationed in the wide Ionian seas,
Long known by Grecian name, the Strophades:
There dwells Celæno with her Harpy crew,

Since angered Phineus drove them from his door,
And from their former haunts in fear they flew.
No loathlier pest and scourge e'er sprang to sight,
Upraised by wrath of gods from Stygian shore;
Winged fiends, with maidens' features; all they touch
Befouled with ordure; taloned hands that clutch;
And famished faces white.

    Anon the port we entered, and were ware
Of cattle that on goodly pastures grazed
And goats that roamed the hills, no herdsman nigh:
Swords drawn, we rushed among them, with a cry
To Jove and all the gods our prey to share;
Then banquet-couches of heaped turf we raised,
Thereon to sit in rustic carnival;
But from the mountains, swooping suddenly,
With hideous clang of wings upon the blast,
The Harpies came, and snatched our rich repast,
With noisome stench and touch polluting all.
Again, 'neath shelving cliff, in hidden cove,
Environed round with trees and sheltering shade,
We spread the board, our altar-fires re-laid:
Again, from some new lurking-place above,
The clamorous taloned troop flew hovering round,
And fouled the feast. My comrades then I bade
Take arms 'gainst that accursed tribe to war;
They, at the bidding, set their swords aground,
And deep in grass their hidden bucklers flung;
So, when Misenus from a lofty scar
His trumpet sounded, and the signal rung
That told their noisy rout was on its way,
Forth rushed our folk, and strove, in novel fight,
Those ocean-vultures with sharp steel to slay.
But little recked they how we showered the blow
On their rank plumage; then in skyward flight
They left, half-gorged, their talon-tainted prey:
All save Celæno; perched on craggy height,
Dread prophetess, she croaked these words of woe:

"Is't war ye threaten, Trojan warriors bold?
War, that ye thus may slay our ravaged herds,
And drive the guiltless Harpies from their realm?
Then hark, and give full heed to these my words!
What Jove revealed, what Phœbus' voice foretold,
I now, your Fury, this dark doom declare.
Ye seek Italia. Borne by breezes fair,
Italia shall ye gain; there moor your fleet:
But never shall embattled walls enfold
The city of your hopes, till, starved for meat—
This outrage ye have done us to repair—
Your very tables ye are fain to eat."

So saying, she winged it back to dusky wood:
But we—with sudden fear our blood grew chill,
Our spirits sank; to arms we turned no more,
Rather with sighs and prayers for peace we sued,
If god she were, or bird of omen ill.
Then did Anchises the great powers implore,
And suppliant bids his folk due offerings pay:
"Ye gods, avert such threats, such ills forfend,
And blessings on a pious people send!"

Therewith were cables loosed and canvas spread.
Strong blew the South, as o'er the foam we sped
Where wafting wind and pilot guided us.
Soon rose Zacynthus' forests o'er the tide;
Dulichium, Samé, and steep Neritus;
Safe past the rocks of Ithaca we glide,
And curse the land that fell Ulysses reared;
Anon Leucate's cloudy crags are spied,
Where frowns Apollo's temple o'er the main,
And warns of sunken reefs by sailors feared:
Weary and worn the little port we gain;
There, anchor cast, our ships in haven ride.

Debarked at length on scarce-expected land,
To Jove, with lustral rites, our vows we pay;
And there, in Trojan games on Actium's strand,
Our youths contend, as did their sires of old,

Wrestling with naked limbs. Right glad were they,
Who from the midst of foes had won their way,
Past many a Grecian shore that threatened death.
And now the sun his yearly round had rolled,
And seas were roughened by keen winter's breath;
'Twas then I fixed on front of temple door
The brazen shield that once king Abas bore,
With verse that thus the trophy witnesseth:
    These arms Æneas, from Greek conquerors won.
Then bade I launch with speed and ply the oar:
With lusty strokes the harbour-mouth we clear;
Soon the Phæacian heights from view are gone;
In onward course we skirt Epirus' shore,
And to Buthrotum's stately port draw near.
    Then wondrous tidings brought they to mine ear:
How Priam's son, sage Helenus, was crowned
King over Grecian land, in Pyrrhus' stead,
Of throne, of queen, possessed; and once again
Andromache to Trojan lord was wed.
Amazed I stood; my burning heart was fain
To greet the chief, and his strange fortunes hear;
So landward from the shore and ships I strode.
It chanced that nigh the town, in wooded dale,
Where to the sea a second Simois flowed,
With sad commemorative rites the queen
At Hector's tomb to her lost husband cried;
A cenotaph it was, with grave-mound green,
And altars twain where Grief might weep its fill.
But when my sudden coming she espied,
And guard of Trojan arms, pale grew her cheek,
Rigid she stood, with wonder terrified,
Then swooned, and scarce at last found voice to speak:
    "Is't thy true self I see? And hast thou brought
True tidings, goddess-born? Dost breathe life's breath?
Then speak! Or, if thou com'st from realms of death,
Say, where is Hector?" Then with clamorous grief
Her tears fell fast, and as she raved distraught,

In broken faltering words I answered brief:
"Ay, sure, I live; and life with me, long while,
Drags on through utmost sorrow and distress:
'Tis truth; this doubt not thou.
O robbed of thy great lord, hath fortune's smile,
Full well deserved, returned, thy heart to bless?
Once Hector's bride, art wed to Pyrrhus now?"
With downcast eyes, and in low tones, she spoke:
　"Nay, blest that royal maid, blest above all,
Whose doom it was, beneath Troy's lofty wall,
To die at foeman's tomb; who suffered not
The slave's estate, the casting of the lot,
Nor to the victor's couch was captive borne!
Myself from burning Troy was sent, a thrall,
O'er distant seas, made subject to the scorn
Of him I served, the great Achilles' son,
And here a child in bondage did I bear.
But soon, intent on Spartan union,
Enamoured of Hermione the fair,
He yielded me to Helenus for wife;
So captive unto captive was I given.
But mark! Orestes, frenzied with desire
For his lost bride, and by the Furies driven,
Struck Pyrrhus down with sudden murderous knife,
Ta'en unawares at altar of his sire.
Then Helenus as monarch was acclaimed;
And he, from Trojan Chaon, newly named
The land Chaonia, and on yonder steep
Built Pergamus, our Trojan citadel.
But thou—what winds have blown thee o'er the deep?
What god's dark will hath brought thee to our coast?
How of the young Ascanius? Thrives he well?
And she?...I guess thy word!
Mourns he for that fond mother he hath lost?
Or fame in deeds heroic would he win,
By noble heritage to valour spurred,
Child of Æneas and great Hector's kin?"

So cried she, and with lamentation vain
Long parleyed; till there came, in royal state,
Lord Helenus, begirt with courtier train,
And knew his friends, and welcomed us with joy,
Yet stanched not, as he spoke, the falling tear.
So on I pass, and find a lesser Troy,
With lowly citadel that mimicks great;
A streamlet which by Xanthus' name they call;
And there I clasp anew a Scæan gate.
Nor do my comrades, housed in spacious hall,
Lack hospitable welcome of the king;
High are the dainties heaped on golden plate,
And Bacchus' gifts long hold them revelling.
    So day chased day; and still the strong South-West
Called soft, and set our swelling sails astir,
When, doubtful, thus the prophet I addressed:
    "Sage son of Troy, the gods' interpreter,
Who read'st the will of Phœbus, and the skies,
And voice of birds, and omens of swift wing!
This tell me—for oracular replies
All grant me prosperous voyage, all gods command
To seek fair Italy's secluded land:
None but Celæno spake of evil thing,
A direful retribution, with dark threat
Of grisly famine—this, I charge thee, say:
By what grim perils is my path beset?
How through such labours shall I win my way?"
    Then Helenus, with blood of victims shed,
Implored the favour of the gods divine,
And loosed the sacred fillets from his head;
So, guided by his hand, I drew anear
O'erwrought with holy awe, to Phœbus' shrine,
And thus, with lips inspired, outspake the seer:
    "Hark, goddess-born! for, sure, some mightier power
Grants thee auspicious passage o'er the deep;
So heaven's high monarch guides the fates' decrees
On ever-circling course from hour to hour;

Such order doth their mighty sequence keep.
How thou mayst sail secure o'er alien seas,
And in Italian harbour find repose,
Brief is my counsel; for the rest Fate's screen
Hath hidden, and Juno bids me not disclose.
But first: this Italy thou deemest near,
And fondly think'st ev'n now to touch its shores—
Long leagues of lands untraversed lie between:
In waves Sicilian must thou bend thine oars;
Ay, thou must traverse the Ausonian foam,
Avernus' lakes, and isle of Circe fell,
Ere thou shalt build in peace thy promised home:
This sign I give thee—do thou mark it well.
When by a lonely river thou shalt stand,
With anxious heart, and see, 'neath ilex-bough,
Of bulk immense, recumbent on the ground,
With brood of thirty young, a mother sow,
White, with her offspring white her dugs around—
There rest thee; there at last thy city found.
Nor by the Harpy's menace be dismayed;
The Fates shall find a way, and Phœbus aid.
But that Italian coast which nearest lies,
Washed by the flow of our Ionian tide,
Touch not; 'tis peopled by Greek enemies:
There have the Locri reared their fortress tall;
There doth thy foe Idomeneus bestride
All Sallentinum's plain with men of Crete;
There stands the Greek Petilia, city small,
Shielded by strength of Philoctetes' wall.
But when thy keels have crossed yon waters wide,
And on the shore thy vows thou wouldst complete,
With purple robe thy temples must thou veil,
Lest, 'mid the rites on altars purified,
An hostile face thy worship should assail
And mar thine hopes and prayers with omens ill:
This usage thou and thine shall cherish still,
Therein devoutly shall thy sons abide.

"Now hark! when hence thou'rt parted, and canst sight
Sicilia's headlands, and the opening gates
Where high Pelorus towers above the straits,
Sail leftward in wide circuit; to the left
Thy course is; shun the perils of the right.
'Tis said, these lands, in bygone ages cleft
By some vast shock—so potent is the might
Whereby through lapse of time earth's face is changed—
Were rent asunder, where before had been
One continent; then rushed the sea between,
With narrow tide disparting shore from shore,
And town from town and field from field estranged.
There, to the right, sits Scylla; leftward raves
Charybdis unappeased, and evermore
Sucks down to sunless depths the boiling waves,
Then skyward flings them back from the abyss,
Lashing the stars of heaven with salt sea spray.
But Scylla in dark cave imprisoned is,
Wherefrom her mouth she thrusts, if so she may
Draw passing ship to ruin on her rocks.
Above, her form is human—to the waist
Shaped comely as a maiden's—but below
Naught but a loathly monster of the sea,
A wolf-bitch, dolphin-tailed; so foul is she.
Wiser it were, though urgent be thy haste,
Far circling round Pachynum's cape to go,
Than once cast eye on the deformity
Of Scylla, where that craggy cave resounds
With bark and bellow of her fierce sea-hounds.
  "Next, if true seer I be, if aught I know
Of prophet's art, if Phœbus be my lord,
One thing above all else I charge thee, one,
Again and yet again, leave not undone;
Be Juno's dread divinity adored;
To Juno vow glad vows, till thou prevail
O'er heaven's great queen; thus victor at the last
To those Italian borders shalt thou sail.

There, when to Cumæ's city thou hast passed,
Where lie the haunted lakes and rustling grove
Of dark Avernus, fail thou not to seek
The wild-eyed priestess who in rocky cove
Foretells the fates; her wont is to consign
To fragile leaves the message she would speak:
That sacred script she ranges, line by line,
And in the hollow of her cavern hides;
There fast, awhile, and motionless it bides:
But when a light wind through the opening door
Has stirred the leaves, and marred their order due,
No thought hath she to stay them as they flit,
Or backward bring, or link their lines anew;
Her suppliants go their ways, illumed no whit,
And loathe thenceforth the Sibyl's mystic lore.
But thou, dread no delays, how long soe'er—
Albeit thy comrades chide, thy voyage impel,
And favouring breezes still thy canvas swell—
So thou approach her shrine, with humble prayer
That she will deign herself her tale to tell,
Herself in gracious speech the fates declare;
Thus from her lips foreknowledge shall be won
Of tribes Italian, mighty wars to be,
What toils thou must endure, what perils shun;
Thus thy long travail shall be crowned with joy.
This is the counsel thou mayst learn of me:
Go, then; exalt to heaven our fallen Troy!"
      Thus friendly spake the sage, and bade them bear
Rich presents to our ships, of massive gold,
And ivory carved, then store within the hold
Much silver, and Dodona's caldrons rare;
A gold-linked coat of triple mail he sent,
And helm with flowing crest and lofty cone,
Arms worn of late by Pyrrhus in his pride;
Such gifts he gave, nor lacked my sire his own:
Steeds, too, and pilots, and fit armament
For seamen's use his lavish hand supplied.

Then, as Anchises bade us hoist the sail,
That we should hinder not the prosperous gale,
The seer addressed him in high courtesy:
"O thou whom Venus, peerless deity,
Found worthy of her love; thou blest of heaven,
Twice saved, when Troy was ravaged by the foe!
There lies Italia: grasp what fate hath given!
But yon less distant region pass thou by,
And onward sail where Phœbus points thee. Go,
Glad father of true son! No more say I,
Nor hold thee back when kindly breezes blow."
    Then likewise, as approached the hour to part,
Andromache, in tears, rare raiment brought
Broidered with thread of gold, and Phrygian cloak,
For young Ascanius, gifts of generous heart;
Works of her loom they were, so richly wrought,
She lavished on the lad, and fondly spoke:
    "Thou, too, child, take these gifts; and may they prove—
These keepsakes of my craft—the changeless love
Of Hector's wife! Take, from Andromache,
These last gifts of thy kindred! Thou alone
Bring'st back the lost Astyanax, my son:
Such eyes, such hands, such countenance had he;
And now his youthful years had matched thine own."
    Then spake I, parting, as the tears fell fast:
"Live happy, ye, whose perils now are past
While we from fate to fate are called to roam!
For you is rest secured; no fields of foam
Your keels must plough, nor must ye ever seek
Far western shore that ever fades away.
Ye look on Troy, Troy's image, which your hands
Have built—'neath better auspices, I pray,
And less at mercy of the vengeful Greek.
If e'er I come to Tiber's distant lands,
And see the destined city of my race,
Then shall our folk unite in kinsmen's ties—
Epirus and Hesperia shall embrace—

Sprung from one sire, and stricken by one fate;
So, in our hearts, one single Troy shall rise:
Such pious tasks our children's care await."
   So on we sail, past those Ceraunian heights
Whence points the nearest course toward Italy.
Now sinks the sun, the hills are shrouded deep;
There, by the wave, where earth's sweet breast invites,
We seek repose in turn, our oars anigh,
And weary limbs in restful slumber steep.
Nor yet Night's car hath climbed the middle sky,
When Palinurus, starting from his sleep,
Catches with straining ear the doubtful breeze;
The stars he notes that glide in noiseless flight—
Arcturus, and the rainy Hyades,
The Wain, and great Orion belted bright;
Void are the tranquil heavens of cloud or gale;
Then his loud-sounding signal bids us rise,
And soon, with canvas spread, our way we wing.
Set were the stars, and Dawn was reddening,
When far dim hills and lowly shore we see,
Italia—"Italia," first Achates cries;
"Italia," all our comrades hail with glee.
'Twas then my sire a brimming wine-cup twined
With flowery garlands, and made haste to pray,
As high on stern he stood:
"Ye gods of sea, and sky, and stormy wind,
Waft us on prosperous voyage and be good!"
Thereat the fair breeze freshened, and the bay
Oped to our vision, drawing near; and lo!
High on the summit stood Minerva's fane;
Then prows to shore were pointed, canvas furled.
Bent was the port from seaward, like a bow,
And round its jutting cliffs the salt spray swirled;
The harbour lay aback, 'twixt headlands twain
That stooped to fling their rocky arms below;
The temple on the slope receding far.
Here met our sight four chargers, white as snow—

First omen—grazing free along the plain.
"Strange shores," cried sire Anchises, "bring ye war?
Ay, war yon steeds forebode; yet oft men train
The horse's strength, obedient to the rein,
To draw in harmony the peaceful car:
Of peace, too, hopes we have." Therewith we prayed
The holy power of Pallas, warrior maid,
Who first beheld us as we greeted land:
Then heads we veiled, that naught the rites should mar,
Enjoined as chiefest by the seer's command,
And honours due at Juno's altar paid.

That duty done, we tarried not, nor stayed,
But canvas-covered yards to seaward turned,
Mistrustful of the haunts of Grecian foes;
And soon Tarentum's bay our eyes discerned,
Beloved, 'tis said, by Hercules of yore;
In front, Lacinian Juno's temple rose,
And Caulon's heights, and Scylaceum's shore,
Whose perilous reefs the wary seaman knows:
Then did far Ætna from the waves upsoar;
Heard was the sea's vast moaning, and the roar
Of rocks forever smitten by the surge;
Hoarse broken voice of billows on the strand;
And depths that seethed with mingled surf and sand.
Then spake my sire: "Here, certain, is the verge
Of dread Charybdis; here the rocky steep
Whereof the sage forewarned us. Haste ye now,
Comrades, with steady strokes the seas to sweep,
And save us from this death!" Straight, ere the rest,
To larboard Palinurus swung his prow;
To larboard all, with sails and oars, we plied,
Now towering high upon some billow's crest,
Now deep descending where the waves subside:
Thrice did the rocks resound with hollow cry;
Thrice flew the foam and drenched the streaming sky;
Then sank the sun, the wind, as on we pressed:
So darkly to the Cyclops' shores we glide.

A spacious port there is, from stormy blasts
Secure; but Ætna, with dread earthquakes riven,
Now to the skies her pitchy cloud upcasts
In eddying fumes, with glowing coals besprent;
And flings forth balls of fire that kiss high heaven:
Now rocky fragments from her entrails rent
She belches forth, and groaning in her toil
Hurls molten crags aloft in burning showers,
As from her depths the fiery surges boil.
'Tis whispered, 'neath that mighty mountain cowers,
Scorched by the vengeful thunder-bolt of Jove,
The bulk of huge Enceladus; above,
Flaming from lidless forges, Ætna rests;
And when his weary limbs he fain would move,
Sicilia trembles to her utmost bound,
And all the heaven in murky smoke invests.
That night, with sheltering forests compassed round,
Bewitched we lay by fearful prodigies,
Nor knew from what dark source arose the sound:
The stars had quenched their fires; no silvery gleam
Illumed the pole; o'erclouded were the skies,
And sullen night had dimmed the pale moonbeam.
  Scarce had the morrow mounted to her throne,
And dewy darkness from the sky expelled,
When from the woods appeared a form unknown,
Gaunt, famished, piteous in his dire distress;
So came he forth, with suppliant hands upheld.
We marked his abject squalor, beard unshorn,
Rent garments rudely stitched with points of thorn;
Yet Greek he was, in all things else, no less
Than when 'gainst Troy he marched, a foeman armed.
He, when he saw our Dardan swords and dress,
Gazed mute awhile, by that strange sight alarmed,
And halted; then, in sudden recklessness,
He flung him in our midst with prayers and tears:
  "Now by the gods I pray—the heavenly spheres,
And this sweet vital air that men respire—

Take me where'er ye will; so it be hence,
I care not! Yea, in Grecian fleet, 'tis true,
I came to sack your homes with sword and fire:
Wherefore, if naught can purge that past offence,
Slay me—upon the deep my dead limbs strew;
So dying, to die by human hand were sweet."
   He spake, and clasped our knees, and at our feet
Fell prone, and grovelled. We, to soothe his fear,
Bade him his name, his race, his woes repeat;
Nor did Anchises long his hand withhold,
By that firm pledge the stranger's heart to cheer;
So reassured at length this tale he told:
   "From Ithaca I sprang, and long have shared
Ulysses' luckless wanderings o'er the wave.
Named Achemenides, to Troy I went,
Son of a humble sire, content till then—
Would with that fortune I had stayed content!
For when my comrades fled, distraught and scared,
The grisly horrors of the Cyclops' cave,
Here was I left forgotten. Huge his den,
Reeking with gore, and gloomy as the grave;
Himself so monstrous, to the stars he towers
(Ah, spare our suffering earth, ye heavenly powers!),
High o'er the sight and speech of mortal men.
Poor flesh and blood this ogre foul devours:
Myself have witnessed how, with giant hand,
As backward leaning in his cave he sate,
He clutched two fellow-captives of our band,
And brained them on the rocks, till walls and floor
Were splashed with blood; and dripping with dark gore
Their still warm bodies quivered as he ate.
Yet did he rue the deed; for swift to act,
At that most perilous moment of his fate,
Naught of his wisest self our leader lacked:
So, when o'ergorged with flesh, with wine o'ercast,
The monster bowed his head in bestial swound,
And flung his hideous bulk along the ground,

Belching the vomit of his foul repast,
Then we, with prayers to the great gods on high,
Each in our ordered place, crept silent round,
And blinded with sharp stake the single eye
That lurked half-hid beneath his scowling brow,
Huge as a shield, or orb that lights the sky:
Thus were our comrades' ghosts avenged enow.
    "But ye—fly hence, poor wanderers, fly amain;
Wrench cables from the shore!
For not alone within these rocky cells,
Pens Polypheme his flocks, their milk to drain;
Ev'n such, nor less in height, an hundred more
This region haunt, and roam o'er fields and fells.
Thrice hath the waxing moon enlarged her light
Since thus my life drags on in thickets dense
'Mid lair of savage beasts, from craggy height
Watching those monsters as they rove immense,
And trembling at their voice and ponderous tread.
Thus have I lived, with cornel-berries fed,
And on wild woodland roots subsisting ill;
Then, as the seas I scanned, by yonder cape
I saw your ships approaching. Now I yield,
Nor care to whom I yield me, so I 'scape
That foul inhuman crew 'gainst pity steeled:
Take ye and slay me by what death ye will."
    Scarce said, when lo! adown a rugged hill,
Descending massive toward the ocean tide,
We saw, amidst his flocks, that shepherd grim;
Huge, gross, misshapen, eyeless; in his hand
A pine he grasped his darkling steps to guide,
Nor, save his fleecy sheep, sole joy and pride,
Was aught to solace him:
But when he passed the breakers on the strand
And reached the main, he washed the streaming gore
That ever from his blinded socket fell,
And groaned, and gnashed his teeth, as on he paced
Through deep mid-sea that wetted not his waist.

Then fled we from the spot, in terror sore,
Nor left that suppliant who had served us well.
All silent, cables cut, we plied the oar,
With eager strokes that drove us through the brine:
This heard he, and did straight his steps incline
To meet the sound; but when his power was past
To gripe our boats ere seaward they could sweep,
Nor those Ionian wavès could he o'ertake,
A roar he raised that made old ocean quake
In all its depths; Italia shook aghast,
And Ætna's inmost caverns bellowed deep.
Then did the Cyclops' kin, from hill and wood,
Rush wildly to the shore in angered crowds:
We watched them, Ætna's monstrous brotherhood,
As frowning in fierce impotence they stood
And reared their towering foreheads to the clouds;
A dread assemblage: so, the skies anear,
Dark cypresses or giant oaks may stand,
In forest aisles to Jove or Dian dear.
We, panic-stricken, loose the sheets and shrouds,
Nor reck what breeze our hurried flight befriends;
But soon, admonished by the seer's command—
To shun that channel, where, on either hand,
'Twixt Scylla and Charybdis, death impends—
Our course we shift; and at the nonce springs forth,
Due from Pelorus' straits, the welcome North,
And wafts us southward on our destined way,
Past where Pantagia's slender streams out-flow
Through reefs of solid stone; past Megara's bay;
Past Thapsus on its foreland lying low:
Such lore from Achemenides we gain,
As now his earlier wanderings he retraced,
Companion of Ulysses' storm-tossed train.

There lies an isle by fair Sicilia's side,
Fronting Plemmyrium's breakers, early named
Ortygia; thither 'neath the sea, 'twas famed,
Alphæus' stream by hidden passage flowed,

With Arethusa's fount to mix his tide.
Here worship we, forewarned, each local god,
Then skirt Helorus' rich well-watered meads
To where Pachynum's lofty headlands frown;
Thence seen afar is Camarina's town,
Which ne'er—so fate had willed—might suffer change,
And Gela, dreaded for its tyrants' deeds;
Then stately towers of Acragas appear,
Once glorious birthplace of high-mettled steeds;
Next, past Selinus and its palms we range,
Past Lilybæum's sunken ledges steer,
To rest awhile in Drepanum's bleak port.
'Twas here—of winds and waters long the sport—
I lost the surest solace of my pain,
My sire Anchises. Best of fathers, here—
Saved from unnumbered perils, but in vain—
He left his careworn son; nor had the seer,
In all his warnings, nor the Harpy dread,
Presaged that heaviest anguish of my soul.
Such was my crowning sorrow; such the goal
Whereto my long and weary wanderings led:
Thence, by god's guidance, to your shores I sped.

Thus did Æneas all his listeners hold
Entranced, intent, the while of fate's decrees
His speech was, and of traversed lands and seas.
He stopped, and silence fell: his tale was told.

BOOK IV

ARGUMENT

DIDO, now deeply enamoured of the Trojan chief—their love being encouraged, for different reasons, by both Venus and Juno—endeavours to detain him at Carthage; but Mercury is sent by Jupiter to remind him of his great destiny, and to command him to depart. Æneas, preparing to obey, is beset by Dido's pleadings and reproaches, but persists in his purpose; at which the queen, passing from anger to despair, dies by her own hand, as the Trojan ships are sailing from her port.

But now the queen, by love's wound sore distressed,
Feeds in her veins the blind consuming fire:
Much o'er his valour, much his pride of race,
She broods; and, graven in her heart, his face,
His accents, cheat her fevered limbs of rest.
So, when the morrow's dawn was mounting higher
And from the sky had chased the dewy night,
Wildly her loving sister she addressed:
  "Anna, what dreams my bodeful soul affright!
This stranger chief, our guest from oversea,
How noble of mien, in heart and hand how bold!
He springeth, sure, from some divinity.
The craven spirit is marked by fear; but he—
Fate-buffeted—what tale of wars he told!
Were not my purpose firmly set and steeled,
To live my life from yoke of marriage free,
Since my first love was slain and left me lone—
Were not my mind of wedlock weary grown—
Perchance to this one weakness would I yield.
Anna, 'tis truth that since Sychæus' blood,
Spilt by a brother's hand, our palace dyed,
None else hath stirred my heart to softer mood;
Yet now I feel that spark of former flame.

But may the earth beneath my feet yawn wide,
And Jove's bolt dash me down to nether gloom—
The gloom that folds the kingdom of the Dead—
Ere modesty by me be put to shame!
My faith was given to him whom first I wed:
'Tis his: still let him keep it in the tomb."
So spake she, and the o'erflowing tear-drops shed.
    "Dearer than life," cried Anna, "sister mine,
Lonely through youth's fair season must thou pine,
Nor children know, nor the glad gifts of love?
Can this bring comfort to thy buried spouse?
What though no suitors thy sad heart could move,
Libyan, nor erst in Tyre? though scorn and slight
Thy pride flung on Iarbas, and the vows
Of Afric's conquering sons who sought thy hand?
Still 'gainst an happier marriage must thou fight?
Bethink thee what fierce tribes beset this land.
Here, the Gætulian cities hem thee round,
And lawless Numidæ, and Syrtes wild;
Yonder, the desert spreads its parching sand,
And rude Barcæi roam unreconciled:
From Tyre thou know'st full well war's surging sound,
And kinsman's enmities.
Kind were the gods, methinks, and Juno smiled,
When to our shores these Trojan vessels sped!
Sister, how great an empire shall arise
From such an union! Linked with yon allies,
How high our Punic pride shall lift its head!
Seek but the aid of heaven, due offerings make;
An hostess fond, contrive thy guest's delay,
While still the storm-clouds vex the watery way,
Nor yet his battered ships their course can take."
    These words her glowing heart to love incite,
Make bold her wavering will, subdue her shame.
First, in the sacred courts, heaven's grace they pray,
And victims choice before each altar slay,
While Ceres, Phœbus, Bacchus, they acclaim,

And Juno most, who rules o'er wedlock's rite.
There, from her chalice, Dido, fairest dame,
'Twixt horns of snow-white heifer pours the wine,
Or moving stately to each laden shrine
Her daily gifts renews, and gazes deep
Into the heaving breasts of slaughtered sheep.
Blind prophets! How can prayers or altars quell
That frenzy? Love's soft flame devours her heart,
And deeply throbs the pang invisible.
Poor Dido! Through her city, far and near,
She roams, as roams some arrow-stricken deer,
Pierced unaware, in distant Cretan dell,
By herdsman who hath sped the winged dart
Heedless; she, wounded, flies through wood and wold,
And still the deadly shaft is in her side.
Full oft the lovelorn queen her guest would guide
To view her new-planned walls, her Tyrian gold;
Then speak—but on her lips the speech hath died:
Oft calls anew for nightly festival,
Still craving for the tale of Ilium's fall,
And on his words still hangs unsatisfied.
Then, when they part, and the moon's radiance mild
Is quenched, and setting stars invite to rest,
Alone through lonely halls she wanders wild,
Or flings her on the couch he late hath pressed
(Absent, his absent form she hears, she sees),
Or still detains Ascanius the child,
Clasping the father's image to her breast,
If so her speechless passion she may ease.
Unbuilt, the while, her towers; untrained her band
Of warrior youths; nor ports nor ramparts rise;
But high impending walls neglected stand,
With engines idly reared toward the skies.
   Now when Jove's consort saw her grievous plight,
By love distraught, and reckless of fair fame,
To Venus thus did mighty Juno speak:
"Much honour, sure, ye win from this brave fight,

Thou and thy son, a great and glorious name,
Two gods, outwitting thus one woman weak!
Nor this escapes me: fear hath made thee hate
My Carthage, and distrust its friendly homes:
But think! what end shall be to such debate?
Shall we not rather seek, in fair accord,
A lasting peace by marriage of those twain?
Ev'n now thy dearest wish thou canst attain,
For Dido burns with love infuriate:
Come, let us rule one race with equal power,
And Dido, subject to a Trojan lord,
Bring thee her Tyrian people as a dower."
    But Venus—for she saw the masked desire
On Libyan coasts to plant the Italian throne—
Thus parleyed: "Who so mad as to disown
Thy friendship, or would choose to brave thine ire,
If fortune shall but crown thy wise design?
But fate is dark: I know not if the Sire
Vouchsafe to Trojan folk, to folk of Tyre,
One home, one common fortune to fulfil.
His spouse thou art, 'tis thou must learn his will.
Lead thou; I follow." "Be that labour mine,"
Said Juno: "Wherefore hark, and thou shalt know
How what we fain would compass can be done.
Their whim it is, when next the rising sun
Illumes the fair earth with its earliest sheen,
A-hunting in the greenwood glades to go,
The lord Æneas and the lovesick queen.
Then, while they scare the prey with feathery screen,
And through the woods the hunter's nets are wound,
My storm-cloud blackening o'er their heads shall break,
And thunder jar the startled firmament.
Their followers fled, with darkness curtained round,
Shall Dido and the chieftain refuge take
In the same cavern. There will I preside—
If thou be gracious still to mine intent—
And in sure wedlock stablish her his bride:

This be their marriage." Venus naught denied,
But saw the sleight, and smiling gave assent.
   Now o'er the ocean wave the Dawn appears;
Forth from the portals issue chosen bands,
Equipped with nets and toils and broad-barbed spears,
And swift Massylian horse, and deer-hound keen;
At palace-port the chiefs await their queen
Still tarrying; and her eager palfrey stands
Superbly trapped, champing the foam-flecked bit.
Soon with attendant train she comes in state,
Her mantle rich with gay embroidered fold;
Gold-quivered, she hath coiled her locks in gold;
With golden buckle is her red robe knit.
There joyful, with the Trojan troop, see ride
The boy Ascanius; there, o'er all elate,
Æneas leads his courtiers to her side.
So goes Apollo, when from Xanthus' tide,
And snowy Lycian plain, to Delos fair,
His own maternal isle, he doth repair,
The dance renewing; and around his shrines
Cretans and Dryopes, in mingled crowd,
And painted Agathyrsians murmur loud:
Himself the Cynthian height he treads, and twines
With sprays of foliage soft his flowing hair
In golden plaits, while on his shoulders proud
Rattle his arrows. So, with godlike air,
Went forth Æneas, with like grace endowed.
   A lofty range they reach, a pathless waste;
Here from the craggy crests the wild goats fly,
Scouring the slopes; there startled deer go by,
In dust-compelling herds, with headlong haste
Down-rushing where the wider vale invites.
Full well the young Ascanius delights
On fiery steed his comrades to outpace;
And oft, 'mid that poor prey, aspiringly,
A prayer he breathes some foaming boar to face,
Or ev'n a tawny lion from the heights.

But now the sky resounds with thunder's roar;
Then falls the gathering storm its rage to wreak:
Tyrians and Trojans, all are fled in fear,
And that Dardanian boy, to Venus dear;
None linger; down the hills the torrents pour.
Then Dido and the chief one cavern seek:
By Earth and Juno, nuptial queen, is given
The signal; flash strange lights i' the conscious heaven,
And wild the Nymphs from mountain summit shriek.
Of death and sorrow was that day the first;
Naught recked she, now, of good or evil fame;
Nor secret was the love that Dido nursed:
She sought her guilt to hide with wedlock's name.
    Straightway through Libya's realms doth Rumour spring—
Rumour, more swift a pest was never bred—
On speed it thrives, and waxes as it runs;
First small and cowed; then skyward towering
It spurns the soil and hides in clouds its head.
Our Earth, incensed against the Gods, 'tis said,
For Cœus and Enceladus her sons,
Brought forth this latest child, fleet-foot, fleet-winged,
Huge, monstrous, awesome; 'neath each plume outspread
A watchful eye there lurketh (strange to tell),
A tongue, a blatant mouth, a listening ear.
'Twixt heaven and earth it flies when night is near,
Loud-babbling, nor with sleep its toil relieves:
By day, on roof or spire perched sentinel,
Great towns with panic terrors can imbue;
Nor ever to the false and froward cleaves
Less fondly than to message of the true.
    So Rumour, many-voiced, filled all the land,
Eager to cry what was, and what was not;
How came Æneas, prince of Trojan race,
To whom fair Dido deigned to give her hand;
And how, the winter long, in dalliance base,
They cherished lawless love, their realms forgot.
Such tale that loathly goblin scattered wide,

Then to the court of king Iarbas hied,
And soon his jealous heart to fury fanned.
  In his far borders (Ammon was his sire;
A nymph his mother, whom the god had wooed)
For Jove an hundred spacious temples stood,
An hundred altars; there the sacred fire
Before the gods burned watchful, night and day;
Steeped was the soil in sacrificial blood,
The portals wreathed with many a garland gay.
He, when that bitter news inflamed his ire,
Standing distraught within the holy place,
Thus cried to Jove with suppliant hands outspread:
"Almighty sire, to whom our Libyan race
At banquet-table pours the meed of wine,
Seest thou these things? Or dost thou hurl for nought
Thy lightnings? Are those dreaded bolts of thine
Blind fires, thy thunder but an empty din?
This woman, wandering to our coast, who bought
A scanty tract, and built her town therein,
To whom we ceded shoreland for the plough,
And royal rights, hath spurned us in disdain
And lord Æneas o'er her kingdom set:
And he, this Paris with effeminate train,
His turbaned hair with Phrygian unguents wet,
This thief hath won her. We—behold it, thou!—
Make sacrifice, and worship thee in vain."
  As thus he clasped the Almighty's shrine and prayed,
Jove heard, and turned his eyes where tarried still
Those lovers, heedless of their fair renown;
Then this behest on Mercury he laid:
"Go, son, bid Zephyrs waft thee on thy wing,
Where loiters Trojan chief in Tyrian town,
Nor cares his destined greatness to fulfil:
Him seek, and swiftly bear my mandate down.
Not such did Venus picture him, her son,
Whom twice she rescued from Greek foeman's hate,
But born to rule Italia big with fate

And rent with wars—yea, destined to transmit
Old Teucer's line till all the world were won!
If this great glory warm his heart no whit,
Nor aught for his high calling will he dare,
Shall he begrudge Ascanius, his heir,
The lordship of the citadel of Rome?
Why lingers he 'mid foes? What hopes he there,
Forgetful of the Italian race to come
And rich Lavinian fields beyond the foam?
Let him set sail. Enough! This message bear."

This said, the god bestirs him to obey
The mighty Father's bidding. To his feet
He girds, for golden wings, those sandals fleet
That bear him high aloft o'er ocean spray,
High o'er the land, companioning the gale;
Then takes that wand wherewith he summoneth
From Hades' house the crowd of spectres pale,
Or drives them down to dreary Tartarus;
Sleep gives, withholds; and opes men's eyes in death:
Such power it has, he rides the whirlwind's breath,
Nor fears athwart the rolling rack to sail.

And now the crest and craggy slopes he sees
Of Atlas, whose strong cliffs the heaven sustain;
Old Atlas, oft his piney head is crowned
With vapours dark, or lashed with gusty rain;
Snows drape his shoulders; down his cheeks amain
Rush torrents; on his beard the glaciers freeze.
Here first Jove's wingéd herald trod the ground,
Poised on light pinions; then adown the breeze
He dived, as fish-hawk, rocky shores around,
Skims low anigh the surface of the deep:
Ev'n so, from where his grandsire Atlas stood,
He clove the air in flight, 'twixt sky and flood,
And down to Libya's sandy coast did sweep.

There, lighting by the hamlet, soon he spied
The chief, intent on forts and walls new-planned;
Studded with yellow jasper was his blade;

And from his arm, in Tyrian purple dyed,
There hung, rich gift, a cloak by Dido made—
Its fine gold threads inwoven by her hand.
Straight spake he, chiding: "Dost thou linger here,
To found the towers of Carthage and uprear
A beauteous city, slave to woman's whim,
Ah, shame, forgetful of thy destined crown?
From bright Olympus am I sent, by Him,
The Lord, whose bidding all creation sways;
From Him in speed I bear this mandate down.
What dost thou here? What hope thy voyage delays?
If thou no whit art moved for glory's sake,
Nor aught for thine high calling wilt thou dare,
Yet of the young Ascanius, thine heir,
Bethink thee, since to him by fate is due
That Roman kingdom." Thus Jove's herald spake;
Then, ev'n in speaking, lost to mortal view,
He vanished, fading ghostlike in thin air.

Speechless, aghast, the chief that vision saw;
Bristles his hair with dread; his accents fail;
Fain would he fly, fain quit that cherished scene,
So stern the warning fell, so fraught with awe.
What shall he do? How bring the infatuate queen
Those tidings? How make preface to such tale?
This way and that he turned his subtle mind,
Gave heed to many a project, pondering all,
Ere to this wiser counsel he inclined:
That Mnestheus and Sergestus he should call,
And brave Serestus—bid them quick prepare
Their ships, their comrades summon, nor declare
Wherefore that secret deed their chief designed;
Himself, since Dido wist not of his will,
Nor severance of their dear love could forebode,
Would wait, the while, for some occasion fair
To speak, or haply find more gracious mode
His purpose to pursue. They, made aware
Of such commands, gladly their part fulfil.

But she—for what can 'scape a lover's eye—
Foresaw his wiles, divined his purposed flight;
That calm distrusting. Then rushed Rumour in;
The self-same pest, her madness to incite,
With tale of vessels manned, of parting nigh.
Helpless, she roamed the town distractedly,
Like some bewildered Thyiad, when with din
Of Bacchus' name at midnight echoing wide,
Cithæron calls, and frantic rites begin.
Thus crazed, his words she waited not, but cried:
    "And didst thou hope, dissembling this foul wrong,
Traitor, to steal in silence from my land,
Unhindered by our love, by plighted hand,
By thought of Dido left to lonely death?
Ev'n wouldst thou sail when stormy winds blow strong
On waters chilled by winter's icy breath?
Cruel; for if no new home were thy plea,
And thy familiar Troy were left thee still,
Not Troy itself would lure thee o'er such sea.
Me dost thou fly? Nay, by these flowing tears—
Thy troth (since now, alas, naught else is mine)—
Our nuptials past, our wedlock that should be—
If aught my love has given thee that endears,
If thou dost owe me aught of solacement—
Pity my failing fortunes, and relent,
If prayers still move thee, from that harsh design!
For thee each Libyan tribe, each Nomad king,
Hates me; my Tyrians are estranged; for thee
Have I betrayed that cherished modesty,
Whereby alone my fame could heavenward spring.
To whom, thus dying, wilt thou leave me, Guest—
Thou who by husband's name wert once addressed?
Why wait I? Till my brother's hatred bring
His armies for my city's ruining,
Or fierce Iarbas take me for his thrall?
I would that ere thy flight I had conceived
A child of thee—that sporting in mine hall

A young Æneas might thy face recall;
Ev'n thus I were less utterly bereaved."
   But he, of Jove forewarned, with sad, fixed eyes,
And stifling the remorse within his breast,
Made answer brief: "How great to thee my debt,
Wert thou to name thy countless services,
By me, fair queen, stands evermore confessed.
Never Elissa's name shall I forget,
While memory lasts, while life still stirs this frame.
Few words I speak. Think not my hopes were set
On stealthy flight; with no false suitor's face,
Or covenant of marriage, here I came.
My foremost thought, had fate vouchsafed me grace
Henceforth my life to order as I willed,
And freedom this grief-laden heart to cheer,
Had been for Troy—to save that remnant dear,
My kinsmen, and with duteous hand rebuild
Great Priam's stronghold for our vanquished race.
But now to far Italia am I led,
Such was the Lycian oracle's command:
Italia—there my love is fixed, there lies
My country. If for thee, Phœnician-bred,
Thy Libyan Carthage hath such tender ties,
Grudge not the Trojans their Hesperian land:
We, too, seek foreign realms, nor less our right.
To me, in dreams, oft as the dewy night
Shadows the earth, and fiery stars arise,
My sire's sad ghost speaks warnings that affright;
In dreams the child I wrong, yet fondly love,
Points to his lands withheld, his promised crown.
Now, too, Jove's trusted herald from above
(Be witness, either god, to this true word!)
Hath swiftly borne the mighty mandate down.
Myself his form I saw in daylight plain,
Within these walls; myself his voice I heard.
Cease, then, to vex our hearts with outcry vain.
Full loth I quit thy shore."

Long, as he spoke, she watched him from aside
With roving eyes, and scanned him o'er and o'er
In silent scorn; then flushed with anger cried:
"Deceiver! thee no goddess-mother bore,
No hero, thou, of Troy's true lineage bred!
Of flinty Caucasus wert thou begot,
And at the dugs of savage tigers fed.
Why should I mask my wrath? Why worse await?
Sighed he in sorrow for his lover's lot?
Or flinched, or shed one tear compassionate?
All, all alike are false. Ev'n heaven's great king,
Ev'n Juno, views me not with candid eyes:
Nor faith, nor hope is left me. Outcast, lone,
Madly I made him partner of my throne,
His scattered ships, his comrades, succouring.
What fury goads me? Now grim auguries
Of Phœbus threaten; now from ruthless skies
Jove's herald must the cruel mandate bring.
Forsooth such tasks the immortal gods engage,
Ruffling their blissful calm! But thou—begone!
I keep thee not; no wordy war I wage.
Go, seek through winds and waves thine Italy!
Yet this, if righteous gods have power, I pray;
To the last dregs thy guilt shalt thou atone,
Wrecked on avenging rocks, and ofttimes cry
Vainly on Dido's name. I, far away,
With funeral fires thy presence will pursue;
And when these limbs are loosened from life's breath,
My ghost shall haunt thee. Yea, this deed thou'lt rue;
And I shall know it in the dark of death."

Abruptly thus she ceased; in sick disdain
From sunshine turned, nor tarried in his sight,
Leaving him awe-struck, hesitant, yet fain
To speak. Her swooning form her maids sustain,
Then within marble chamber lay her light.

Much though Æneas longed, in gentle speech,
To find some solace for her grievous cares—

And sighed, for love had strength to shake his heart—
Yet to his fleet, as heaven ordained, he fares.
Then stoutly toil his Trojans; from the beach
The tarry keels are launched and ride the brine:
Rough logs and leafy boughs must furnish oar;
Such haste is to depart;
Still from the gates they stream in lengthening line.
Ev'n so, when prudent ants, for winter store,
Their nests refill from heap of plundered grain,
Continuous through the fields a sable train
By narrow grassy track the spoil conveys;
Some, heaving weighty burdens, march and moil,
Some rally them that lag, or chide delays;
Till all the path is glowing with their toil.
   What thoughts were Dido's, when, from high watchtower,
With many a groan forth-gazing, she descried
The shore in busy tumult surging wide,
And din of voices from the sea upswelled!
Ah, Love, what human heart can brave thy power?
Again to tears, again to prayers compelled,
Her passion makes surrender of her pride,
Lest aught, before she die, be left untried.
   "Anna, thou seest that concourse by the shore
Far mustering: now the canvas craves the wind,
And garlands on the sterns glad sailors bind.
This anguish I had strength to see before,
And strength shall find to bear it. Yet do thou
One crowning boon to thy sad sister grant!
Since none that wretch revered but thee alone—
To thee his inmost counsels would avow,
His gentler moods, his better self, make known—
To this proud foe be thou my suppliant!
No share had I with Greeks in that fierce oath
At Aulis sworn, to wreck the Trojan race;
No ships of war to Ilium's coast I sent,
Nor from the tomb his father's ashes rent:
Why, then, to hear my pleadings is he loth?

Why hastes he? I but crave this one last grace:
Let him await fair breezes that shall aid
His onward course. No more am I intent
On marriage, since that pledge he hath betrayed,
Nor that his cherished realms he should forgo:
Mere time I ask—a respite for love's pain—
Till, chastened, I shall learn to bear my woe.
Thou, of thy pity, this last favour gain:
Dying, I shall repay thee all I owe."

Such prayers her sister bore, such tale of tears,
Again and yet again; but he, unstirred,
Implacable, nor tears nor pleadings heard;
Fate bound him, and to pity closed his ears:
As when some massive oak, made strong by years
Which Alpine winds, in ever-shifting blast,
Strive to o'erthrow—the while with straining sound
Trembles its trunk, and scattered leaves fall fast—
Still grips the rock, and high its head uprears,
And thrusts as deep its roots beneath the ground:
Ev'n so their windy words the chief assail,
Ceaseless; his soul with sorrow is o'ercast;
Unmoved his will, nor aught their sighs prevail.
    Then Dido, scared by Fate's unkindness, prays
For death: she loathes the sunny vault of sky;
And quickened is her dark resolve to die;
For when on incense-burning shrine she lays
Her gifts, death-black the holy waters grow,
And wine transformed to blood her gaze appals,
Which sight not ev'n her sister's self may know:
Ay, and from marble shrine within her walls,
Deep-reverenced in remembrance of her spouse,
And decked with snowy fleece and festal boughs,
Are voices heard, as her dead husband calls
And claims her, 'neath sad midnight's canopy;
Oft on her roof the solitary owl
Chants dirge of death with long-drawn wailing cry:

And many an old terrific prophecy
Sore startles her. Himself, with angry scowl,
Æneas haunts her dreams; oft must she stray
Forsaken; oft, companionless and lost,
She seems to pace some never-ending way,
And seek her Tyrian folk on desert coast.
So Pentheus, frenzied, sees a growing host
Of Furies, two-fold Thebes, two suns o'erhead;
So, in the tragic scene, Orestes quakes,
Pursued by wraith of her whose blood he shed,
His mother, girt with fire and baneful snakes;
And on the threshold sit the Avengers dread.
　　Then frantic grew her heart, by grief possessed:
Die must she, yet betrayed not when nor how,
As thus her weeping sister she addressed,
Veiling dark purpose 'neath unruffled brow:
　　"Sister—share thou this joy—a way is found
Which shall restore my love, or liberty.
Yonder where sinks the sun, near ocean's bound,
Stretches the far, strange Æthiopian land,
Where Atlas on his shoulders wheels the sky
Studded with burning constellations bright.
Thence came an Afric priestess to my sight,
Who watched the temple of the Hesperides;
And fed the dreaded dragon, so to keep
Safe guard o'er golden fruit on sacred trees,
Sprinkling sweet honey-dew and poppied sleep.
She by her spells one soul in joy can steep;
On others, toil and tribulation send;
Can stay swift streams, or turn the stars aside;
Ay, she can raise the dead at midnight lone,
And 'neath thy feet the quaking earth shall moan,
And mountain-ash its native slope descend.
Full loth I am in witchcraft to confide:
This by the gods I swear, and thy sweet love;
Yet midst our inner court I pray thee spread
A secret funeral-pyre, and range above

Those arms the traitor hung within mine hall,
His garments, and that luckless bridal-bed
Which saw my ruin: so shall perish aught
That his most impious crime might e'er recall:
Thus hath the priestess warned, this cleansing taught."
She spake; then stood in silence, pale and still.
    But Anna, guessing not what mortal ill
'Neath that strange mask of magic she could hide—
What frantic purpose in her mind embrace—
Nor dreading worse than when Sychæus died,
Bowed to her sister's will.
Soon, in that inmost courtyard's roofless space,
A pyre, piled high with faggots and sawn pines,
The queen o'erstrews with garlands, and entwines
With sad sepulchral boughs; then lays, o'er all,
Her bridal-bed, his robes, his imaged face,
The sword he left—nor doubts what shall befall.
Around are altars raised, whereat the seer,
Dishevelled, thrice with ringing voice appeals
To Hades' hundred gods—bids Chaos hear,
And Erebus, and dreaded Hecate;
The virgin Artemis, whose forms are three.
Then waters, fabled from Avernus' stream,
She sprinkles; and bespeaks, for magic use,
Gross herbs, exuding black envenomed juice,
Reaped with brass sickle 'neath the pale moonbeam,
And love-charm torn from brow of colt new-foaled.
Herself, fair Dido, by the sacred shrine—
One foot unsandalled, loose her vesture's fold—
In her pure hand the holy cake must hold,
Then call the gods to witness, ere she die,
And stars that wot of human destiny,
And most, if such there be, those Powers benign
That keep ill-mated lovers in their care,
Faithful and just—to them she makes her prayer.
    'Twas night. Earth's weary creatures, far and wide,
Slumbered; wild woods and waters lay unstirred;

At that still hour when stars serenely glide
In their mid course; when all the land hath rest;
And flocks are hush'd, and every bright-winged bird,
Haunting the limpid lake, the bosky plain,
Is lulled to sleep beneath the silent spell;
And suffering hearts have respite of their pain.
But not sad Dido. Ne'er can slumber blest
Soothe her, nor night's soft balm on eyes and breast
Fall welcome; still love's bitter pang renewed
Torments her, tossed on passion's stormy swell;
Still ceaseless o'er her sorrows must she brood:
　"What way is left me? Shall I seek, forlorn,
My former lovers—beg from Nomads rude
An husband, where so oft I flung my scorn?
Or follow these proud Trojans to the last,
Submissive; since, forsooth, for favours past
They cherish yet such gentle gratitude!
Ev'n if I would, methinks my hated face
Scant welcome on their haughty ships would meet.
Ah, simple Dido! Wilt thou never know
What treachery lurks within that perjured race?
How then? With those glad sailors shall I go,
Alone? Or chase them with my Tyrian fleet?
Bid folk, who scarce from Tyre obeyed my call,
Turn seaward now, and hoist their sails anew?—
Nay, die, as thou deserv'st: the sword ends all.
Sister, 'twas thou my courage didst undo,
When yielding to the tears my madness shed,
Thou laid'st me open to mine enemy!
Shame, that I might not live my life unwed,
Like some wild guiltless thing, from sorrow free!
Now to my buried spouse I die not true."
Such sighs in anguish from her bosom broke.
He on his lofty ship brief slumber wooed—
His sailing fixed, all planned in order due—
When lo, in sleep, the god's same presence stood
Before him, and the same stern warning spoke:

'Twas Mercury's self; his voice, his features fair,
His comely youthful form, his golden hair.
  "Rise, goddess-born! Canst slumber at such hour?
Art blind to perils dread that o'er thee lower?
Mad, that thou hearest not the prosperous wind?
She, sworn to die, hath mischief in her mind
And murderous thoughts on tide of passion tossed.
Fly hence in haste, while flight be in thy power.
Soon shalt thou see her prows the waters part,
And angry torches blaze along the shore,
If dawn shall find thee loitering on this coast.
Rise, then, nor brook delay; for woman's heart
Fickle it is, and changeful evermore."
He spake, and in the gloom of night was lost.
  Quick, by that sudden apparition scared,
Æneas starts from sleep, and hails his crew:
"Awake, and rouse ye, mates! Let oars be bared,
Sails spread! Again, sent down to mortal view,
The god commands us to unmoor apace,
And in swift flight our seaward course pursue.
Behold, we follow thee, thou form divine,
Whoe'er thou art, and glad thy bidding do!
O, be thou nigh, and help us, of thy grace,
And grant the stars in heaven may friendly shine!"
So saying, he plucked his falchion from its sheath
With lightning swiftness, and the cable clove:
One impulse urged them all; they strained and strove.
The shore recedes; hid are the waves beneath,
As with swift strokes they lash the sea to spray.
  Soon, with the first beam of the dawning day,
Aurora from her saffron couch did spring.
But when, 'neath whitening heavens, the queen espied
The ships with square-set sails fast voyaging,
The beach deserted, and the port left bare,
Thrice, and again, she tore her amber hair,
And beat her bosom, as in wrath she cried:
"'Fore God, shall he sail scatheless, and deride

Our realm that gave him refuge? Are ye slow
To make pursuit with all our arméd force?
Doubt ye to launch our swiftest vessels? Go,
With fire and sword! Spread sails, and stoutly row!—
Words, words! Where am I? By what madness plied?
Ah, Dido! now too late thou know'st remorse,
More fitting when thou yieldedst him thy throne!
Behold his plighted troth! A saint, men say,
Who o'er the main his household gods could bring,
And bore his age-worn father from the fray!
Had I not power to rend his body, and fling
In fragments o'er the waves? his mates to slay?
Ev'n 'gainst Ascanius might have raged mine ire,
And served his dead limbs when his father dined.
The chance of war were doubtful? Be it so!
Dying, need I have feared his camp to fire,
To burn his decks, extirpate son with sire,
And on that flaming mass myself to throw?
O Sun, that seest the deeds of all mankind!
Thou, Juno, judge and witness of my woe!
Dread Hecate, with midnight moans adored!
Ye vengeful Furies, and ye deities
That watch o'er lost Elissa as she dies!
Give heed to these dark wrongs, and hear my word!
If he must reach that refuge of his race,
Curst renegade, and bring his ships to shore—
If such the will of Jove, the end decreed—
Yet grant that smitten by the foeman's sword,
An exile, severed from his child's embrace,
He may go forth strange succour to implore,
And, humbled, see his hapless kinsmen bleed!
On him may ignominious peace be thrust!
Him may no joys of kingly life await,
But death untimely, and for final fate,
To lie unburied in the desert dust!
This parting curse with life's last blood I pour.
But ye, my Tyrians, turn your bitterest hate

'Gainst his detested tribe for evermore;
Be this fierce feud your offering at my tomb!
In love or peace ne'er may these nations blend;
But from my blood may some Avenger spring
Red ruin on the seed of Troy to bring,
Now, or whene'er the power to smite shall be!
Let shore to shore stand adverse, sea to sea,
And race to race—fulfilling thus their doom,
They and their children's children—to the end."

   She spake, and pondered in her anguish lone,
How soonest life's loathed bondage she could break;
Then thus to aged Barcé briefly spake,
Nurse of her lord Sychæus, for her own
Long since in native land was slumbering:
"Hither, dear nurse, my sister Anna bring;
Go, bid her haste, with lustral water sprayed,
And fetch those offerings that for sins atone;
Thou, too, thy brows with pious chaplets bind.
For now to Stygian Jove these rites delayed
I would fulfil, that so my task be done,
And the false Trojan's pyre to flames consigned."
She spake, and on her errand sped the crone.

   But Dido, shuddering at the deed she dared,
With bloodshot rolling eyes, wan cheeks that glowed
With fevered spots, and in death's presence pale,
Burst through the inner doors, nor feared to scale
The lofty pyre, then, wild, his falchion bared,
(Not for such usage was that gift bestowed!)
And gazing long on that familiar bed,
Those Trojan robes, while soft the tear-drops fell,
She paused, and on the pillow laid her head,
Ere yet she sadly spake the last farewell:

   "Relics I loved, while still approved of heaven,
Receive my soul, and quit me of this woe!
I have fulfilled the life by fortune given,
And queenly to the phantom world I go.
For I have seen the city that I planned

Rise glorious; fulness of revenge I know
For husband slain by faithless brother's steel;
Happy, ah, more than happy, had my land
Ne'er felt the treacherous touch of Trojan keel!"
The couch she kissed: "Though unavenged I die,
Yet die I will; thus, thus I yield my breath:
Soon may that wretch my funeral flames espy,
And take, for omen on his way, my death!"
   Thus crying, the sword to her own heart she set.
But when her scared attendants saw her fall,
Saw reeking blade, and hands with blood-drops wet,
Aghast the cry arose in lofty hall,
And Rumour wild went raging through the crowd.
With sobs, and sighs, and women's wailing loud,
The palace shook, and heaven the tale retold.
It seemed some conquering host, in ruthless war,
Great Carthage sacked, or ancient Tyre; and far
O'er roofs of men and gods the fierce flames rolled.
   All faint with fear, that cry the sister heard,
And rushed with tremulous steps, beating her breast,
And thus aloud the dying queen addressed:
"Sister, was this thy purpose? False thy word?
This did that pyre, that altar-flame portend?
What plaint can tell my loneliness? Wast loth,
Dying, to see thy sister at thy side?
Would thou hadst summoned me to share thine end:
One sword, one pang, one parting hour for both!
With mine own hands thy pyre I built, and cried
Loud on ancestral gods their aid to lend,
Yet failed thee in thine anguish at the last!
Sister, thou hast destroyed thyself, and me,
Thy town, thy Tyrians all. Bring water, ye!
That I may wash her wounds, and ere she die
May catch, perchance, her life-breath fleeting fast."
   As thus she spake, the lofty steps she passed,
And that pale form in fond embraces bound,
And groaned, and with her garments stanched the gore.

She, fain to lift her heavy lids once more,
Fell back, the blood-stream bubbling from her wound:
Thrice, on her elbow stayed, she strove to rise:
Thrice, sinking on her couch, with wandering eyes
Heaven's light she sought, and sighed when it was found.
  Then Juno, pitying her slow decease
And pain prolonged, sent Iris from above,
Her struggling breath from bondage to release;
For since she perished, ere her day was due,
In ruin undeserved and frenzy of love,
Not yet had Proserpine from her fair head
Severed the lock and doomed her to the dead.
So Iris, dewy-bright on saffron wing,
Trailing her rainbow robe of changeful hue,
Glides down, and o'er her stands: "To Hades' king
This sacred tress, by high command, I bear:
And thus thine earth-bound soul I liberate."
She cut the lock; then sank life's fire; and straight
The troubled spirit passed in empty air.

BOOK V

ARGUMENT

THE Trojans, having left Carthage, are driven by a storm to Sicily, and again take shelter at Drepanum, where, in the friendly kingdom of Acestes, Æneas celebrates the anniversary of his father's death by instituting games—boat-race, foot-race, boxing-match, archery, and an exhibition of horsemanship by the Trojan boys. Meanwhile the women, weary of their long voyaging, set fire to the ships, four of which are destroyed. Warned by Anchises in a dream, Æneas decides to take with him to Italy only the strongest of his followers, and to leave behind in Sicily the women and the weak. He is granted a fair passage by Neptune, but loses his pilot, Palinurus, on the way.

And now Æneas clove the watery ways
Through billows darkened with the North's keen breath,
His purpose firm, yet backward turned his gaze
To walls illumed by hapless Dido's pyre.
What cause had lit those soaring flames of death
They knew not; but the bitter grief that sways
A wounded heart when ties of love are rent—
The strength of woman desperate in her ire—
This filled their minds with dark presentiment.
    The deep they gained, where land was none to view;
Around, above, lay naught but seas and skies:
Then high o'erhead the gathering rain-squall flew,
In lurid storm, and 'neath that sombre shroud
The waves were ruffled in the growing gloom.
Ev'n Palinurus, dauntless pilot, cries:
"Alas, what vapours dense the welkin cloud!
Say, father Neptune, what portends such gale?"
Then bade he trim the rigging, and make room
To ply the oar; and as, with slanting sail,
They tacked and veered, his lord he thus addressed:
    "Great-hearted chief, not ev'n at Jove's behest
Such passage at such season would I dare!

Changed is the wind, and sprung from murky West
Blows hard athwart us through the rayless air.
No strength we have such boisterous foe to face;
Wherefore to Chance, our mistress, let us bow,
And follow where she calls; nor far, I trow,
Stands friendly Eryx o'er his harbour fair,
If rightly ways remembered I retrace."
  Then spake Æneas: "Yea, long time I see
How tyrant winds thy baffled efforts scorn.
Change, then, our course. Can shore more welcome be,
Or where our battered keels may fitlier rest,
Than that which holds Acestes, Trojan-born,
And clasps my father's ashes in its breast?"
So port they seek; and soon their sails are fanned
By prosperous breeze, as o'er each billowy crest
They ride in joy to that familiar strand.
  Meanwhile Acestes, as they hove anear,
Had watched in wonder from a lofty mount;
And soon he met them, armed with huntsman's spear,
And in rough Libyan bearskin rudely clad.
Of Trojan mother born, for sire he had
The god that watches o'er Crimisus' fount:
Nor heedless was he of his Dardan birth,
But welcomed their return, and made them glad,
With wealth of rustic hospitality
In friendly solace for their toils gone by.
  Soon as the dawn has put the stars to flight,
Æneas bids his trusty folk draw near,
And proclamation makes from rampart's height:
  "Brave Trojans, sprung from heaven-descended line!
Well-nigh complete is the revolving year,
In all its months, since to the grave were borne
The last remains of my dead father dear,
Bewept at many a consecrated shrine.
Soon comes the day that I must ever mourn—
Since thus the gods have willed that it should be—
In bitter grief, yet ever must revere.

Yea, should I spend it as an exile lone
'Mid far Gætulian quicksands, or at sea
In Grecian waters, or unwary thrown
Ev'n by Mycenæ's walls, those duties still
With sad funereal pomps would I fulfil,
And with due gifts the solemn altars heap.
Now hath chance led us to this tomb once more—
Yet not, methinks, without some heavenly will—
Where rest my father's bones by friendly shore.
Come, then! that day in honour let us keep;
And seek fair winds, that so, our city gained,
These annual rites be evermore ordained
In temples where his memory shall abide.
But hark ye this! Our host, true son of Troy,
Sends for each ship two steers, a generous gift;
Call ye your gods to share this festal joy,
And be Sicilia's gods with ours allied.
Next, when, to bless mankind with light anew,
The ninth day dawns and flings her radiance wide,
I will appoint you games—ye shall contend
In lusty boat-race first, crew matched 'gainst crew;
Then let the fleet of foot, the champions keen
Most skilled the spear to hurl, the bow to bend,
Or with rude glove untanned to dare the fight,
Claim each his meed as each hath victor been.
Fair silence now, and wreathe your brows aright!"
    He spake, and decked his temples, in their sight,
With garland of his mother's myrtle bound;
So Helymus, so grave Acestes crowned,
So young Ascanius with his fellows stood.
Then, with great concourse thronging him around,
He passed to where Anchises lay at rest;
And goblets twain of wine he poured on ground,
With twain of milk, and twain of sacred blood,
And scattering purple flowers his sire addressed:
    "Hail, thou! Again I greet thee, parent blest!
Hail, ashes, rescued once, yet rescued not!

Since fate forbids thy son to seek, with thee,
Those realms Italian that the fates allot,
And Tiber, wheresoe'er his waters be."
  Scarce had he spoke, when from the altar's base,
With sevenfold coil immense, a snake uprose,
And gently clasped the tomb in lithe embrace.
Along his back with blue and golden sheen
The bright scales glimmered, as a rainbow throws
Its countless shifting hues across the sky.
Amazed Æneas stood; then, sinuously,
Gliding the bowls and polished cups between,
The serpent sipped the cates, and slid unseen
Back from the shrine innocuous to his lair.
Thereat the more his ceremonial rite
The chief renewed, yet guessed not if it were
The genius of the place, or friendly sprite
Attendant on his sire; then victims twain,
Ewe-sheep, and swarthy steers, and bristling swine,
He slew, and from the chalice poured the wine,
And called aloud upon Anchises' ghost,
Released awhile from Acheron's domain.
So bring they all, as each the means can boast,
Fair gifts to load the shrines, or oxen slay;
Some range the brazen caldrons on the plain,
Or, stretched in groups along the greensward, lay
Hot embers 'neath the spits, the flesh to roast.
  Now was the ninth day nearer, and the Dawn
Rose calm and fair, by Phœbus' coursers drawn:
Allured by rumour and Acestes' fame,
To watch, or some perchance to join the fray,
The neighbouring folk in glad assembly came.
There were the prizes spread in all men's sight;
Steel armour, sacred tripods, garlands gay;
And palms, that noblest meed by victor won;
Talents of gold, of silver; rich array
Of vestments purple-dyed. From central height
The trumpet's blare announced the games begun.

First court the combat, by strong oarsmen manned,
Four ships, well-matched, select from all the fleet:
Bold Mnestheus' mariners the Dolphin sail;
Mnestheus, whom soon Italian shores shall greet,
And house of Memmius as its founder hail:
O'er huge Chimæra's bulk Gyas presides;
Vast as a city, deck o'er deck she soars,
Propelled by triple bank of Trojan oars;
Sergestus, whence the Sergian line began,
Rules o'er the Centaur; on green Scylla rides
Cloanthus, parent of Cluentian clan.

Fronting the foamy shore an islet lies,
Oft by the scourge of swollen waves o'errun,
When northern blasts have veiled the starry skies;
In calm, it lifts o'er tranquil tides a shoal
Beloved of seafowl basking in the sun:
Thereon was fixed a leafy bough, for goal
And guide to sailors, thence their prows to turn,
And homeward on their circling course to bear.
Now drawn are lots for station: high astern,
In gorgeous guise the captains pace apart;
Plain poplar wreaths the stalwart oarsmen wear;
On bared anointed arms the sunlight plays:
So, seated all, they wait the sign to start,
With hands outstretched: quick beats the panting heart
With breathless zeal and eager lust of praise.

Clear pealed the trump; and, instant, forth they broke,
While seamen's clamour smote the firmament:
Churned were the waves to foam 'neath sturdy stroke;
Each keel a furrow clove; the watery waste
In yawning gaps by blade and beak was rent.
Not swiftest chariots make such headlong haste,
When in mid course they race across the plains,
And eager drivers shake the wavy reins,
Or bend above their steeds to ply the lash.
Then, as men roared applause, their friends to cheer,
Answered the grove and hollow shore around,

And loud the echoing hills rolled back the sound.
First Gyas darts ahead, with sudden dash,
'Mid shouts and cries; Cloanthus follows near,
With oars more skilled, but hampered in his speed
By weight of timber; next, at equal space,
Dolphin and Centaur strive for prior place:
Now Dolphin, now huge Centaur hath the lead;
Now level is the contest, prow by prow,
As with long keels the briny waves they plough.
    And now the rock was nigh, the goal at hand;
When Gyas, victor still, his race half sped,
Menœtes, timorous pilot, thus upbraids:
"To left! Why thus to starboard swerve we wide?
Steer left; and let the oar-blades graze the strand:
The deep let others sail." But he, in dread
Of hidden shoals, still circled seaward far.
Again: "Stay; swerve not; skirt the rocks!" he cried;
Then, backward glancing, saw Cloanthus fast
O'erhaul him, as the shorter course he kept:
But he, 'twixt rival boat and seething bar,
Turned leftward, and on inner passage swept,
Clear through to foremost place, the beacon past,
And safe o'er tranquil waters homeward turned.
Then deep in Gyas' heart resentment burned;
Wet was his cheek with tears: forgetful he
Of comrades' safety, of his own renown,
From lofty steerage flung Menœtes down,
And cast him, sluggard, headlong to the sea:
Himself, the tiller seizing, cheered his mates,
Pilot and captain both, and shoreward made.
But when Menœtes slow to surface rose,
Nor young he was, in dripping garb down-weighed,
Striving to scale the rock and there recline,
Loud laughed his fellow Trojans at his woes;
Sank he, or swam he, naught their laughter stayed;
Naught, when he sputtered forth the bitter brine.
    Thereat those hindmost twain with hope were blest

The balked and faltering Gyas to outstrip.
Now, as they neared the rock, Sergestus led,
Yet, leading, led not by full length of ship,
But part; the Dolphin's prow o'erlapped the rest;
Then Mnestheus in his crew new courage bred,
Passing from man to man: "Now, now, I pray,
Rise stalwart to the stroke; now prove your worth,
Great Hector's henchmen once; since Troy's dark day
My chosen comrades! That grand strength put forth,
That dauntless spirit, which did never tire
'Mid Afric sands, or where, in dense array,
By Malea's cape, Ionian billows roll!
No more to victory's meed do I aspire—
Ah, if I might! but done be Neptune's will!—
To lag the last, 'tis this that shames my soul.
Come, sirs, defeat this worst, most grievous ill,
Nor brook not such disgrace!" Then they, the more,
Bend zealous to their task, with heart firm set:
Quivers the boat beneath the straining oar,
The sea reels past, as still they struggle sore,
Panting and parched, and copious flows the sweat.
   'Twas chance that proffered them the prize they sought:
For, fain to pass where space would scarce allow,
As in wild haste Sergestus steered within;
On jutting reef, his luckless keel was caught.
Loud rang the shock, as on the sharp-edged shoal
The oar-blades smote, and shattered hung the prow.
Up leapt the baffled crew with clamorous din,
And many a boat-hook plied and pointed pole,
The floating wreckage from the waves to win.
But Mnestheus, gladdened now, since fate was kind,
With rapid strokes, and aid of friendly wind,
Down open seas on shoreward current rode.
As when a rock-dove, scared from her abode
On crannied ledge, where her loved nestlings lie,
Speeds forth with noise of startled flutterings,
Then, gliding peaceful through the liquid sky,

Sails on, with scarce a tremor of her wings:
So sailed the Dolphin toward her journey's bound,
Borne by the strong momentum of her flight;
And first Sergestus' ship she distanced quite,
Battling with broken oars in shallow sound,
Where help was none to mend such grievous plight;
Next was Chimæra's mighty bulk o'erhauled,
And vanquished soon, of pilot's skill bereft.
And now Cloanthus, and none else, was left;
Him Mnestheus followed close, with utmost might,
While loud, and yet more loud, men's clamour grew,
As shouting comrades cheered them to the chase.
So strive they—those, the still unconquered crew,
Disdaining aught below the foremost place,
And bartering life for glory; these, success
Hath lent new courage: what they dare they do.
And so, perchance, might both have victors been,
With level prows; but in that crowning stress
Cloanthus o'er the waves did suppliant lean,
And prayed aloud, and called on heaven to bless:
    "Gods of the sea, o'er whose domain I race,
If now my prayers ye heed, on yonder shore,
Before your shrines for victim will I place
A snow-white bull, and wine in plenty pour."
He spake; and deep below the ocean floor
The Nereids all gave ear unto his word;
Fair Panopea, and old Phorcus heard;
And sire Portunus with a god's strong hand
Pushed Scylla to the fore—so sped she on,
More swift than wind or arrow, to the strand,
And there to haven came, her voyage done.
    Forthwith the chief, when all his folk were met,
Proclaimed Cloanthus by the herald's voice
Victor, and wreathed with laurel green his brow;
Then, crew by crew, rich prizes for their choice—
Oxen, and wines, and solid silver set:
Nor lacked the captains recompense enow:

A cloak of gold the proud Cloanthus won,
Round which was broidered deep, in double line,
A glowing fringe of purple, serpentine,
With wondrous picture, deftly worked thereon,
Of Ganymede, in Ida's leafy dale,
Chasing the stag with foot and javelin fleet,
Keen, panting, life-like; him with taloned feet
The mighty bird of Jove did heavenward hale,
The while his agéd guards in mute amaze,
All impotent to help, their hands upraise,
And hounds with angry bark the skies assail.
Anon, a gold-linked coat of triple mail
He gave to second champion in the fight—
For pride and sure defence of valiant knight—
Which erst from Greek Demoleus he had ta'en,
What time his foe he slew by Simois' wave:
So massy 'twas, his stalwart henchmen twain
Scarce bore it; yet therein accoutred light
Demoleus drove the Trojans o'er the plain.
Third prize, two goblets rich-embossed he gave,
Of silver wrought, two brazen caldrons bright.

   Now each had honours gained in ample store,
And proud they went, with rosy ribbons crowned,
When mocked and jeered, with many a broken oar,
'Scaped from the reef whereon she lay aground,
Sergestus brought his luckless boat to land:
As when a snake, o'ertaken on the path,
O'er whom an iron-shod wheel has passed aslant,
Or wayfarer with stone hath mangled sore,
And left to crawl half-dead, yet drags in wrath
His sinuous coils, uplifting sibilant
A threatening neck, and eyes still flashing bold,
Albeit his wounded parts he scarce can trail,
Twisted in knots, and writhing fold on fold;
Thus rowed Sergestus slow, yet, hoisting sail,
At length with canvas spread to harbour pressed.
Nor did his chief the due reward withhold,

Since ship and crew he lacked not power to save:
His, skilled with spindle, was a Cretan slave,
A mother, with twin infants at her breast.
    That contest done, Æneas went his way
To grassy plain, where, girt with hill and wood,
Midmost the vale a level race-course lay:
There, round him, surged a mighty multitude,
As seated in the centre, high o'er all,
He summoned in swift foot-race to compete
Whoe'er by prize was lured or glory's call.
Therein did Trojans and Sicilians meet:
First Nisus and Euryalus;
Euryalus, for youth and beauty famed;
Nisus for his fond love: then, nothing loth,
Diores, sprung from Priam's royal clan;
Salius, and Patron—one Acharnian,
One of Arcadian blood; next, Helymus
Stepped forth, and Panopes, Sicilians both,
Acestes' comrades, learn'd in woodland lore;
And many another, known to fame no more.
Then, from his station, spake the chieftain thus:
    "List now, and let my words rejoice your hearts!
None in this struggle shall unhonoured be;
To each a pair of polished Gnosian darts,
With silver-graven axe I give for meed;
Such honours all shall share: the foremost three
With chaplets of green olive shall be crowned:
Who fleetest runs shall earn a gay-trapped steed;
The next, an Amazonian quiver, bright
With Thracian arrows, and encircled round
With golden belt by jewelled buckle bound;
The third, this Grecian helmet shall delight."
    This said, their posts they take, and at the sign
Leap forth, with speed tempestuous, from the line,
Fixing their gaze where distant goal is seen.
First Nisus, from the start, outstrips the rest,
Swifter than thunder-bolt or wingéd wind;

And next, but next with mickle space between,
Comes Salius; then, of them that lag behind,
Third runs Euryalus,
Euryalus, by Helymus hard pressed;
And him Diores doth so hotly chase,
Heel grazing heel, as step by step they race,
That if the course were closed not by the plain,
Perchance his rival he would yet outpace,
Or leave the combat doubtful 'twixt the twain.
   But when, with goal in view, and strength far spent,
They neared the end, it chanced, by fortune's spite,
That Nisus stumbled, where the grassy floor
With blood of slaughtered victims was besprent;
Unhappy youth, till then so confident!
His steps he stayed not, but in woful plight
Fell headlong, plunged in mingled mud and gore.
Yet still his cherished friend in mind he bore,
And, rising in the path where Salius sped,
Him also in the slippery mire he cast:
Whereat, by comrade's help inspirited,
Euryalus, 'mid shouts and glad acclaim,
Leapt forth, and so to goal a victor passed;
Next Helymus, and third Diores came.
   Then Salius fills the concourse with his cries,
Sad tale to foremost ranks he hath to tell;
His rights, by treachery lost, demanding back;
Yet doth Euryalus no favour lack,
So seemly are the teardrops in his eyes,
And prowess, matched with beauty, pleadeth well:
Loud, too, protests Diores; for in vain
Had been the struggle for his hard-earned prize,
If Salius still the winner's place retain.
Then spake Æneas: "Nay, your honours won
Await you, lads; of that be sure; for none
Shall shift these prizes from their order true:
Yet may I give a luckless friend his due."
So saying, a lion-skin, with shaggy mane

And golden claws, in Salius' hands he placed.
Then Nisus: "If the vanquished thus be graced,
And they who stumble win thy pity most,
What gift hath Nisus, who the palm hath lost,
Because, as Salius fared, so fared he ill?"
He spake, and showed how muddy filth defaced
His visage and his limbs. Fair smiled the king,
And called for buckler carved with craftsman's skill,
From Greeks at Neptune's sacred temple snatched;
Such gift he gave for Nisus' comforting.
    The foot-race ended, the rewards assigned,
He bade new warriors venture in the lists,
Whoe'er they be that craft and courage find
To wield the heavy gauntlet on their fists:
For prize, a steer with golden garlands twined;
A glittering casque and sword for whoso fell.
Nor long they wait, ere growing murmurs tell
That Dares in his might hath drawn anear;
None else of Paris had been deemed the peer;
'Twas he by Hector's tomb had strength to stand,
And smote great Butes, giant son of Thrace—
From far shores come, in vaunted pride of race—
And stretched him, dying, on the yellow sand.
So, towering for the combat, Dares rose,
With sinewy shoulders, and with glancing hand,
Now right, now left, that clove the air with blows.
But who might meet him? Who, of all the band,
'Gainst such a foeman dared the gloves to don?
He, thinking his proud victory foregone,
Before Æneas stood, full well content,
With hand on horn of steer, and thus bespake:
"Say, chieftain, since antagonist is none,
Why wait we more? This guerdon shall I take?"
Then all the Trojans shouted in assent,
Claiming such promise for their champion.
    But grave, in chiding tones, Acestes turned
To old Entellus, seated by his side

On couch of grassy turf: "Entellus, say,
Thou bravest hero, but of bygone day,
Wilt thou see yonder prize thus lightly earned?
Where now is he, thy Master deified,
Great Eryx? Where thy fame, so widely spread,
And glorious trophies hanging in thine hall?"
Then he: "Nay, glory doth in no wise pall,
Nor coward fear hath robbed me of my pride;
But numbing age has power the blood to chill,
And frozen is the strength I once could wield.
Ah, if that braggart's youth were in me still!
If mine it were, and still this pulse it stirred,
'Twould need no prize to draw me to the field;
Naught reck I of such gifts." And, at the word,
Full in the midst those ponderous gloves he flung
Wherein great Eryx, eager for the fray,
Had once been wont his mighty hands to dight.
In awe men gazed, where seven huge bull-hides lay,
With lead and iron in rigid bosses strung;
Gazed Dares most, recoiling from the fight.
Then, as Æneas felt the massive might
Of those stark coils, and turned them o'er and o'er,
Spake old Entellus in such words as these:
   "How if the gloves of godlike Hercules
Thou'dst seen—the very gauntlets that he wore
In that calamitous fight by yonder shore!
These gloves ye view, on Eryx' hands were braced
(Still may ye note the stains of sprinkled gore);
In these the great Alcides' self he faced;
In these I, too, was skilled, while youth was mine,
Ere envious age had streaked my temples hoar;
But if your Dares yon dread arms decline,
And both our monarchs this resolve approve,
Equal the fight; this gauntlet shall be spared—
Fear not—and thou shalt doff thy Trojan glove."
He spake, and from his neck his mantle flung;
And there, with arms and joints and shoulders bared,

Forth to the ring, a stalwart champion, sprung:
Then brought Æneas gloves of equal weight,
And with fair-balanced weapons bound their hands;
And straightway each, intent, on tiptoe stands,
Dauntless, with head thrown back, and arms elate,
As, fist with fist engaged, they feint and spar;
One confident in youth, and nimbler far;
One huge of bulk, but panting 'neath the strain,
For slow and slack with age his movements are.
Full many a blow they launch, but launch in vain;
Full many a sounding stroke on breast and side;
Round ear and temple busy fists are plied,
And oft on stricken jaw and cheek-bone jar.
Firm stands Entellus, watchful, motionless,
Foiling the foe with steady poise and eye;
But he—as men with siege and battery press
On some proud town or mountain-fortress high—
Now here, now there assays, tho' baffled oft,
A new approach, and tries each inch of ground:
But when Entellus, lunging from aloft,
Flings out his right, that other, warily,
Foresees the blow and 'scapes it at a bound.
Then, on the winds his giant strength misspent,
Huge form, in ruin huge, Entellus fell,
As from its roots some hollow pine is rent
'Mid Erymanthus' rocks or Ida's dell:
Sicilians, Trojans—all arose, to swell
The rival shouts, as king Acestes lent
Compassionate hand his fallen friend to aid.
But he, no whit disabled or dismayed,
By wrath aroused, and lusting for the fight—
His strength by shame and conscious valour fired—
Drove Dares headlong o'er the field, nor tired,
As stroke on stroke he dealt, with left, with right;
No pause, no rest: like hailstones falling fast
On rattling roof, the hero showered his blows
With busy hands, nor ceased to thrust and smite.

But now Æneas, lest the bounds be passed
Of wrath and passion, bade the combat close,
And rescuing Dares from his weary plight
Spake these consoling words from kindly heart.
  "What wouldst thou, madman? Overbold thou art.
Seest not the gods themselves against thee stand?
Then yield, since heaven so wills it, and depart."
Therewith the fight was ended, and a band
Of faithful friends their champion shoreward led;
Scarce could he drag his failing limbs; his head
Swung to and fro; his lips were wet with blood.
The sword and helmet, at the chief's command,
They take, and to Entellus leave the prize.
Thereat victorious, in exultant mood,
"See goddess-born, and Trojans all," he cries,
"What strength in youth I had, nor now I lack;
And from what death ye drew your Dares back."
Fronting the steer, the victor's meed, he stood,
And poised his mighty hand, thick gauntleted,
Between the horns; then, rising to the stroke,
Through skull and brain with crashing blow he broke:
Sank to the ground the quivering victim, dead.
Then gravely o'er the corse this word he spoke:
"Eryx, not Dares' life, but this, I bring,
To praise thy name, a fitter offering;
And now, unconquered still, in power and pride,
The gloves I doff, and lay mine art aside."
  Then forth are brought new guerdons, to be won
By whoso craves the dexterous archer's fame.
Ta'en from Serestus' ship, a lofty mast
Is reared by stalwart arm, and tied thereon
Flutters a dove, the mark for bowman's aim.
The champions meet: in brazen helm are cast
Their lots for vantage; first, 'mid loud acclaim,
Is drawn precedence for Hippocoön;
Then Mnestheus, honoured late in boat-race keen,
Mnestheus, still garlanded with olive green;

And next in order comes Eurytion,
Brother to far-famed Pandarus, who durst
Defy the truce that Troy respected not,
And hurled 'gainst Grecian foes his spear the first:
Last in the helmet lurked Acestes' lot;
Bold veteran, still in youthful pastime versed.
    Then stoutly man by man, the bow they bend,
And each an arrow from the quiver draws;
And first Hippocoön's, from the twanging string,
Speeds on aerial course without a pause,
Till in the tremulous mast its flight hath end:
Whereat the startled dove on restless wing
Flutters, and shouts the concourse in applause.
'Twas Mnestheus next his lusty bowstring drew,
His soaring arrow guided by his eye;
Yet luckless; for it left unscathed the dove,
But cleft in twain the hempen bond, whereby
Her foot was tethered to the spar above:
She, 'mid the winds of heaven, unfettered flew.
Then, quick, Eurytion, in whose hand the shaft
Ev'n now to ready string was fitted tight—
Invoking brother's name to bless his craft—
Marked her up-soaring skyward from men's view
As wings she clapped in free and joyous flight,
And pierced her, at far range, beneath the clouds:
Falling, she leaves her life at starry height,
And brings to earth his arrow as she dies.
    Still was Acestes left, tho' lost the prize;
Natheless he sped one skyward shaft, to show
A master's skill and bend the sounding bow:
Whereat a sudden marvel met their eyes,
With solemn awe by seers and sages hailed,
And fraught with fate no less in the event;
For lo! his arrow kindled, as it went,
And marked a fiery track that slowly paled,
Lost in the clouds; as when through fields of air
Some wandering meteor is transversely trailed.

Amazed men stood, then cried to heaven in prayer,
Each folk alike; nor did the Trojan lord
Distrust that portent, but in glad accord
Sicilia's chief with generous gifts embraced:
"Sire, since Jove wills thee, by these fiery signs,
Honour exceeding great, I bid thee take,
As from Anchises' self, this cup, enchased
With graven figures, rare memorial,
Which Cisseus gave my sire for friendship's sake."
So saying, he wreathed his brow with verdant bays,
And loud acclaimed him victor over all:
Nor did Eurytion grudge that higher praise,
Though to his bow alone the dove did fall.
Next prize was his who cleft the cord; his, last,
Whose wingéd arrow trembled in the mast.

 Therewith the chief, ere yet the sports had end,
Called Periphas, and whispered him in ear,
The young Iulus' trusty guide and friend:
"Go, seek Ascanius, if, in armed array,
With mounted troop of friends, he waits anear;
And in his grandsire's honour bid him speed,
And boyish feats of horsemanship display."
Then, at his word, the surging crowd made way
That thronged the course, and left the spacious plain.
On come the lads, controlling each his steed,
Before their fathers' eyes, with bit and rein,
Watched with admiring murmurs, as they wheel,
By all the hosts of Sicily and Troy.
Bedecked with close-trimmed garlands, boy by boy,
They bear two cornel javelins tipp'd with steel;
Some, polished quivers; all, a golden chain
That from the neck in pliant coil is tied:
Three troops there are, three leaders; in each train
Twelve bright-clad squires in separate squadrons ride.
One band 'tis youthful Priam's joy to lead,
Polites' son, from royal grandsire named,
Thereafter in Italian annals famed;

A piebald Thracian charger is his steed,
With pastern white, white forehead high uplift:
Next Atys, sire of Attian line to be,
Young Atys, dear to young Iulus' heart:
Last, and of all that troop the comeliest,
Mounted on proud Sidonian horse, the gift
Of beauteous Dido's love and courtesy,
Iulus rode, to play his princely part;
On native steeds the rest.
    Thus pass they, breathless, 'mid applauding cries
From Trojan parents gladdened to behold
Their sons the likeness of their sires of old,
And traverse all the field in all men's eyes;
Till Periphas gives signal from afar
With shout and crack of whip, when lo! each band
Disparts itself in triple companies,
Through shifting groups disposed, and as in war
Wheels swiftly back, and charges at command.
Then some advance impetuous, some retreat,
Troop facing troop; and so they move and meet
In ever-varying evolutions blent,
And matched in stern similitude of fight:
Anon their backs they turn in seeming flight,
Yet, as they fly, sharp-pointed spears present;
Then, peace restored, their squadrons reunite.
And as of old was built in lofty Crete
That fabled Labyrinth, with dark alleys pent
'Twixt dubious walls, and teeming with blind ways.
Where every clue brought failure and defeat
In trackless and irremeable maze:
Ev'n so those boys their movements intertwine,
Now feigning flight, now war, in mazy play,
Like dolphins diving sportive through the brine
Of deep Carpathian gulf or Libyan bay.
Nor did Iulus let those games decay,
When Alba Longa by his power was walled,
But bade his Latin folk that usage learn

Wherein himself was skilled in boyhood's day:
Their sons the Albans trained; and thence, in turn,
To Rome herself that age-long custom came;
Ev'n to this hour "the Trojan sport" 'tis called,
And honoured still in sire Anchises' name.

But now no more is fickle Fortune kind;
For, while those funeral rites they solemnize,
Great Juno, still resentful in her spleen,
Still plotting harm, sends Iris from the skies
Down to the Trojan fleet on prosperous wind:
She, gliding swift with many-tinted bow,
Treads her steep path, by mortal eye unseen,
And marks that concourse round the tomb, but lo!
The port deserted, and the ships unmanned;
And there, secluded by the lonely strand,
The Trojan dames bewail Anchises dead,
And as they gaze on the great deep outspread,
Fast fall their tears. Alas, the toil, the pain,
That still await them on those leagues of sea!
One cry, one prayer, have all—their promised home—
Respite from labours of the weary main.
So Iris—in such guile no novice she—
Glides in their midst, and doffs her form divine;
Nor goddess now she seems, but Beroë,
Doryclus' agéd spouse, to fame once known
For noble rank and sons of Thracian line;
Thus to those Trojan dames was access won.

"Alas," she cries, "good cause ye have to weep,
Who died not, stricken 'neath your native wall!
Poor souls, what worse destruction waits you yet!
Wanes now the seventh summer since Troy's fall;
Yet still we roam sea, land, and stony steep;
Still by the stars our weary watch we keep,
Still toward a phantom shore our course is set.
Cast here, 'mid kindred folk, on friendly ground,
What hinders us our city's walls to found?
Gods of our country, were ye saved for naught?

Ne'er shall we see our Troy renamed? ne'er know
Banks of new Xanthus and new Simois, fraught
With memories of great Hector's conquering spear?
Come, let us burn these ships that work us woe!
Ev'n now Cassandra in my sleep I saw;
A blazing torch she brandished: 'Troy is here;
Here is your home,' she cried. Why wait we, then?
Haste, for such dreams no loitering permit.
See, Neptune's altars four, with flames new lit!
Fire, and fierce passion, from the god we draw."
So saying, a fiery brand she grasped, the first,
Then wildly waved it, high in air upraised,
And hurled. Long time they stood, perplexed and dazed,
Those Trojan dames, till spake a beldam old,
Who once the sons of Priam's house had nursed:
"What think ye? 'Tis not Beroë ye behold,
Doryclus' wife; for mark that godlike grace,
How proud her step, her tone of voice, her face,
Those eyes that glow like fire—her mien how bold!
Myself but now left Beroë, as she lay,
Grieving that sickness held her from her place,
Where thus our tribute to the dead we pay."
Such thoughts did she declare.
They, doubtful first, upon the vessels glare
With evil eye, divided 'twixt desire
Of present home, of realms decreed by fate;
But when the goddess spreads her vans in air,
And trails her glittering rainbow high and higher,
Then, by such portent scared, infuriate,
With one wild cry they rush to snatch the fire
From hearth and home, or spoil each sacred shrine;
Branches and boughs they fling, the flame to feed;
Rages the fire-god with ungoverned greed
O'er thwarts and oars and sterns of painted pine.

　　The ships a-flame! such news Eumelus brings
To crowded concourse by Anchises' tomb;
And gazing back, men see the fiery pall

Drift on the wind and fill the sky with gloom.
Iulus first, from those feigned skirmishings—
Ere yet his breathless guardians could recall—
Straight to the troubled camp on horseback flies:
  "What rage is this? what would ye now?" he cries:
"No Grecian host, no foemen's camp, ye view:
Your surest hopes ye burn! 'Tis I, your own
Ascanius!" At their feet the helm he threw
That masked his boyish face in mimic war:
Nor lagged Æneas and his host behind.
But they, those guilty dames, scattered in flight,
Where'er they may, seek woods or caverns far:
Remorseful for their deeds, they loathe the light;
Their friends they know, and brought to saner mind
Thrust Juno's deadly promptings from their breast.
Yet not one whit subsides the quenchless flame:
'Neath sodden planks still burns the smouldering tow,
Forth-belching stubborn smoke; and sure, but slow
The fire consumes the hulls; that deep-sunk pest
Nor strength of man, nor water's help, can tame.
  Then did Æneas rend his robes, and cry
Aloud to heaven with palms outstretched, and prayed:
"Great Jove—unless thou hatest utterly
Our Trojans all—if still thine ancient grace
The sorrows of mankind considereth,
Grant that this fury from our fleet be stayed,
And save the piteous remnant of our race!
Else what is left me, but to die the death,
If so I merit, by thy lightning stroke?"
Scarce uttered, when from bursting storm-clouds broke
A furious tempest; far o'er hill and plain
Clattered the thunder, and the heavens were drenched
From murky South with rush of roaring rain:
That downpour swamped the decks; the beams half-charred
Still smoke till all the vaporous heat is quenched,
And from the ships, save four, the flames debarred.
  Yet bitter was the blow; long time the king

His shifting purpose pondered o'er and o'er;
Should he, forgetful of fate's ordering,
Rest on Sicilian soil, nor voyage more?
Or seek, still seek, the far Italian shore?
'Twas then old Nautes, by sage Pallas taught—
For skill he lacked not of interpreting
Gods' wrath, or fate's demand, by mystic lore—
Thus to the chief his cheering counsel brought:
  "Sire, tho' Fate drive us on, or drag us back,
Still must we follow faithful in her track!
He masters best his lot, who best can bear.
Take thou, a willing friend, thy thoughts to share,
Acestes, Trojan-born, of blood divine;
To him the crews of those lost ships assign,
With folk that weary of thine arduous quest,
And all that fearful are and weakliest;
The greybeards old, the womenfolk who crave
Repose and respite from the wandering wave:
In this calm region let them bide unblamed,
And hence Acesta shall their home be named."
  Warmed by the wisdom of his agéd friend,
Fresh counsel with his heart he fain would take:
But now Night's dusky car had climbed the sky;
When, gliding from some blest abode on high,
It seemed he saw his father's ghost descend,
And thus in sudden speech the silence break:
  "Son, in life's hour more dear than life to me!
Son, harassed long by Troy's distressful fate!
By Jove's command I come; thus wills it He
Who from thy ships has thrust the fiery foe,
And heard thee from his throne compassionate.
Obey wise Nautes' words: with thee shall go
None but the stoutest hearts of all thy band;
Stubborn and strong the race thou must o'erthrow;
But first shalt thou draw nigh to Death's dark land,
And in Avernus' realms my presence seek:
No captive I, 'neath impious depths of hell,

'Mid woful shades, but where the just and meek
Sweet converse hold, in blissful haunt I dwell,
By fair Elysium. Thither, to my side,
If many a sable ewe for victim bleeds,
The Sibyl, priestess pure, thy steps will guide,
Then of thy sons, thy cities, shalt thou hear;
But now, farewell! for Midnight's hour is near,
And Dawn breathes on me with his panting steeds."

So saying, he passed from sight like smoke in air.
"Where art thou? Whither gone?" the chief exclaims:
"What power withholds thee from thy son's embrace?"
Then doth he stir the embers' slumbering flames,
And supplicate his Trojan gods, nor spare
Incense and grain in Vesta's holy place.

Next, to Acestes, and his comrades true,
Of high Jove's edict, of his sire's behest,
And of his own intent, his tale he told,
And ready pledge they gave his will to do.
To that new township all who fain would rest
Were straight transferred—the womankind, the old,
The souls that listed not for glory's call.
Themselves their fire-charred benches they renew,
And planks repair, and oars and tackle test;
Brave band in numbers few, but bolder none.

Meanwhile Æneas marks the city's zone,
With ploughshare traced, apportioning streets and sites;
Here Troy he names, and each remembered spot:
Nor less content Acestes mounts his throne,
A senate summons, and new laws indites.
Then, nigh the stars, must Eryx' crest make room
For Venus' temple; nor is priest forgot,
Nor sacred grove, to guard Anchises' tomb.

Nine days their feast they held, their offerings made;
But when soft-whispering breezes lulled the deep,
And fresh from southward piped the prosperous wind,
Then by the shore they 'gan to wail and weep;
Night fell, yet still that parting they delayed.

Women, ay men, who shunned the waves unkind,
And scarce had borne old ocean's name to hear,
Now for the toils and tasks of exile prayed.
Soft words Æneas spake, their hearts to cheer,
And to Acestes' charge his folk consigned.

Then bids he offer to the Storm God's might
A lamb, three calves to Eryx on his hill,
And loose the cables from each ship outright;
Himself an olive garland hastes to don,
And standing nigh the prow a goblet fill,
And on the briny waves the bright wine pour:
Rising astern, a fair gale wafts them on,
As zealously they ply the sweeping oar.

But Venus, sore distressed, and torn with care,
To Neptune now her tale of sorrow brought:
"'Tis Juno's ire, her unrelenting rage,
Compels me thus to stoop to lowliest prayer.
Nor time, nor pious vows can move her aught;
Nor Jove, nor fate, her bitterness assuage:
No whit content is her malignant mood
To have wiped our Phrygian city from earth's face,
And dragged its suffering folk from woe to woe:
Behold, the very remnant of our race,
Troy's bones and ashes, by her hate pursued!
The cause of such wild wrath herself may know.
Be thou my witness how, on Libyan wave,
In sudden turmoil sea and sky to whelm,
And loose the winds, tho' vainly, from their cave,
She dared, in thine own realm!
And lo! Troy's women, by her dastard deed,
The ships have burned, and now, on foreign strand,
Are comrades left forlorn and desolate.
Grant thou that who survive may scatheless speed
Where Tiber rolls his tide by Latin land:
Thou know'st I ask but what is willed by Fate."

Then spake the lord of ocean, Saturn's son:
"Fair Cytherean, ample right thou hast

To put thy faith in my dominion,
Whence thou didst spring. Nor do I merit less,
Who oft have quelled the fury of the blast
And all the boisterous rage of sea and heaven;
Yea, and on land—let Simois' banks confess—
Saved thy Æneas, when Troy's warriors fled,
In breathless haste before Achilles driven,
'Gainst their own ramparts dashed; when thousands fell;
When groaned the flooded rivers, choked with dead;
And Xanthus scarce found passage to the sea.
Then round thy son I cast my cloudy spell,
And drew him from the fight—o'ermatched was he,
Pitted 'gainst great Achilles—though my joy
Had been to raze and ruin ruthlessly
Those walls I built, the towers of perjured Troy.
So fear not thou; for still unchanged I keep
My purpose; granted is thy heart's desire;
Safe to Avernus' port he sails the deep:
One soul, one only, shall the gulfs destroy;
One life the fates require."
   When thus the goddess' sorrow is consoled,
His steeds he yokes in harness all of gold;
Then adds them foamy bits to curb their pride,
And from his potent hand shakes loose the rein:
Light skims his azure chariot o'er the main;
Beneath its thundering wheel the waves subside,
And clouds fly scattered from the firmament.
Motley the troop that followed in his train:
Huge whales and dolphins sported on the tide;
There nimble Tritons with old Glaucus went,
There Phorcus, with his mermen all arrayed;
To left, in merry band, the sea-nymphs played,
Thetis, Thalia, with fair Melité;
Nor far was Panopea, beauteous maid;
Nesæe, Spio, and Cymodocé.
   Now strange sweet joys the chieftain's heart uplift.
He bids them raise the masts, the canvas spread:

Then all, as one, set sail; the bellying sheet
They loose, to left, to right; and now they shift,
And now reverse, the yard-ends overhead.
Soft glide the ships, by wafting wind caressed,
With Palinurus leader of the fleet;
And as his course he steers, so steer the rest.
　　And now had dewy midnight scaled the sky,
And toil-worn mariners lay slumbering
Along the benches bare, their oars anigh,
When down from starry spheres, on noiseless wing,
Slid Somnus, diving through the dusky air.
Thee, Palinure—nor blame was thine—he sought;
To thee, on poop alit, sad slumber brought.
A god, in Phorbas' garb, and spake thee fair:
　　"See, friend; the waves themselves thy vessels bear!
Calm breathes the wind. Come, rest thee for a space,
And from their labours steal those weary eyes;
Myself will guard the rudder in thy place."
But he, with scarce uplifted look, replies:
"Me dost thou bid forget yon ocean's guile?
Me, put such faith in yonder monstrous deep?
And trust Æneas to the fickle skies—
Me, who so oft have rued their crafty smile?"
So saying, the helm he closer clasped the while,
And steadier watch upon the stars did keep.
　　But lo! the god waves lightly o'er his brow
A slumbrous wand, with Stygian spells imbued,
And steeped in dripping dews from Lethe's flood;
And seals his swimming eyes, o'ermastered now:
Then, as in earliest sleep relaxed he lies,
Swift o'er him stoops, and to the glassy wave
Hurls him, with steerage flung in disarray,
Headlong, and crying on his friends to save;
Himself on airy pinions heavenward flies.
Natheless the fleet still held its destined way,
On course assured by Neptune's high command;
And soon the Sirens' rocks it passed, long known

To evil fame, and white with many a bone;
Where loud the salt surf thundered on the strand.
'Twas then the chief, his trusty pilot gone,
Himself was fain the drifting barque to guide,
And groaned, his comrade's loss lamenting sore:
"Ah, Palinure! o'ermuch didst thou confide
In calm of sky and sea: now stark and lone
Thou'lt lie, a naked corse, on what wild shore!"

BOOK VI

ARGUMENT

HAVING arrived at the port of Cumæ, in western Italy, where, at the cave of Avernus, was the fabled entrance to Hades, Æneas consults the Sibyl, priestess of Apollo and Hecate, with the purpose of meeting the spirit of his father Anchises, and after the performance of sacrifices he is permitted to visit the world of the dead. There, under the Sibyl's guidance, he converses with the ghosts of former friends, and is shown the several precincts and divisions of Pluto's kingdom. In a lengthy discourse, Anchises informs him of the great future awaiting the Trojan race, and points out some of the individual souls destined to be famous in the annals of Rome. In the end, Æneas and the Sibyl pass out of Hades through the ivory gate of dreams.

Weeping he spake, and to the fleet gave rein,
And soon at Cumæ's coast they glide to land.
Seaward the prows are turned; then the anchor's tooth
Fast moors them, and the good ships fringe the strand
With their curved sterns. Forth leap the expectant youth
In eager troop to range the Italian shore;
Some seek the sparks of fire in flinty vein
Deep-hidden, some the forest-glades explore,
Haunt of wild beasts, or hail new streams in sight.
But grave Æneas hastes to that stern height
Which lofty-throned Apollo reigneth o'er,
And secret cave, the dreaded Sibyl's shrine,
To whom the god has given the sense divine
And oped the mysteries of the future's lore:
Ev'n now they pass her grove and golden door.
    When Dædalus, 'tis famed—from Minos fled—
On pinions light made bold to scale the sky,
Far through the strange chill sea of air he sped,
Till poised o'er Cumæ's towers he hovered high:

There lit, to Phœbus he would consecrate
His oarlike wings, and massy temple built,
And pictured on the porch that tale of guilt,
Androgeus' death, and Athens' piteous fate,
The sevenfold yearly tribute of her blood:
There stands the urn—drawn is each fatal lot.
And lo! where Crete looks back across the flood,
The savage lust of the Bull, the foully wed
Pasiphaë, and that monster misbegot,
The Minotaur, of impious union bred.
See, too, that marvel of the Master's toil,
The inextricable Maze, revealed to none,
Till, pitying a lovelorn maiden's vow,
Himself resolved the labyrinthine coil,
Guiding her blind steps with a thread. Here thou,
Lost Icarus, a foremost place hadst won
In that heroic work, would grief allow:
Twice did the father, sorrowing for the son,
Strive to portray his hapless fate in gold;
Twice fell his hands unnerved. This pageantry
Their eyes were still surveying, when behold!
Achates, sent before on solemn quest,
And at his side the Sibyl—priestess she
Of Phœbus and the Stygian Hecate—
Wise Glaucus' child, who thus the chief addressed:
    "No time is this to gaze at yon fair sight:
'Twere fitter now, from unpolluted flock,
Seven steers, seven ewes, the appointed death should die."
Therewith (the while they haste the sacred rite)
She bade them to her lofty hall draw nigh,
A cavern hewn from vast impending rock,
Whereto an hundred spacious entries led,
And from the shrine an hundred voices dread
Rushed outward when the Sibyl made reply.
The threshold reached, she greets him, passionate:
"'Tis time to ask the riddle of thy fate:
Behold, the god, the god!" and with the cry,

Changed instant is her face, her colour fled,
Her locks dishevelled; then quick pants her breast;
And beats her shuddering heart; her stature grows;
Louder she speaks than mortal, as possessed
By the god's nearer presence: "Hast delayed
Thy prayers, Æneas? 'Tis by prayer alone
This spellbound temple will its doors unclose."
She ceased: fear chilled the Trojans to the bone,
And from his inmost heart their monarch prayed:
    "Phœbus, for thou hast pitied from of yore
Troy's wrongs, and didst direct the Dardan hand
Of him whose shaft the great Achilles smote—
Guided by thee, round many a wave-worn strand
Have I adventured, to the far remote
Massylian tribes and Afric's shoaly seas:
Now, when we grasp Italia's fleeting shore,
Oh, may Troy's fortune follow us no more!
Ye, too, I pray, be ruthful to our race,
Each god and goddess Troy did erst displease
By its exceeding glory! And thou, blest seer,
Wise prophetess, grant thou this boon, that here—
No realms I ask, save those that fate decrees—
Here may the Trojans find their resting-place,
With all their wandering storm-tost deities!
To Phœbus then, and Trivia, will I raise
A shrine of solid marble, and ordain,
In the glad name of Phœbus, festal days.
Thou, too, with us shalt sanctuary find;
Thy revelations, thy dark oracle,
For me and mine shall evermore remain,
A gracious charge, to chosen priests consigned.
But now entrust not thy prophetic strain
To leaves that flit the playthings of the wind:
Speak thou thyself, I pray." Then silence fell.
    But she, inspired, yet unsubmissive still,
Raged in her cave with frenzy maddening,
The sway of Phœbus from her breast to fling;

While he, the more, her wild heart dominates,
And tames her wandering utterance to his will:
Then, lo! untouched, the temple's hundred gates
Roll open, and the awful résponse bring:
   "O saved at last from perils on the brine!
Yet worse remain by land. Thy Trojan line,
Doubt not, shall reach Lavinian realms afar,
But yet shall rue their coming. War, fierce war,
And Tiber swol'n with bloody foam I see:
New Simois and new Xanthus wait for thee;
New Dorian camp, and Latin foemen led
By new Achilles; he, too, goddess-bred;
Nor Juno, scourge of Troy, shall plague thee less.
Ah, then, what tribes, what towns, in thy sore stress
Wilt thou not woo, to win them to thy side!
Again a foreign courtship works thee woe;
Again a foreign bride.
Thou, yield not to such threats, but bolder go
Where fortune points thee. Safety's path thou'lt trace
Whence least thou thinkest, from a Grecian race."
   Thus from her hollow shrine, with echoing cries,
The Sibyl chants her wild ambiguous lore,
Truths veiled in darkness; so Apollo plies
His bit and spur within her goaded breast.
Soon as her rage is spent, her lips at rest:
"To me no toil, no grief time holds in store,"
The hero says, "can unforeseen appear;
All have I felt, all braved in thought before.
One boon I ask thee: since the gate lies here,
So fame avers, of that dark monarchy
Where Acheron's waters flood the shadowy mere,
Fain would I pass my father's face to see,
An thou wilt guide, and ope the guarded door.
Him, through war's flames and many a hurtling dart,
In these strong arms I saved from stricken field,
And he in my wild wanderings bore his part,
Nor to the frown of sea or sky would yield,

Albeit his age might gentler lot desire;
Nay, that I thus should seek thy grace revealed,
'Twas his command, his prayer. On son, on sire,
Have pity, O gracious priestess, for thou art
Most mighty, nor hath Hecate in vain
Set thee to rule o'er that her dark domain.
If Orpheus, for the love of his lost bride,
Her spirit could raise, so sweet his harp he strung;
If Pollux, to redeem his brother, died,
And trod the paths of death and life in turn;
If Theseus, if great Hercules, could earn
This privilege—I, too, from Jove am sprung."
    He prayed, with hands outstretched, clasping the shrine.
To whom the seer: "O, born of blood divine,
Troy's lord, full easy is the downward way;
Death's sombre door stands open night and day:
But to return—to gain the light above—
This is the task, the toil. Those few, whom Jove
Held dear, or ardent virtue raised to heaven,
To them alone, gods' sons, such strength was given.
O'er the mid regions drowsy forests brood,
And black Cocytus coils its sluggish flood:
But if thou feel'st desire so great, so fond,
Twice to be wafted o'er the Stygian pond,
The gloomy depths of Tartarus twice to see,—
If this mad labour hath such joy for thee—
Know first: a tree there is, whose shades enfold
A branch with leaf and supple stem of gold;
To Hades' queen 'tis sacred, and the ground
Stark woods and shadowy glens encompass round:
But none may view the hidden world below,
Save he whose hand hath plucked that glistering bough.
This Proserpine demandeth as her meed;
And fast as branch is torn, doth branch succeed,
Golden, and twigs that sprout with metal bright.
Go, then, this treasure seek, and, found aright,
Grasp it amain: if so the fates command,

Freely 'twill follow; else, no mortal hand
With strength nor steel can sever it by force.
Mark, too, where outcast lies a comrade's corse,
Unknown, and brings pollution on thy ships,
Whilst here thou wait'st on these prophetic lips.
Him in fit tomb behoves thee first to lay,
And, for atonement due, black oxen slay:
So shalt thou see those Stygian mansions dread,
And ghostly realms no living wight may tread."

Therewith, her message done, was silence wrought.
Forth from the cave, perplexed, Æneas fares,
With downcast eyes, and plunged in silent thought,
Pondering those hidden issues. At his side
Achates, trusty friend, his trouble shares,
O'er many a theme their converse ranging wide:
Of what dead comrade did the priestess speak?
Whose houseless corse to burial must be brought?
When lo! ev'n as they passed, Misenus lay
There on the barren shore, untimely slain.
Misenus! ne'er had trumpeter such pride
To fire, inspire, men's ardour for the fray.
Great Hector's henchman once, in Hector's train
With trump and spear he gloried in the fight;
But when his chief had felt Achilles' sword,
Æneas next he served, this fearless knight,
Nor found less valour in his later lord.
Now, while his clarion sounded o'er the deep,
And, reckless, with the ocean-gods he vied,
If true the tale, 'twas Triton's jealous spite
Had caught him on the shoreland's rocky steep,
And drawn him under in the foamy tide.

There stand they round, with murmurs of dismay,
Æneas foremost; then, with tears on cheek,
They haste the Sibyl's bidding to obey,
And with heaped boughs an altar high uprear.
An ancient wood, the wild beasts' lair, they seek;
Then stricken fall the pines, the axe rings clear,

Stout oak and ashen beam, with wedges rent,
And stately rowans down the slopes are sent;
Nor fails the chief such busy work to lead
And girded with like tools his comrades cheer:
Yet, sad at heart, that riddle would he read,
Seeing the wood so vast, and prays aloud:
"Oh, if that golden branch would now unshroud
Its splendour to mine eyes in this dense brake!
For, sooth, too true all else the priestess spake."
Scarce said, when lo, twin doves before his eyes,
From out the sky down-sailing on swift wing,
Light on the grassy turf; then, gladdening,
The hero knows his Mother's birds, and cries:
    "Guide ye, and point my path, if path there be,
To where that rich branch casts its mellow shade;
Nor fail me, Thou, in this perplexity,
My goddess mother!" Then his steps he stayed,
Watching what signs they give, what course pursue:
They, feeding as they go, such distance fly
As he who follows still their flight may view,
Then, where Avernus' noisome jaws they sight,
Soar swift, and gliding through the liquid sky,
Ah, joy, the twain on that one tree alight,
Where through the dark boughs flashed the golden sheen.
And as, when winter broods o'er woodland scene,
Fresh blooms the foliage of the mistletoe—
Which in an alien tree hath fixed its root—
And wreathes the smooth trunks with its yellow fruit,
Thus on swart ilex did the live gold show,
Thus tinkled in the breeze that metal fine.
Eager he grasps and plucks it, yielding slow,
And bears his treasure to the Sibyl's shrine.
    Meantime the Trojan mourners on the shore
Bring their last tributes to the heedless clay:
A mighty pyre they raise, of oak and pine,
Its sides with sad sepulchral boughs intwine,
Then range the sombre cypresses before,

And, high o'er all, his glittering armour lay.
Some, where the brazen caldrons throb with heat,
Lave the cold corse, and dress with unguents sweet,
Loud wailing; then, their weeping done, the dead
On his last couch they lay, 'neath wonted pall
Of flowing purple tapestries o'erspread.
Some to the ponderous bier their shoulders set—
Sad service—and by olden rite apply
The torch, their eyes averted; over all
Pure oil and cates and frankincense are thrown.
But when the embers sink, and flames down die,
The remnant of parched dust with wine they wet;
And Corynæus next—his task it is
To enclose in brazen urn each scattered bone—
And bear the lustral water thrice around,
From olive branch besprinkled—and anew
His comrades cleanse, and speak the last adieu.
There built Æneas a memorial mound,
With trump and oar to mark the hero's fame,
Where towers the Cape that as Misenum known
Forever through the ages keeps his name.
    This done, he acteth as the Sibyl bade.
A cave there was, with gaping gorge deep-rent,
Rock-strewn, by black tarn guarded and dark shade,
O'er which scarce bird unharmed its way could wing,
So fierce from that dark cleft the fumes upspring,
And drifted high toward heaven's pure firmament.
Here hath the priestess set four swarthy steers;
Now on their shaggy brows she pours the wine,
And 'twixt their horns the topmost bristles shears,
Flung as first-offering on the flame divine—
Dread Hecate with cries petitioning,
Mighty in heaven above, in hell below—
Then knife to throat is laid; warm blood-streams flow,
Caught in the bowls beneath. With sword the king
A black-fleeced ewe-lamb slaughters, to appease
The Night, dread mother of the Eumenides,

And Earth, her mighty sister; next implores
With barren cow the power of Proserpine;
Last Pluto with dark sacrifice adores,
With flesh of bulls the altars cumbering,
And flaming oil upon the entrails pours.

But, hark! Anigh that hour when dawns the day,
The earth groans underfoot, the forests quake,
And hell-hounds through the gloom are heard to bay.
She comes—the goddess! Then, "Avaunt, avaunt,
Ye uninitiate!" loud exclaims the seer;
"And from this hallowed grove your presence take;
Thou, warrior, draw thy sword, and onward press:
No terrors now must thy firm spirit daunt."
So saying, she flings her in the cave's recess;
He with unwavering footsteps follows near.

Ye gods who o'er the Shades dominion hold,
Chaos, and realms that boundless silence keep,
Grant me to tell the tale as erst 'twas told.
Grant me your grace those secrets to unfold
In earth's abysmal darkness buried deep!

Dimly they went, where there was naught but night,
Through the empty halls and kingdoms of the Dead;
As when, by the stray moonbeam's niggard light,
Men trace some forest-path, and a black spell
Of hueless gloom the landscape hath o'erspread.
And there—in the very gate and gorge of hell—
Sat Grief, and Care who tracks her prey afar,
And pale Disease, and Age, with looks unkind,
And Fear, and Famine that dishearteneth—
Shapes hideous to behold—and Dearth, and Death;
Death's cousin, Sleep; ill joys, of Passion bred;
And full in front the grisly form of War:
There the iron Furies couched; and Discord dread,
Her viperous locks with gory fillets twined.

Midmost, an aged elm spreads ghostlike arms,
Huge, shadowy—haunt primeval, 'tis averred,
Of fickle Dreams that 'neath its foliage cling—

There, likewise, many a fearful, monstrous thing,
Centaurs and Scyllas, in hell's doorway herd;
Vast Briareus, and that Snake from Lerna's hold,
Fierce-hissing; the Chimæra ringed with flame;
Gorgons, and Harpies, and the bulk three-fold
Of mighty Geryon's gigantic frame.
In sudden fear, Æneas grips his sword,
On that advancing rout its edge to turn;
Then by his guide was bidden to discern
Mere fleeting forms, of life and strength bereft;
Else had he rushed upon the phantom horde,
And with vain strokes their ghostly substance cleft.
    Hence leads the downward way, where Acheron's flood,
Turbid with eddying tides that swirl and spin,
In slow Cocytus spews its silted mud.
O'er these dark pools keeps watch a boatman dread,
The grim and squalid Charon; from his chin
Straggles the unkempt grey beard; dull gleam his eyes;
Looped from his neck a sordid cloak hangs long.
Himself the sail he trims, the pole he plies,
And on his dusky barque transports the dead;
Old is he; but a god, still hale and strong.
Here to the banks flock all that lifeless throng—
Matrons, and men, and many a silent ghost
Of mighty heroes, boys and girls unwed,
And slain youths buried in their parents' sight—
Countless as leaves that 'neath autumnal frost
Fall withered, or as birds in huddled flight,
That from the deep main seek the sheltering coast,
When winter scares them sunward o'er the sea.
Here stand they, palms outstretched, in rivalry,
For distant bank of river yearning sore:
But that stern boatman, moved no whit is he;
Now these, now those, he taketh sullenly,
And others drives forbidden from the shore.
    Then spake the king, on that strange scene intent:
"What means the concourse by the dark stream-side?

What seek yon shades? By whose arbitrament
Far from the bank must some rejected bide,
While others o'er the livid pool are sent?"
Thereto brief answer did the priestess make:
"Anchises' son, of heaven the offspring sure,
Thou seest Cocytus, and that Stygian lake
Which ev'n the gods fear falsely to adjure.
Yon piteous crowd are they that lack a grave;
The boatman, Charon; they who ride the wave,
The buried; on none else is grace bestowed
To cross yon dreary bank and moaning flood,
Save when their bones lie peaceful in the ground:
An hundred years they flit these shores around,
Then, late, win access to the stream they crave."
   His step Æneas stayed, and full of care
Stood sorrowing, by their hapless lot distressed.
There saw he with Leucaspis, mournful pair,
Orontes, captain of his Lycian crew;
Whom both, from Troy embarked, the strong South-West
Had spared not, ships and sailors, to o'erwhelm.
Next, Palinurus, guardian of the helm,
Who late, while on the stars he fixed his gaze,
From the high stern fell headlong to the sea.
Him, wandering woful through the murky haze,
The chief accosts: "What cruel god was he,
That snatched thee from us 'neath the watery floor?
This tell; for here Apollo spake not sooth—
Here only, who did ne'er deceive before—
That thou, unscathed, shouldst 'scape the waves, and gain
The Italian borders. Lo, is this his truth?"
   But he: "Nor spake the prophet's voice in vain,
Nor sea-god dragged me 'neath the ocean tide.
I fell; and hurled with mighty force aback,
The helm whereto I clung, our course to guide,
Went with me. By those surging seas I swear,
Not for myself high courage did I lack,
But for thy ship, left rudderless and bare,

Its pilot lost, at mercy of such foes.
Three stormy nights across the waters wide
The fierce wind drove me; when the fourth day rose,
Italia from the wave-tops I descried.
Landward I swam; ev'n then my toil was o'er;
When, as I stood with dripping robe down-weighed,
And clutched with straining hands the cliff's sharp face,
The savage folk their murderous onset made,
And slew me as fit prey for their dull race:
Now winds and waters toss me by the shore.
But, by the heaven's sweet light, the blessed air,
I pray thee—by thy sire, and by thy son,
The youth Iulus, and his promise fair—
Save me from this foul plight, thou fearless one!
This canst thou; back to Velia's harbour go,
And earth upon my outcast body throw;
Or, if thy goddess mother point a way—
For not, I trow, without such grace divine,
To cross the Stygian mere dost thou essay—
Reach hand, and lift me o'er yon stream of woe,
That thus at least in death may peace be mine."
  "Ah, Palinure," thus quick replied the seer;
"Whence comes on thee this craving overbold?
Wilt thou, unburied, sail the Stygian mere?
The Furies' awful river dar'st behold,
Or ev'n beside its bank, unbidden, fare?
Nay, cease to hope that fate can yield to prayer.
But hark thou this, thy sorrow to beguile:
The neighbouring tribes of them that slew thee there,
By portents driven, thy bloodshed shall atone,
And where thy tomb they build, and offerings make,
As Palinurum shall the place be known."
Her words his grief console; his heart awhile
Joys in the land thus titled for his sake.
  So on they went, and to the stream drew near;
Whom when the boatman from his post had scanned,
Pacing through silent grove to river-marge,

In chiding tones rang forth his challenge clear:
"Whoso thou art, that armed approachest here,
Halt, and thine errand tell, where thou dost stand.
Here dwell the Shades, and Sleep, and drowsy Night;
Nor aught that lives may journey on this barge.
And, certes, it did bring me scant delight
To have borne the great Alcides on his way,
And Theseus and Pirithous withal,
Though sons of heaven, and matchless in their might;
His feat it was hell's watch-dog to enthrall,
Ev'n at our monarch's throne, all cowed with fright;
Theirs on Death's wedded queen rash hands to lay."
    Whereto the priestess with few words replied:
"Fear not; no treason in our hearts we hide;
This sword shall smite not. Bellowing in his hold,
Your guardian hound may still the pale ghosts scare;
Still in chaste home may Proserpine abide.
Æneas, faithful son and warrior bold,
Here in the depths of Hades seeks his sire.
If by such pious deeds unmoved art thou,
Let this"—from 'neath her robe she bared the bough—
"Convince thee." Then at once down sank his ire:
No more he spake, but eyed with wondering look
That mystic branch, after long ages seen;
And his dark prow the middle stream forsook.
The phantom forms that on his benches sate
He chased aside, and cleared the thwarts between,
As on his vessel's fragile planks he took
The tall Æneas. Groaning 'neath the weight,
The leaky craft much ooze and marsh did drink,
Till safe they stepped upon the sedges green,
Priestess and chieftain, by the miry brink.
    Here Cerberus makes dread din, with triple bark,
In his confronting cavern couched enorm;
But when the Sibyl saw the serpents stark
Rise on his bristling neck, a sop she cast,
With honey drugged and herbs of slumbrous power.

Ravenous he rushed, her bounty to devour,
With jaws agape; then stretched his monstrous form,
Strewn in unwieldy bulk athwart the cave.
The watch-dog thus in slumber's chains made fast,
Æneas quick the entry gained, and passed
The border of the irremeable wave.

   Forthwith are voices heard, and loud lament,
The souls of infants wailing at the gate:
Snatched from the breast—from life's sweet portion rent—
The dark day whelmed them in untimely fate.
Anear are those unjustly doomed to death;
Nor without strict allotment here they stand:
'Tis Minos shakes the urn, and summoneth
That silent crowd his judgment to await,
And of their lives, their sins, makes stern demand.
Next are the sufferers slain by their own hand,
Who, guiltless—for mere hatred of the light—
Their lives abandoned. Gladly now would they
Bear dearth and sorrow in the world of men!
It may not be: the sullen, stagnant fen
Winds its detested wave across their way,
And Styx with nine-fold coil precludes from flight.

   Nor long the road, ere wide outspread they find
The Mourning Fields—such name those meadows own.
Here those who in love's cruel pangs have pined,
By secret paths with myrtle boughs o'ergrown
Walk hidden, nor ev'n in death has grief surcease.
Here Procris, and here Phædra saw he plain,
And Eriphyle by her son's hand slain,
Still pointing sadly to that wound abhorred;
Evadne, and Pasiphaë; and with these
Was Cæneus, once a man, now changed again
To woman, and her former shape restored.

   Midst these, still smarting from her deadly wound,
Went Dido, wandering that sad woodland through:
Whom when Æneas, close approaching, knew,
Dim through the shadows that enwrapped her round—

As when, through stormy scud that veils the skies,
One sees, or deems he sees, the young moon rise—
He wept, and thus with love bespake her fair:
"Unhappy Dido! So the tale was true,
That thou hadst laid the sword to thine own heart!
Diedst thou for me? Nay, by the stars I swear,
By heaven—by aught held sacred here below—
Full loth I was from thy kind shore to part.
But 'twas the gods, by whose divine command
I traverse now this waste and sunless land,
Imperious drove me forth; nor could I know
That I was leaving thee to grief so great.
O stay thy steps, nor draw thee from my gaze!
Know'st not whom thou dost shun? 'Tis fixed by fate
These words I now would speak thee are the last."
Her passionate, frowning spirit thus he prays
In gentle tones, the while his tears fall fast.

But she, averse, with unuplifted eyes,
Heeded no more his speech than if she stood
Carven of flint or hard Marpesian stone;
Then hied her, sullen, to a thicket lone,
Wherein the faithful spouse whom erst she wed
Soothes grief with grief, to love with love replies:
Nor ceased Æneas o'er her woes to brood,
But watched her far, and pitied as she fled.

Then on he fares, till further fields they gain
Where warriors famed in battle roam apart;
Here meet him Tydeus; here, of valiant heart,
Parthenopæus; and pale Adrastus' shade;
Here many a chieftain of the Trojan line,
His comrades much bewept, in battle slain,
He groans to see in ranks of death arrayed:—
Glaucus, and Medon, and Thersilochus;
Antenor's sons; the priest of Ceres' shrine;
Idæus, henchman still, still charioteer.
So stand their shades around innumerous;
Not sated with one look, but, lingering near,

Converse, and causes of his coming seek.
Not so the hosts and squadrons of the Greek:
They, when the presence of their foe they spy,
Scared by his arms that glimmer through the night,
Tremble in sudden fear; some turn in flight,
As erst their ships they sought; some raise a cry
In phantom tones that mock their efforts weak.
    Here Priam's son, Deiphobus, he found,
Sore mangled; with fierce cuts deformed his face,
His face and hands; his ears from temples torn;
His nostrils slit with ignominious wound.
Thus cowering, so to hide his foul disgrace,
Scarce did Æneas know so changed a wight,
Yet straight in well-remembered accents spake:
"Brave warrior-prince, of Troy's high lineage born,
What foe had wish this fell revenge to take?
What fiend had power? To me, on that last night,
News came that thou, with slaughter's work outworn,
Hadst fallen on serried heap of foemen killed;
Myself on shore thy cenotaph did build,
And thrice I called aloud upon thy ghost:
Thy monument remains; thou, friend, wert lost;
Thy tomb on native soil is yet unfilled."
    Then to the king made answer Priam's son:
"By thee no friendly deed was left undone;
Whose care it was those funeral rites to pay.
'Twas fate, and the Greek woman's fell intent,
That dragged me to this dire disfigurement:
These were her tokens ere she went her way.
In what false joys that last dread night we spent
Thou knowest, nor can its memory e'er decay:
But when the fatal Horse o'erleapt Troy's wall,
With those armed warriors in its secret hold,
She, feigning dance, in Bacchic festival
Led forth the Trojan women, and made bold,
Midmost herself with blazing torch held high,
From Trojan citadel the Greeks to call.

But I, with drowsiness and cares oppressed,
In my ill-fated chamber chanced to lie,
Sunk in a spell of sweet, deep, deathlike rest;
Then did my gentle partner, craftily,
All weapons from within our walls remove,
And stole from 'neath my head my trusty blade:
Then Meneläus to the door she bade,
Hoping, forsooth, that, through such gift of love,
Noise of her earlier guilt might be forgot.
So in they rushed—why should I tell it not?—
With him, Ulysses, ever prompt in crime.
Ye gods, upon the Greeks like ills requite,
If with pure heart for just revenge I pray!
But thou—come tell thy tale in turn, and say
What chance hath brought thee, living, to this clime;
Art still a wanderer o'er the ocean foam?
Comest thou by will of heaven, or fortune's spite,
This sad, unrestful, sunless land to roam?"
    Thus parleying, till the rosy car of Day
In its high course had topped the dome of heaven,
Soon had they spent such time as fate had given,
Had not the seer's brief warning brought an end:
"Night speeds, Æneas; we weep the hours away.
Thou standest where the branching path is cleft:
Here, by the right, past Pluto's lofty throne,
Elysium waits us; yonder, by the left,
The wicked to their hell of pain descend."
She spake, and thus Deiphobus replied:
"Be wroth not, priestess. Back my way I wend
To those dim shades whereof I am but one.
But thou—a fairer fate be thine, Troy's pride!"
No more he said, but turned him, and was gone.
    A sudden backward glance Æneas throws,
And sees, to left, beneath a height profound,
A city, girt with triple rampart round,
Nigh which a raging fiery torrent flows,
Fierce Phlegethon, and whirls loud rocks along.

Huge the confronting gate, with pillars strong
Of solid adamant, which no mortal might
Can storm by force, nor ev'n the great gods' power;
And high o'er all up-soars an iron tower,
Where the dread Fury, clad in blood-stained shroud,
Sits sleepless o'er the entrance day and night.
Thence groans they hear, the savage thud of blows,
The creak of iron, chains that clank aloud:
Aghast Æneas stands, so dread the din:
"This tell me, prophetess; what crimes are those?
What penalties? What mean such anguished cries?"

    "Renownéd chief, know this," the seer replies,
"No righteous foot may pace that house of sin;
But She who set me o'er her dark domains
Herself these terrors showed, and taught me all.
O'er this curst realm 'tis Rhadamanthus reigns;
He hears each charge, each crime he chasteneth,
Compelling to his stern confessional
The rogue who, laughing in his vain conceit,
His deeds hath hidden till the day of death.
Then will the avenging Fury, scourge in hand,
Trample such guilty sinners 'neath her feet,
While, in her left, grim snakes she brandisheth,
And calls her Sisterhood's remorseless band.
Lo! on its creaking hinge the infernal gate
Swings open. Mark what guard the doorway keeps!
What shapes of hell upon the threshold lie!
See, with her fifty throats the Hydra wait,
A fiend still fiercer! Tartarus, hard by,
Yawns twice so far toward the nether deeps
As upward towers the Olympian height of sky.

    "There the young Titans, Earth's primeval brood,
Lie weltering, hurled by thunder-bolt to hell:
There, too, the huge Aloïdæ I viewed;
To storm the Almighty's realm who durst aspire,
And drag Jove down from his high citadel.
Nor with less anguish hath Salmoneus rued

His aping of the dread celestial fire:
With waving torch, on four-horsed chariot fleet,
Through Grecian Elis in proud pomp he went,
And dared, as god, men's worship to demand:
Fool, who with din of brass and horse-hoofs' beat
Would mock the inimitable levin-brand!
For swift, through gathering clouds, the Omnipotent
His lightning launched—no torch with smoky glare—
And dashed him to his death on whirlwind wild.
   "See Tityos, too, the great Earth-Mother's child!
O'er acres nine his mighty bulk lies bare;
The while yon ravening vulture with crooked beak
His never-dying liver still must tear,
And on his fertile flesh new vengeance wreak,
And probes, and lodges in his hollow breast,
Where still the fibres grow, but find not rest.
What boots it of the Lapithæ to speak,
Ixion, or Pirithous? o'er whose head
A dark crag hangs, as though ev'n now it fell;
Or golden banquet-couch they see with zest,
And regal sumptuous fare before them spread;
In vain; for yonder sits that hag abhorr'd,
The Fury, and ever scares them from the board,
Rising with torch aflame and thunderous yell.
Whoso did hate a kinsman in life's day,
A parent strike, a client's honour sell,
Or gotten wealth in selfish avarice hoard,
Nor share with poorer kin (as oft befell);
The adulterer slain; the traitor, who drew sword
'Gainst brethren, or did master's hand betray—
Here wait their penance. Bid me not recite
What forms of vengeance whelm them in the pit.
Some roll great·boulders; some to wheels are bound,
Pendent; here sits, and shall forever sit,
Doomed Theseus; here, through dolorous gloom of night,
The warning cries of Phlegyas resound:
Learn justice, all; nor mock the great gods' might.

One for a bribe his country's freedom sold,
Made and unmade her laws with base design;
One to defile his daughter's bed was bold:
All some accursed deed did do and dare.
Not if an hundred tongues and mouths were mine,
An iron voice, their crimes could I unfold,
The full tale of their punishments declare."
    Such were the words she spoke, the long-lived seer:
"And haste," she cries, "ere yet the time grow late,
Our duty to discharge; ev'n now appear
Those walls in Cyclopean forges wrought;
And lo! in front, that massy high-arched gate,
Whereto the goddess bids her gifts be brought."
Then side by side they tread the shadowy way,
And cross the middle space, and draw anear.
Sprinkled with water pure, he enters straight,
And fixes on the porch the sacred spray.
    This done, and thus fulfilled that high behest,
They pass to pleasant scene of sunny glade
And joyful grove, the mansions of the blest.
An ampler ether hath these fields arrayed
In purple lustre; and who here have rest,
Their own sweet daylight know, their starlight sweet.
Some on the grassy sward in games compete,
And wrestle sporting on the yellow sand;
Some to the dance beat time, or swell the song.
Here sacred Orpheus, robed in vesture long,
Striking his lute-strings, now with ivory wand,
Now with deft fingers, tuneful music plays;
Here Teucer's seed, to perfect beauty grown,
Bold-hearted heroes, born in statelier days;
Here Ilus resteth, here Assaracus,
And Dardanus, the sire of Trojan throne.
Here, too—strange sight—their phantom chariots are,
The lances fixed in earth, and o'er the meads
The horses pasturing free. What love they gave
In life to burnished armour and bright car,

What glory felt in strength of glossy steeds,
Such pleasures still attend them in the grave.
See, on the grassy lawns some feast in mirth,
Or glad triumphal chant in chorus sing,
Through groves of odorous laurel, whence to earth
The full founts of Eridanus upspring.
Here they who for their country fought and bled;
Priests who, in life, were ever pure of mind;
True bards, whose singing brought their lord no shame;
Whoso by fruitful thought enriched mankind,
Or from his fellows earned unending fame—
All such with snow-white wreaths go garlanded.

    These, grouped around, the Sibyl thus bespake,
But to Musæus, most, her words addressed,
While to his towering form up-looked the rest:
"Ye happy souls, and thou, blest singer, say,
Where dwells Anchises? Hither, for his sake,
O'er hell's dark torrents have we won our way."
Then did the hero-bard brief answer make:
"We dwell in leafy wood; fixed home is none:
By cushioned bank, or vale-refreshing rill,
Our haunt is. But if this your heart content,
Yon easy path shall guide you o'er the hill."
Ahead he stepped, and where the fair fields shone
Gave signal; thence on downward course they went.

    There sire Anchises, deep in grassy glen,
Mused thoughtful on the yet unfettered bands
Of souls predestined to the world of men—
Recounting all his kin that should succeed,
Their fates and fortunes, every mood and deed.
But when his son's advancing steps he spied,
In eager haste he rose, with outstretched hands,
And wet with tears his cheeks were, as he cried:
"Hast come at last, ev'n as my heart foretold,
With love victorious over toil and pain?
Have I this joy, to see thy face again,
To hear thy voice, and answer, as of old?

Thus did I dream, nor doubt that it would be,
Counting the days, nor was my thought in vain.
But what wild lands, what waters, hast thou crossed
To greet me! By what stormy perils tossed!
Ay, much those wiles of Libya did I fear."
But he: "Nay, father, 'twas the thought of thee,
'Twas thy sad, haunting image led me here.
My ships at anchorage ride. But thou, a space,
Give me thine hand to hold, and draw more near,
Father, nor shrink not from thy son's embrace."
Such words he spake, nor could forbear to weep;
Thrice in his arms to fold him he assayed;
Thrice did the phantom form his grasp evade,
Like fleeting wind or airy shape of sleep.
　　Then saw Æneas, by lone valley-side,
A sheltered woodland, whispering in the breeze,
Where flows, past quiet homesteads, Lethe-tide,
Round which unnumbered forms were fluttering wide,
As when, in summer's tranquil season, bees
Flit round the gaudy flowers and lilies white,
And all the fields are filled with murmuring sound.
Struck with amazement at the sudden sight,
The name of that far stream he fain would know,
And who the folk that flock its banks around.
Then said his sire: "Those souls, whom fate doth owe
New incarnation, first at Lethe-brink
The fount of deep forgetfulness must drink.
Long have I yearned their destiny to show,
And teach thee the far future of our kin;
That thus the more with me thou mayst delight
O'er that Italian kingdom thou shalt win."
　　"Say'st thou that souls rise hence in earthward flight,
To that dull mortal body to return?
Why crave they thus life's sorrows to renew?"
"This straightway," quoth Anchises, "shalt thou learn,"
Then thus expoundeth all in order due:
　　"Know, first, that sky, and earth, and ocean fields,

The shining globe o' the moon, the day-star fair,
An inner spirit, deep pervading, wields,
And all their mighty mass by Mind is stirred.
Thence spring the tribes of man, and beast, and bird,
And monstrous beings that the dark depths bear.
A fiery strength these heaven-born seeds possess,
Save when sore trammelled by the body slow,
And deadened by the mortal clay's distress:
Hence fear they feel, and love, and joy, and woe,
Yet still, in gloom of prison-house held fast,
What lies beyond the darkness may not know.
Ev'n when the latest ray of life hath passed,
That curse they can escape not, nor lay by
All earthly taint; so wondrous deep within
Must many a long-implanted blemish lie:
Wherefore they now pay forfeit for past sin
With full atonement; some extended wide
To searching winds, some 'neath the vasty tide
Cleansed of inveterate guilt, some purged by fire.
Each his own spirit's penance we endure;
Then through Elysium sent, a scanty band,
We reach the Happy Fields of our desire:
Till agelong time, fulfilling fate's demand,
The fleshly stain has banished, and left pure
The ethereal sense and spark of heavenly flame.
Such souls, when thousand years have passed them o'er,
Flock, at the call divine, to Lethe-strand,
To drink oblivion ere they rise once more
And crave anew to dwell in mortal frame."
    So spake Anchises as he led the twain
Through that loud spirit-concourse, to a height
Whence he could scan their slow-advancing train,
And read each hero's countenance aright.
    "List now, what glory waits our Dardan line,
Those far descendants of Italian birth—
Illustrious souls in whom our name shall shine—
All this, by fate predestined, shalt thou hear.

That youth thou seest, who leans on bloodless spear,
Next to life's threshold stands—he first to earth,
Of Trojan and Italian marriage, springs;
Silvius his Alban name, thy last-born son,
Whom, in thine age, shall queen Lavinia rear
'Mid sylvan haunts, a king, and sire of kings,
Whence for our race is Alba Longa won.
See Procas, pride of Trojan line, appear;
Next Capys, and next Numitor draw near;
And he in whom thy name shall live again,
Silvius Æneas, famed in heart and hand,
If e'er upon his Alban throne he reign.
Brave heroes all; behold how strong they stand,
And their calm brows with civic garlands crown:
'Tis these shall build thee fortresses well-walled;
Nomentum, Gabii, and Fidenæ town;
Collatia's stronghold, set on mountain height;
Pometii, and the Camp of Inuus called;
With Bola, Cora, and many a land that lies
Now nameless, but shall bask in glory's light.
Nay, more; for in his grandsire's steps shall tread
Great Romulus, Mars' son, of Ilia bred:
Seest not twin plumes upon his helm upright,
Wherewith his Father marks him for the skies?
Lo! his the name whence glorious Rome shall rise,
To o'ercome the world and soar in heart to heaven,
Girding with single wall her summits seven;
Rich in her sons; like that great Mother-Queen,
Wont, chariot-borne, through Phrygian towns to ride,
Clasping her children's children in her pride,
All gods, all dwellers on the heights serene.
  "Now turn thee hither, and yon host survey,
Thy Romans—Cæsar, and Iulus' line—
Who yet shall issue to the light of day.
This, this, is he, thy kinsman oft foretold,
Augustus Cæsar, of descent divine,
Who shall restore the fabled age of gold

To Latian realms where Saturn reigned of old,
Ay, and o'er Garamant shall spread his sway
And India, ev'n to the utmost boundary,
Beyond our stars, beyond our sun's far flight,
Where Atlas on his shoulders wheels the sky,
Studded with flaming constellations bright.
Now, ere he cometh, mystic voices fright
The Caspian realms and far Mæotian lake,
And thrill the banks of sevenfold Nile with fear;
Not ev'n Alcides roamed the world so wide,
Albeit he pierced the brazen-footed deer,
And stilled the Erymanthian forest-side,
And with his arrows bade all Lerna quake;
Nor He, whose reins of vine his chariot guide,
Bacchus, by tigers drawn from Nysa's brow:—
But we—why strike we not for valour's sake?
Why fear to tread the promised land ev'n now?

"But who stands there, with olive chaplet crowned,
At sacrifice? That grey-haired king of Rome,
Who first our settled state with laws shall found,
Called from his township small, and humble home,
To wield the imperial power. To him succeeds
One who breaks sluggish peace with warlike deeds,
Tullus, and wakes the Roman ranks again
To high triumphal hopes long laid aside;
Then follows Ancus, monarch over-vain,
And courting much the fickle popular breath;
The tyrant Tarquins; and that soul of pride,
The avenger, Brutus—he that rescueth
The people's fasces, by the despot ta'en.
He first the Consul's awful powers shall hold,
Himself his own rebellious sons reprove,
And doom them, for fair freedom, to the death:
Unhappy sire, howe'er the tale be told;
Athirst for honour and a patriot's love.
Mark, too, the Decii and the Drusi bold:
Torquatus, fierce with battle-axe high-waved;

Camillus, conqueror, with the standards saved.
"Two spirits, see, that in like armour shine!
At concord here, in ante-natal night:
Alas! if e'er they live, what strife malign,
What armaments, what bloodshed will they breed!
For one shall sally down from Alpine height,
One to the fray the embattled Orient lead:—
Nay, sons, steel not your hearts, if pity plead,
Nor mass 'gainst mother-land that murderous might!
Thou first, be ruthful, thou of race divine;
Unarm thee, child of mine!
    "See one, renowned from Corinth's overthrow,
Borne high in triumph, conqueror of the Greek;
One lays proud Argos and Mycenæ low,
Exacting vengeance on Achilles' race,
For wrong to Troy and Pallas' injured fane.
Of Cato, Cossus, who shall spare to speak?
The Gracchi, and that scourge on Libya sent,
War's thunder-bolts, the fiery Scipios twain?
Fabricius, rich in poverty's content;
Or thee, Serranus, busy with the plough?
Breath fails me, ye great Fabii—Greatest thou,
Who by thy tarrying shalt the day regain!
    "More deftly some the breathing bronze shall mould—
I doubt not—carve in stone the lifelike face;
More eloquently plead; more surely trace
The heavenly chart, the rising stars foretold.
Thou, Roman, to a sterner task art vowed:
For thou must lord it o'er thy vanquished foes;
These be thine arts—the rule of peace to impose,
To spare the meek and subjugate the proud."
Then, as they marvelled, still he mused aloud:
    "Marcellus, see, with princely spoils elate,
Strides victor, towering o'er his clansmen all!
He that, in treason's hour, shall stay the State,
Trampling the Punic foe, the insurgent Gaul,
The third great trophy so to dedicate

High in our sire Quirinus' sacred hall."
   Here spake Æneas—for he saw, hard by,
A youth of beauteous form, in armour sheen,
But sad of visage and of downcast eye:
"But say, who follows yonder chieftain nigh;
Son is he, or of later lineage bred?
How throng his comrades round, how proud his mien!
But sombre night flits bodeful o'er his head."
Then sire Anchises, as he dropped the tear:
   "Son, ask not of thy children's grief supreme.
Scarce shall earth see this peerless youth, ere fate
Claims him. Too mighty would the high gods deem
Our manhood, if 'twere grudged not gifts so great.
But now what sobs of sorrow shall Rome hear
From her wide Camp of Mars! what pageantry
Of sad funereal crowds shall Tiber see,
As past that new-raised grave he rolls his stream!
Never shall child of Troy such hopes excite
In Latian sires, nor ever Roman land
In scion of her blood such glory feel.
Alas, his loyal heart, his strong right-hand
Invincible, for scatheless none could stand
His onset, if on foot he waved his steel,
Or spurred his foaming charger to the fight!
Poor youth! if fate's harsh ban thou canst defy,
Thou'lt be Marcellus. Heap me lilies high,
For I would fling the flowers that brightest are,
And to my kinsman's soul this tribute pay,
How vain soe'er the gift!"
                         Thus roam they far
Around that ghostly plain, in wide survey.
But when Anchises thus hath trained his son,
And fired his heart for glories to be won,
Next he recounts each circumstance of war,
What powers the Latin tribesmen shall array,
What labours must he dare, what perils shun.
   Two gates there are of Sleep; one carved of horn,

Which opes, 'tis said, to none but visions true,
One white with polished ivory, wherethrough
From the under-world delusive dreams are borne.
There, 'mid such converse, did Anchises guide
The chieftain, with the Sibyl at his side,
And gave them exit by the ivory gate.
Then back to ships and friends Æneas hies,
And to Caieta's port sails onward straight:
There, anchor cast, the fleet at moorage lies.

BOOK VII

ARGUMENT

SKIRTING the shore of Italy, Æneas arrives at the mouth of the Tiber, whence he sends envoys to Latinus, king of Latium, whose daughter Lavinia is sought in marriage by Turnus, prince of the Rutuli. Warned by an oracle, which has foretold the coming of a foreign chief, Latinus welcomes the Trojans, and is disposed to receive Æneas as son-in-law in place of Turnus; but Juno, intervening, causes a quarrel between Trojans and Latins which leads to war. The book closes with an enumeration of the Italian chieftains who come to the aid of Latium.

Thou, too, Caieta, nurse of Trojan king,
Dying didst give these shores a lasting fame;
Ev'n now the place is honoured, and thy name
Still marks the foreland where thine ashes bide,
In proud repose, on great Hesperian land.
There funeral rites he paid, and sorrowing
Her grave-mound heaped; but when the ocean tide
Flowed calm, with hoisted sail he left the strand.
Freshens the gentle breeze when falls the night,
Nor fails the fair moon's guidance, as they glide
O'er waters sparkling 'neath her tremulous light.
 So skirt they close those witching shores along,
Where Circe, wealthy daughter of the Sun,
Makes her enchanted woodlands ring with song,
And nightly, to illume her gorgeous bower,
Burns fragrant cedar, while her fingers run
Swift o'er the slender web with lisping reed.
Heard is the roar of lions, with fierce growl
Chafing against their chains at midnight hour,
And boars, and bears, loud clamouring to be freed,
Wrathful, and monstrous wolfish forms that howl;
For these by potent drugs and magic power
From human shape had suffered bestial change.

But lest the pious Trojans, unaware,
Should drift to perilous port, within the range
Of her damned spells and dread environment,
Kind Neptune filled their sails with breezes fair,
And past those seething shoals their vessels sent.
  Soon flushed the ocean, as with rosy car
Up-soared the Dawn, in saffron vest arrayed:
The soft-voiced wind to sudden silence sank,
And slow through sluggish waters toiled the blade.
'Twas then Æneas sighted from afar
A forest huge, wherethrough, by sunny bank,
Tiber in eddying current seaward sped,
'Mid wealth of yellow sands. Above, anear,
With cries of gladness that most soothing seem,
Wheeled birds that haunt the river's banks and bed:
Then bade he quit their course and shoreward steer,
And came, light-hearted, to that leafy stream.
  Come, aid me, Muse; for now my lays must tell
Of Latium's ancient realm, its powers, its king,
What time that foreign fleet drew nigh our coast;
And how the earliest seeds of strife befell.
Thou, goddess, be my guide! Of wars I sing;
Dread shock of battle; monarchs by fierce ire
To their own ruin hurled, when Tuscan host,
When all Hesperia, met in conflict dire:
Now to sublimer deeds my thoughts aspire;
A greater theme, a grander task I boast.
  Latinus for long years the crown had worn,
And through his quiet kingdom wars were none:
Of Faunus and Laurentine wood-nymph born,
He sprung, so legend tells, from race divine:
His father's sire was Picus, Saturn's son;
Thou, Saturn, wast the founder of his line.
No son Latinus had; the gods so willed,
His son had died, youth's promise unfulfilled;
One only daughter graced his royal hall,
Still mateless, but to wedlock's age up-grown:

And many a suitor did her fame enthrall
Through great Italia's length. Noblest of all
Was Turnus, warrior chief of proud descent;
On him, designed to share her daughter's throne,
The queen with eager love and favour leant:
But now stern warning signs from heaven forbade.
　　Midmost the palace court, in cloistered shade,
A laurel grew, preserved from bygone days
With awe and reverence; this the king had found,
When first his city's strength he planned and walled,
And spared, a sacred tree, for Phœbus' praise:
Laurentines thence his colonists were called.
Lo! strange to tell, its topmost twigs around,
Winging through cloudless skies with murmurous hum,
A swarm of bees flew sudden into sight,
And hung with clasping feet from lofty bough.
Then cried the seers: "A foreign chief shall come,
With foreign host, as comes this bee-swarm now,
And lord it o'er the city's topmost height."
Yea, more; for when the young Lavinia came
With holy torch the altar-fire to light,
And stood beside her sire, a mystic flame
Embraced, with crackling sound, her robes, her hair;
Flashed her long tresses, flashed her coronet,
With many a regal gem and jewel set;
Enwrapped she seemed in lurid vaporous glare,
And far with fiery sheen the palace glowed.
Nor do men's minds those prodigies forget;
Fortune, for her, and glory they forebode,
But bid her kin of mighty wars beware.
　　These ominous sights the monarch's heart appal;
His sire's prophetic guidance he would win,
Beneath Albunea's height, in darksome dale
Where loud the sacred stream is heard to fall,
And sulphurous fumes from forest depths exhale.
Thither, for counsel from the voice within,
Oft came the Italian tribes, by doubts distraught;

And there the priest (his wonted offerings brought)
Must take repose on slaughtered victim's skin,
'Neath midnight's solemn silence, courting sleep,
Till through his vision fleeting forms go by
In strange array, and ghostly words he hears,
And holds true converse with the gods on high,
And those dark powers that dwell in nether deep.
Thus, when Latinus sought to still his fears,
With sacrificial rites his vows he paid,
Then slumbered, stretched on fleeces of slain sheep,
Till sudden résponse rang from sombre shade:
    "Consent not, son, to yield thy daughter's hand
To favoured suitor born of Latin land;
Cometh a foreign bridegroom, from whose blood
A race shall rise o'er all the world subdued:
Where'er the sun looks down upon the sea,
Eastward or westward, shall their empire be."
Such answer 'neath the darkness Faunus gave,
Nor strove the king his warning words to hide;
Long time had light-winged Rumour borne them wide,
Ere came those Trojan wanderers o'er the wave,
And moored their keels to Tiber's grassy side.
    Beneath the boughs of lofty tree reclined,
Æneas with his chosen chieftains sate;
There on the turf a frugal feast was spread
Of viands laid on carven slabs of bread
(So had Celæno the god's will divined),
And sylvan apples piled on wheaten cate.
But when 'neath stress of hunger they were fain
With reckless hand and tooth to violate
The slender gifts of Ceres, nor refrain
From fateful crust that marked the destined hour,
"Why, look, our very tables we devour!"
Iulus cried, in jest. That welcome word
First brought surcease of woe; that word his sire
Upcaught—the heedless utterance of a boy—
And pondered deep, by silent wonder stirred:

Then, "Hail," he cried, "thou land of my desire!
Hail, ye Penates, trusty gods of Troy!
Here is our port, our home. Such secret lore
Erstwhile, it minds me, from my sire I heard.
'Son,' said he, 'when thou'rt cast on foreign shore,
So hungered, thou wouldst fain thy tables eat,
Then mayst thou hope to rest thy weary feet,
There doubt thou not thy city's walls to found.'
This is that hunger, this that last despair;
Our sorrow's utmost bound.
Come, then; at day-dawn let us wander wide,
To learn what folk upon this land abide:
Now pour we Jove's libation; and with prayer
To sire Anchises, pass the wine-cup round."
This said, with leafy spray he decked his brow;
Then to the Genius of the place, and Earth
The primal power, to Nymphs of field and fell,
And streams as yet unknown, he breathed a vow;
To Night, and Stars that in the night have birth,
And Jove, he prayed, and Her, most venerable,
The Phrygian Mother; to his parents twain,
Venus, revered above, his Sire below.
Then did the Almighty thunder thrice, and deign
From sunny skies a luminous cloud to show,
Burning aloft with many a golden ray;
Whereat ran rumour through the ranks of Troy
That now the hour had come, with fate's accord,
Foundation of their promised walls to lay:
So, by great omen cheered, they pledged, in joy,
The flagon, and the brimming bumpers poured.

But when the morrow's dawn illumed the land,
They ranged afield. Here slow Numicus flowed,
Here Tiber's stream, here stood the Latin town.
Forthwith Æneas bade a chosen band,
His hundred envoys, wreathed with olive crown,
Betake them to the king's august abode,
Laden with gifts, his friendship to implore:

They with swift strides on peaceful errand went.
Himself, the while, his future city planned,
Camp-like, with shallow trench beside the shore,
With rampart circled and high battlement.
　　But now the Trojans, journeying on their way,
The royal towers and turrets had espied,
And lofty walls. Upon the fields anear
Tilted the Latin youth in martial play;
Eager the bow they bent, or hurled the spear,
Or in swift chariot curbed their coursers' pride:
Bold champions, as in speed and strength they vied.
Then spurred a mounted courier to the gate,
With news that foreign folk, of stature tall,
And garb unknown, were nigh at hand; and straight
The king bade summon them within the hall
Where on his sires' ancestral throne he sate.
　　High o'er the city, with proud colonnade,
The stately palace of old Picus rose,
Hallowed of old, and dark with solemn shade.
Sceptre and fasces here to Latin kings
Must first be handed; here the Senate met
For counsel; here, at solemn banquetings,
When on the board the slaughtered ram was set,
The feasting Elders sat in lengthy line.
Along the porch their great forefathers stand,
In cedar carved; there Italus hath place,
And old Sabinus, planter of the vine,
Still imaged with keen pruning-hook in hand;
And father Saturn, and the two-fold face
Of Janus, and great kings of long ago,
And dauntless knights that bled for native land.
Nor lacked there trophies on the posts—a row
Of captive chariots, battle-axes bent,
And helms, and bolts from iron gateways rent,
And spears and galley-prows in combat ta'en.
There, famed for horsemanship, sat Picus; clad
In robe of state, his augur's staff he had

In strong right-hand; a targe was in his left;
Picus, whom Circe loved, but loved in vain:
Wherefore her golden wand in sorcery
She waved, and lo! of human form bereft,
A bird with gaily-coloured wings was he.
'Twas there Latinus, on ancestral seat,
Waited, those Trojan messengers to greet,
And, calm of speech, addressed them graciously:
   "Trojans—for not as strangers have ye come,
Nor lack we knowledge of your country's pride—
What seek ye on this far Hesperian coast?
What need hath brought you o'er the boundless foam?
Whate'er your lot—or strayed or tempest-tost,
Ills such as oft to mariners betide—
Since now within our port your keels have rest,
Doubt not our friendship: know, we spring from Him,
Great Saturn's self, a nation calm and kind
By no constraint, but born with gentle mind,
And with that old Saturnian instinct blessed.
I now bethink me, but in memory dim,
If our Auruncan sages spake aright,
'Twas hence that Dardanus, on daring quest,
To Samothracia's isle and Phrygia sailed:
From Tuscan home he crossed the watery ways;
Now sits he throned above the starry height,
One god the more for mortal men to praise."
   Then did Ilioneus in answer speak:
"Famed monarch, by no tempest buffeted,
To this Hesperian coast our ships were driven;
No treacherous skies or shores our course misled:
By fixed and firm design your walls we seek,
Long exiled from a realm once mightier far
Than aught the sun beheld from eastern heaven.
Jove was our sire; from Jove our high estate
We Trojans boast; from Jove our king is sprung,
Æneas, whose ambassadors we are.
What storm of battle, by Mycenæ's hate,

O'er Ida's devastated fields was flung—
Europe 'gainst Asia dashed by will of fate—
Ev'n to remotest shores of earth is known,
Yea, to the fierce heart of the torrid zone.
'Scaped from that ruin o'er the trackless wave,
A little refuge for our gods we pray,
A friendly shore, a guileless harbour crave,
And air and water that to all are free.
Your people's honour will we not betray,
But rather bring you fame abundantly,
With deathless gratitude for service true:
For, sure, that hour Ausonia ne'er shall rue,
When outcast Troy was taken to her breast.
This swear I by our monarch's destiny,
And by his strong right-hand, the trustiest
E'er grasped, in war or peace, by foe or friend.
Full many a people, as we roamed the earth
(Scorn not our suppliant hands, our earnest pleas),
Was fain with Trojan race its race to blend;
But still, by Fate's imperious decrees,
We sought these lands where Dardanus had birth;
Hither our lord Apollo now recalls,
With mighty voice that still more urgent grows,
Where sacred Tiber, where Numicus flows.
Gifts, too, our chief hath sent—poor relics, these,
Of past wealth rescued from Troy's burning walls.
From this gold cup Anchises oft would pour
Libation at the shrines; these Priam wore,
Mitre and sceptre, in his judgment-halls;
These robes our damsels wrought."

   So spake he; but Latinus, plunged in thought,
His gaze fixed on the ground, sat silent there,
With anxious, roving eyes. Small joy had he
In purple-broidered rugs and sceptre gold:
His daughter's marriage still had all his care
And sire's forewarning of the things to be.
Lo, now, that foreign bridegroom, long foretold,

Destined to share his crown with equal right;
Whose offspring, with unconquerable will,
Should make the wide world subject to their might!
Then glad he spoke: "May heaven our hopes fulfil,
And its own tokens! Friends, your wish I grant,
Your gifts I slight not. Never, while I reign,
Lands, rich as erst were Troy's, shall Trojans want.
But let your king in person, if he deign
To test my kindness and be hailed ally,
Speed hither, nor our friendly faces dread;
Hand clasped in hand, we'll pledge our loyalty.
Go now: this message to your chief convey.
A daughter have I, whom I may not wed
To Latin suitor; this the gods gainsay,
This warn me voices from my father's shrine:
Cometh a foreign bridegroom o'er the brine—
For him let Latium look—whose sons shall spread
Our fame o'er earth and heaven. Now draws he nigh,
This prince whom fate demands? Such thought have I;
Such hope, if rightly I forebode, is mine."
    Within the royal stables ranged in line
Full thrice an hundred glossy chargers stood:
Thence, for his Trojan guests, he bade them bring
Swift steeds, in pomp of purple garb arrayed;
Gold necklets from their shoulders swung and swayed;
All gold their trappings were, their bits all gold:
Likewise a chariot for the Trojan king,
Drawn by two coursers of ethereal mould,
Who from their nostrils snorted scornful fire;
Of that mixed race, by mortal mother foaled,
Which Circe, crafty daughter of the Sun,
Bred from the flaming stallions of her sire.
Such gifts, such mandate, did those envoys bear,
As back they rode, elate, their errand done,
Glad news of peace and concord to declare.
    But now, returning from her Argive fane,
Jove's vengeful spouse her airy path pursued,

And soaring o'er Pachynum's headland high
The Trojans' joyful landing chanced to spy:
Past were their perils on the stormy main,
Their ships abandoned. Smit with grief she stood,
And shaking stern her head, cried wrathfully:
　　"Detested tribe, whose fates 'gainst mine conspire!
Could they not perish on Sigean field?
Nor burn with burning Troy? nor, yielding, yield?
Nay, still unscathed through circling sword and fire
Found they their passage! Now forsooth is spent
My godhead's force, and quenched is Juno's ire!
No toil I spared to plague their exiled band;
I barred the deep where'er their course was bent,
And lavished all the wrath of seas and stars;
But naught availed me Syrtes' shifting sand;
Naught Scylla; naught Charybdis' waters white.
Behold them moored by Tiber's promised strand,
Heedless of waves and me! Full power had Mars
The Lapithæ's gigantic race to smite;
Nor did great Jove shield ancient Calydon
From utmost vengeance of Diana's hate:
Such forfeit paid they: was their sin so great?
While I, the consort of the Almighty's throne,
Must leave no shift untried, no deed undone,
Foiled by Æneas! Does my godhead pall?
Naught reck I, then, whence needed aid I seek:
If Heaven will heed not, Hell shall hear my call.
True, naught can shut him from his realm decreed;
His destined bride, Lavinia, must he win;
Yet can I weave impediments, and wreak
Revenge on folk who for their monarchs bleed.
So, by betrayal of their suffering kin,
Let sire and suitor frame their covenant!
Fair maiden, warriors' blood shall be thy dower;
And lo! stern patroness of nuptial joy,
Bellona waits thee! Not Troy's queen alone
Brought forth a fiery brand in childbirth's hour;

Nay, Venus, too, hath borne, in this her son,
A second Paris, a fierce flame, with power
To blight the hopes of rearisen Troy."
    She ceased, and earthward turned her sullen flight,
Then summoned from the blackest pit of hell—
From that dark mansion where the Furies dwell—
The fiend Alecto, whom the woes of war,
Treasons, and threats, and deadly crimes delight:
Loathed is she by her ghoulish sisterhood,
Ev'n by grim Pluto loathed, so countless are
The ghastly forms and fashions she can take,
With vipers crowned that sprout in venomous brood.
Thus, then, her wrath to rouse, the goddess spake:
    "Daughter of Night, I pray thee for that aid
Which none but thou can give; lest men deny
Those honours that to Juno's name belong,
And Trojan wooers cozen with false tongue
The Latin monarch, and his realm invade.
Thou, by thy wiles, canst breed mad enmity
'Twixt fondest brothers; homes with hatred blast;
Red rage and deadliest strife 'mid kinsmen bring;
A thousand names, a thousand plagues, thou hast.
Come, rack thy fertile brain, this pondering—
How thou mayst break two nations' fair accord,
And in their hearts the seeds of fury fling:
So shall impetuous youth demand the sword,
And instant from its sheath the sword shall spring."
    Therewith Alecto, clad in serpents stark,
To Latium speeding, sought the king's abode,
And lighted at Amata's threshold dark.
Ev'n now the queen, for favoured Turnus' sake,
Roused by the coming of a rival love,
With all a woman's fear and anger glowed:
On her the hell-hag threw one gleaming snake
Plucked from the coil, and deep her bosom clove,
That so her madness all the house might scare:
And straight she clasped the monster, unaware,

As 'neath her robe within her breast it wound;
Nor touch she felt, nor in her frenzy knew
What viperish spirit from that pest she drew;
A golden spire it seemed, her neck around;
It seemed a ribbon from her fillet strayed;
It twined among her tresses; or in turn
With sinuous folds along her limbs it played.
But when the stealthy poison thrilled her frame,
And in her very vitals 'gan to burn—
Ere yet her inmost heart had felt the flame—
Gently, as mothers use, her plaint she made,
And o'er those new espousals fain would mourn:
   "How? Trojan exiles? Say'st thou one of these
Must wed Lavinia? Pity hast thou none
For her, thy daughter? for thyself no care?
No care for me, her mother? Let the breeze
Once blow, and straight this pirate will be gone,
And in his barque the captive maiden bear;
As erst that Phrygian shepherd o'er the seas
From Lacedæmon bore his stolen fair.
What of the ties that bind thee to thine own?
Thy pledge so often to my Turnus given?
But if from foreign race a son is sought,
Nor darest thou set old Faunus' words at naught,
All lands methinks are foreign that are free
From scope of Latin lordship: thus I would
Interpret the command thou heard'st from heaven.
Ay, if thou'lt ask what Turnus' lineage be,
From heart of Greece his grandsires drew their blood."
   Vain were her words; unmoved Latinus stood;
And soon the madness in her breast engrained
Sank deep and spread its venom to the core;
Then, mastered by delirious impulse strong,
She roamed the city's borders unrestrained:
So flies a top beneath the curling thong
Wielded by boys on some great court-yard's floor,
Intent on pastime. 'Neath the lash it spins

In widening circles, while the playful throng
Bends o'er the boxen toy in fond surprise,
And from its flight a childish wonder wins;
Such speed their blows impart. In course as fleet
The queen through savage clans and regions flies:
Nay, worse; for feigning Bacchus' sacred rites,
Where sombre forest-depths yield dark retreat,
More daring deeds her frenzy would assay,
To hide her daughter 'mid their leafy heights;
Ev'n thus those dreaded nuptials would she stay;
Loud crying: "Evoë, Bacchus! None but Thou
Is worthy of this maid. For Thee shall glance
Her thyrsus; Thee she shall acclaim in dance;
To Thee her sacred virgin tresses vow."
   Winged Rumour spreads; and soon the matrons all
Are seized with one wild tumult of unrest;
Their homes they quit, and to the breezes, mad,
Their bosoms bare, and let their locks down fall:
Some shriek in frenzy; some, in rough skins clad,
Go waving spear-like wands in vine-leaves dressed.
Herself the queen, with blazing torch held high,
Rolling her bloodshot orbs distractedly,
Proclaims the royal maid to Turnus wed:
"Ho! hear my voice, ye mothers, wheresoe'er
Your footsteps stray," thus rang her passionate cry;
"If aught for lost Amata's misery
Your kindly bosoms are disquieted—
If for maternal rights ye still have care—
Unbind ye each the fillets from her head,
And with your queen these solemn orgies share."
   So 'mid the woods, through many a desert lair,
Wandered the queen in fury uncontrolled;
But when no power could quench the deadly flame
That wrecked those hopes whereon Latinus leaned,
Far on her sooty pinions flew the fiend
To that Rutulian fortress where of old
Fair Danaë with her Argive settlers came,

By boisterous breezes driven: 'twas Ardea hight,
And Ardea still remains the city's name,
Though gone its glory. There, 'neath gloom of night,
In lofty chamber Turnus slumbering lay:
Whereat she doffed hell's dreadful livery,
And cloaked her visage in a beldam's guise:
Wrinkled was that stern brow; her hair was white;
White were her fillets, wreathed with olive spray:
'Twas Juno's priestess, agéd Calybe,
That speaking stood before the chieftain's eyes:
  "Turnus, shall all thy labours be undone?
Wilt see thy sceptre pass to foreign lord?
For now the king despoils thee of thy bride
And royal dowry that thy blood hath won,
And mocks thee, throning strangers by his side.
Go, then—for thine the risk without reward—
Lay low the Tuscan bands, bring Latium rest!
This warning, while thy sleep was tranquillest,
Great Juno bade me speak into thine ear:—
Arm quick thy youthful chivalry thou must,
And lead them forth to battle in good cheer,
Where, by fair Tiber's brink, those Trojans lie.
Go, smite them; burn their painted prows to dust:
So heaven commandeth. Ev'n the king shall know—
If still his plighted promise he deny—
How vain the fight, when Turnus is a foe."
  Thereto the youth in bitter scorn replied:
"Nay, but those tidings have escaped me not
Of foreign galleys banked by Tiber side:
Feign not false perils, nor that heaven's great queen
Her Turnus hath forgot.
Mother, thyself hast long decrepit been;
The truth no more is in thee; but old age
Affrights thy vision, 'mid the strife of kings,
And mocks thee with its vain imaginings.
To guard the sacred temples is thy care:
Let wars be waged by men, who wars must wage."

Then sudden did the Fury's wrath upflare.
Ev'n as he spoke, he shuddered with strange awe;
Dazed were his eyes; such hissing snakes he saw,
So grim a visage faced him. Fiercely burned
Her rolling orbs; and when with faltering tongue
He fain had spoken still, his tale she spurned,
And cracked her whip, and cried, to frenzy stung:
"Behold me—long decrepit! now no more
The truth is in me; but, 'mid strife of kings,
Age mocks me with its false imaginings!
Yet look thou! for I come from that dark shore
Where waits the dreaded Sisters' demon band:
Wars, deaths, are in my hand."
        This said, she flings her flaming torch, and deep
Its murky fires the warrior's bosom pierce:
Then shattered in wild terror is his sleep,
As down his body runs the streaming sweat.
For arms he rages, clamours, near and far,
Craving the sword, with savage lust of war,
And anger crowning all. So, blazing fierce,
Crackle the thorns 'neath bubbling caldron set,
When sobs with heat the water, and anon
Its troubled surface 'gins to foam and fret,
Then 'scaping soars, a vaporous cloud, in air.
Forthwith he bade his trusty chiefs prepare
To face the king; let coward peace be gone,
And smite the foes that wrought Italia shame;
Himself for both their hosts were match enow—
Trojans with Latins. Thus their hearts he fired,
And called the gods for witness to his vow.
So did the Rutuli that war acclaim;
Some by his youth and comely form inspired,
Some by his royal race, his deeds of fame.
        Ere thus his followers' hearts he stirred to flame,
The fiend on Stygian wings her course had bent—
For so with crafty watch she spied the shore—
Where young Iulus, on his sport intent,

Hunted the fleet-foot deer by Tiber's bounds:
Then cast she sudden madness on his hounds,
Tempting their nostrils with the wonted scent,
Till for the quarry's blood they lusted sore.
That fatal chase, with toil and anguish rife,
First roused a peaceful folk to murderous strife.

A stag there was, stately with antlered pride,
Whom Tyrrheus' sons had reared, a nursling fair,
Within their father's gates; for his the care
Of the king's herds and all the woodland wide:
No labour did their sister Silvia spare
To tame her charge; his horns she garlanded
With tender flowers, and combed his shaggy hair,
And washed him with the fountain's sparkling tide.
He, for he loved the fostering hand that fed,
Freely the forest depths would range and roam,
Yet failed not, when night fell, how late soe'er,
To seek the friendly shelter of his home.

'Twas he that wandering in a lonely place,
And drifting down the gently flowing stream
'Mid grassy banks, to shun the noonday beam,
Thus drew Iulus' hounds in furious chase;
And the young huntsman, quick his bow he bent,
Fired with fierce longing for so rich a prize,
Nor missed the mark, for Fortune smiled, and sheer
Through the strong side the sounding arrow went.
Then home, sore stricken, fled the wounded deer,
Back to the stall, and there, with wounds displayed,
Like some sad suppliant with imploring eyes,
Through all the house loud lamentation made;
While Silvia foremost to his rescue flies,
Beats breast, and calls the countryfolk to aid.
Quick came they, ev'n as that foul pest designed,
That lurked in silent woods; for arms, they held
Charred stake or knotted club—what each could find
Was anger's weapon: far in forest glade
Was Tyrrheus, where it chanced an oak was felled;

Thence rushed he, breathing wrath, with axe in hand.
But when, from her retreat, the Fury knew
The moment ripe to work the mischief planned,
High on the roof-top perched, she fiercely blew
Through shepherd's horn her blast, the dolefullest
That ever summoned simple swains to war:
It thrilled the forest to its depths profound;
'Twas heard at Dian's lake; 'twas heard where far
Velinus rolls, and sulphurous stream of Nar;
Yea, many a mother heard that dreary sound,
And, trembling, clasped her children to her breast.

    Soon, at the trumpet's din that broke their rest,
With weapons snatched in speed, from left, from right,
The yeomen ran; nor less the men of Troy
Poured from the camp to shield the princely boy:
Ranged are the ranks; no more in rustic fight
With sharpened stakes or hard-burnt brands they deal;
Now must the sword decide a deadlier fray;
The blades are bared in rigid crop of steel,
And sunlit armour flashes back the ray:
So, 'neath a coming storm the waves gleam white,
As more and more with foamy crests they leap,
Till in one surging mass up-heaves the deep.

    Then flew a droning dart across the strife
And Tyrrheus' eldest son, young Almo, smote;
He fell, the fatal barb within his throat,
Choking with blood the gate of speech and life.
Nor he alone; fell old Galesus then,
Who, standing 'twixt the foes, for peace did plead;
A man for justice famed, much wealth he earned
In former years; still nightly to their pen
His flocks and herds came five-fold from the mead,
And with an hundred ploughs the soil he turned.

    But when the war, thus kindled on the plain,
With equal fortune raged, that Shape abhorred—
Her dreadful pledge performed, for now the sword
With blood was red, and the first death-blow dealt—

Sailed from Hesperian fields to heaven's domain,
And thus to Juno spoke the pride she felt:
  "Look! I have perfected thy work of hate.
Go, bid them now their peaceful pact fulfil,
Since Trojan hand is wet with Latin blood!
Ay, more; for if thy power befriend me still,
Each neighbouring tribe I will exasperate,
Stirring their hearts, with lust of blood imbued,
To join in battle; nor shall weapons fail—
These will I scatter wide o'er field and hill."
But Juno: "Nay, sufficient is thy tale
Of guile and terror. Deep-set discord reigns;
For now in combat hand to hand they meet,
And arms, that chance supplied, their life-blood stains.
Such marriage-rites shall king Latinus greet,
And Venus' son, that prince of virtue rare!
But thou—why roam'st at large through upper air?
So wills not He that rules the Olympian height.
Begone: the future task, how hard soe'er,
Myself will order." Thus Saturnia spake;
Then spread the fiend her snaky wings in flight,
And sank from heaven to gloom of Stygian lake.
  A spot there is, by mountains compassed round,
In fair Italia's midst; to fame far known,
The vale of dark Amsanctus: forests lone
Lie dense on either flank; and deeply pent
'Twixt wild o'erhanging rocks, with roaring sound
Tumbles an eddying torrent. Here are shown
A gloomy cavern, and that yawning rent
Where with o'erflowing flood-gates Acheron
Opes his pestiferous jaws. Therein was hid
The Fury, as she plunged with swift descent,
And earth and heaven of her foul presence rid.
  Natheless, by mighty Juno's ordering,
That feud was fostered. To the city sped
Scared shepherds from the fight, and bore their dead,
Galesus' mangled corse, young Almo slain;

Loudly they cried to heaven, adjured the king.
There Turnus stood, and swelled their fears the more,
As hotly of that wrong he did complain,
With tale of Trojan to the sceptre called,
Their Latin race with Phrygian blood defiled,
Himself an outcast driven from palace door.
There, too, flock they whose womenfolk, enthralled
In Bacchic revels, roam the woodlands wild
With frenzied dance (for still the power is great
Of queen Amata's name): these clamour loud
For war, and yet for war, till all the crowd,
Scorning the signs from heaven, the voice of fate,
In froward mood the curse of war demand,
And eager round the monarch's gateway stand.
He, rock-like, in his place unyielding bides—
An ocean rock, which, steadfast 'mid the din
Of barking billows, fronts the raging tides,
Firm-based; albeit the foam-swept cliffs above
Shriek in the storm, and from its streaming sides
The wrack is dashed rebounding to the main.
But when nor help nor hearing can he win
'Gainst that blind purpose, but those issues move
As Juno wills them, then the sire in vain
Invokes the heedless heaven to hear his vow,
Crying: "Fate breaks us: to the storm I bow.
'Tis ye, poor wretches, with your blood will rue
This sacrilegious deed. Thou, Turnus, thou
Wilt suffer vengeance stern: too late thou'lt cry
To heaven this fatal madness to undo.
For me is rest assured, life's voyage past;
One thing alone I lose—in peace to die."
No more he said, but far from sight withdrew,
And from his hands the reins of empire cast.
    In Latium's realm an agelong custom rose,
Thenceforth through Alban cities handed on,
And cherished still where Rome her way hath won,
Whene'er our folk would light war's dreaded flame,

'Gainst Scythian tribe, or Medes, or Arab foes,
Or eastward press beyond Aurora's throne,
Or back from Parthian hands the standards claim.
Two Gates of War there are (for such their name),
In fear and reverence sacred from of yore:
With hundred bolts of brass they wait fast-barred
And deathless strength of iron, and evermore
Grave Janus at the threshold sits on guard.
Here, when the Senate's will on war is bent,
The Consul, robed and girt majestical,
Himself unlocks each harshly-grating door,
Himself the sword invokes, acclaimed of all,
While brazen trumpets join in harsh assent.
Thus ancient usage bade that agéd king
With solemn voice the god of battle call
'Gainst Trojan foes, and those grim gates unswing;
But from the touch he shrank, and turned away,
Loathing the task, and sought his inmost hall.
Then down from heaven herself did Juno glide,
And pushed the unwilling doors, nor brooked delay,
Till, forced on creaking hinge, they parted wide.
   Soon all is fire, where stillness long hath been.
Some march afoot; some, mounted, gallop light
'Mid surging dust; for battle all prepare.
Smooth shield and gleaming lance they polish bright,
And on the whetstone grind their axes keen,
Or hoist the flag, or hark the trumpet's blare.
Five cities forge new armour for the fight:
Bold Ardea and Atina lend their powers,
With Tibur, haughty on its slope reclined,
Crustumium, and Antemnæ crowned with towers.
Now are strong helmets fashioned, osiers twined
For wicker targe; some carve the steel cuirass,
Or burnished greaves of molten silver mould:
Naught else they heed, whose joy erstwhile it was
To wield the pruning-hook or guide the plough.
Their fathers' swords they forge afresh; and now

The clarion rings, now is the watchword told.
See! one impatient grasps his helm, and one
Yokes his high-mettled steeds with eager hand,
Or buckler stout, or frock of mail would don,
Gold-laced, or gird him with his trusty brand.
  Ope now your Helicon, and stir my verse,
Ye Muses; for in song must I rehearse
What monarchs marched to war, and in their train
What armies met embattled on the plain;
Yea, with what martial spirit glowed, ev'n then,
Italia's soil, fair mother of brave men.
Ye know those chiefs, those bygone deeds can name:
To me hath come scarce whisper of their fame.
  First to the fray, grim lord of Tuscan race,
Who mocked the almighty gods, Mezentius sped,
With Lausus, loyal son, whose bodily grace
No knight, save Turnus only, could excel;
Lausus, that peerless rider—in the chase,
How long soe'er the toil, he ne'er did tire:
Now from Agylla's stately walls he led
A thousand swords (alas, for what befell!),
And, sooth, in nobler cause he merited
To serve, nor own Mezentius for his sire.
  Next, his victorious car with palm-leaf crowned,
Proud Aventinus strode triumphant on;
Of godlike Hercules the godlike son;
Deep on his shield was graved his father's sign,
A Hydra girt with hundred serpents round.
Him, in a secret croft of Aventine,
Rhea the priestess bore—such love she won
From that great hero, when to Latin land
He turned from death of conquered Geryon,
And bathed in Tuscan stream his Spanish kine.
So marched the clansmen, sturdy pike in hand,
Poniard, and Sabine spear, or javelin light;
Himself, rough-clad in skin of lion slain,
Unkempt with grisly shock of tufted mane,

And teeth above his temples gleaming white,
Through palace-gates a savage shape he passed,
His sire's huge mantle o'er his shoulder cast.

Then from high Tibur's walls two brothers wend;
Catillus, Coras, youths with heart aglow,
Rushing impetuous to the foremost field:
So, when two cloud-born Centaurs swift descend
From Homole, or Othrys' peak of snow,
In headlong haste, the boundless forests bend
Before them, and the crashing thickets yield.

Nor doth Præneste's royal founder fail—
By God of Fire 'mid flocks and herds begot,
And found on shepherd's hearth, so ran the tale—.
Great Cæculus. A rustic troop he leads
From Gabian cornlands, from Præneste's hills,
And Anio's cooling waves, and many a spot
Where Hernic rocks are wet with dewy rills;
From vales that father Amasenus feeds;
From rich Anagnia's bounds. Scant arms they boast,
Nor shield, nor rattling chariot; but the most
Sling leaden bullets and with javelins twain
Go armed, their heads in tawny wolfskin dight
For helm; bare feet they plant upon the plain,
The left; rough hides untanned protect the right.

Messapus, lord of steeds, great Neptune's child,
Whom ne'er with fire or sword might mortal slay,
Rouses a folk disused from warfare wild,
And grasps anew his falchion for the fray.
Faliscans, or Fescennia's yeomen they;
Or from Soracte's brow, Capena's grove,
Or far Ciminius and its mountain-mere;
In measured march harmonious they move,
Chanting the praise and prowess of their king;
As when through liquid clouds on snowy wing
A flock of swans their homeward voyage steer,
With necks outstretched, and ever, to their glee,
Caÿster's marshes ring.

Nor wouldst thou deem that in yon serried mass
Were steely swords, but rather, from the sea,
A cloud of clamorous fowl that shoreward pass.
    Lo, Clausus, Sabine chief of long descent,
From whom the Claudian tribe through Latium spread
When Sabine blood with Roman race was blent:
A mighty host—himself a host—he led;
The old Quirites, Amiternum's best,
And dauntless warriors that inhabited
Mutusca's vales with fruitful olives blessed;
Or fair Eretum, or Nomentum town,
Or Rosean pastures; or had hastened down
From crags of Tetric and Severus' crest.
Nor lacked there those that drank of Tiber's tide,
Or Fabaris, or from chilly Nursia came;
And Latin folk, and dwellers by the side
Of Allia, stream of inauspicious name:
Countless as rolling waves on Libyan main,
When fierce Orion sets, and storms begin—
Or ears of corn that bask in summer heat
On Lycia's yellowing fields or Hermus' plain—
They march; their shields resound with brazen din,
And quakes the earth beneath their tramping feet.
    Next rides a lord of Agamemnon's line,
Halesus, foe to Troy implacable:
A goodly troop he brings to Turnus' aid
Of carles that stir the soil and tend the vine
On Massic slopes, or 'mid the mountains dwell,
Sons of Auruncan sires; or where, outspread,
Lies the Campanian plain; from Cales some,
Or from Vulturnus' shoaly waters come,
With warlike Oscan bands. Slim shafts they wield,
Fitted, as custom bids, with pliant thong:
Their left arms wrapped in sturdy Spanish shield,
With scythe-like sword in thickest fight they throng.
    Nor thou, brave Œbalus, in this my song
Shalt go unhonoured. Fame it is that thee

Sebethis, river-nymph, to Telon bore,
What time he ruled the realm of Capreæ,
An agéd king: the son, content no more
With that paternal kingdom, held in fee
The people of the plain by Sarnus fed,
And Rufræ, Batulum, and Celemna's vale,
And high Abella's apple-growing glade:
Barbaric darts, as Teutons use, they hail;
With cork-tree bark their brows are helmeted;
Bright gleam their brazen targe, their brazen blade.

    Thou, too, didst haste from Nersæ's lonely wold,
Ufens, in many a daring foray famed;
Lord of wild tribesmen reared on savage soil,
Inured to hardy chase and woodcraft bold.
Armed in the fields they laboured, nor were shamed
To live by pillage and heap high the spoil.

    With these there came the brave Marruvian priest,
Sent forth to battle by his king's command,
His helm with spray of gracious olive dressed,
Umbro: strange power was his, to lull to rest,
With charm of chanted word and waving hand,
Fierce vipers and the hydra's venomous rage,
And by his skill their deadly wounds to swage:
But for the mortal stroke of Dardan spear,
Stricken, he found no healing cure, nor aught
His magic arts and slumbrous spells availed,
Nor potent herbs on Marsian mountains sought.
Him green Anguitia, him the glassy mere
Of Fucinus bewailed.

    Rode with the rest Hippolytus' fair son,
The princely Virbius, by his mother sent
From grove of wise Egeria; there were spent
His boyhood's years by that calm shore whereon
Stood gracious Dian's tribute-laden shrine.
For when, through guilty step-dame's craft malign,
Hippolytus, by father's curse pursued,
Was dashed to death, from flying chariot cast

By frighted steeds—fame says with life renewed
He rose again to daylight's realms above,
Recalled by healing herbs and Dian's love.
Then Jove, indignant that death's bounds were passed
By mortal man, with his own levin smote
The leech, Apollo's son, who worked such cure:
But Dian bore the youth to bowers remote,
And laid him in Egeria's woodlands lone;
So might he, 'mid Italian woods obscure,
Fulfil his life, by name of Virbius known.
Wherefore the goddess doth nowise endure
Nigh to her sacred shades and chaste abode
The fleet-foot Horse, since by his panic fear
Her favourite from his chariot was o'erthrown:
Yet durst the son his fiery coursers cheer
O'er spacious plains, and swift to battle rode.

   Himself among the foremost, stately, tall,
Grasping his sword and buckler, Turnus goes,
And by a head o'ertops his fellows all.
On his three-crested helmet, dark and dire,
Chimæra sits, forth-breathing flames of fire,
And fiercer still, and still more baleful glows,
As bloodier and more desperate sways the fight.
See! on his polished shield, in gold embossed,
An Io; now, ev'n now, with horns upright,
Her maiden form in heifer's semblance lost
(A strange device), and Argus at her side;
While Inachus, her sire, from sculptured urn
Pours forth, a river-god, his storied tide.
So Turnus goes, companioned by a host
Of shields in dense array, like storm-cloud stern:
His Argive warriors, proud Auruncia's ranks,
And old Sicanian chivalry are there;
And brave Labici with their painted shields,
And folk that till Numicus' sacred banks,
Or Tiber's lawns, or plough with gleaming share
Circæan ridge and steep Rutulian fields.

From Anxur, where Jove's fane o'erlooks the lea,
They come; from Satura's low-lying fen;
From gay Feronia's forest-glades; and where,
Rushing with icy wave through deep-cut glen,
Swift Ufens hastes to hide him in the sea.
    Last marched Camilla, born of Volscian race,
Followed by troop in shimmering steel arrayed.
No woman's work did her fair fingers wield
With distaff or with loom; a warrior maid,
So fleet of foot the winds she could outpace,
She braved the fiercest hardships of the field.
O'er ripening cornlands might she wing her way,
Nor in her passage harm the tenderest blade;
Or glide above the weltering waves so fast,
Her feet were wet not with the flying spray.
Forth came a gazing throng, where'er she passed,
Of youths and dames that watched, in ravishment,
With what proud pomp of purple, as a queen,
She robed her gleaming shoulders—how with gold
Her hair was braided—with what gesture bold
She grasped her Lycian quiver, as she went,
And shaft of myrtle tipped with spear-point keen.

BOOK VIII

ARGUMENT

ADVISED by the river-god Tiber, Æneas seeks the help of Evander,
a Greek prince, whose city Pallanteum was built on the Palatine
Hill, the future site of Rome. An alliance is formed against the Latins;
and Evander sends his son Pallas to accompany Æneas to the war.
At the request of Venus, Vulcan forges for Æneas a shield, on which
are depicted some of the events destined to be famous in the history
of Rome.

When Turnus from Laurentum's towers up-raised
War's signal, and the harsh-toned trumpets rang—
'Mid noise of clattering steeds and armour's clang—
Distracted were men's minds, all Latium lost
In uproar wild, and youthful warriors crazed
With lust of battle. They who led the host,
Messapus, and Mezentius haughty-willed,
Contemner of the gods, fresh levies brought
Of peasants dragged from fruitful fields untilled;
While Venulus from Diomede's city sought
Armed aid, and news of evil import bore:
How men of Troy were camped on Latin shore;
Their chief Æneas, with his gods exiled,
Came self-proclaimed the king foretold of yore,
Nor homage lacked from many a native clan;
Ev'n now his fame through Latium's borders ran.
What hopes thereon he built, if fortune smiled—
What ends pursued by prosperous battle blessed—
Small need was theirs to tell; such Trojan plan
To Diomede's self might be more manifest.

Thus Latium armed; and when Æneas learned
Its purpose, tossed on thought's unquiet stream,
This way and that his subtle mind he turned,
Gave heed to many a project, pondering all:

So, when in brazen caldron waters gleam,
Whereon the sunlight or pale moonrays fall,
Far flits the glint of that reflected beam,
Then, rising, strikes the roof of lofty hall.
   'Twas night: earth's weary creatures, far and near,
Winged birds and fleecy flocks, knew slumber's spell.
There, on the river's marge, 'neath chilly skies,
Perplexed at heart by war's untimely knell,
Æneas courted sleep, how late soe'er.
When lo! in dream, Dan Tiber did appear:
'Mid pleasant poplar grove he seemed to rise;
Of linen fine was woven his glaucous gown,
His temples shaded close with sedgy crown,
As thus the chieftain's grief he strove to cheer:
   "O heaven-born hero, who to Tiber's strand
Bring'st back the race of Troy, from foemen freed,
Proud city of lofty towers, redeemed for aye:
Hail, long-expected lord of Latin land!
Here, certain, is thy home by fate decreed;
Here, doubt not, sure abode thy gods shall find.
Nor fear war's menace; now hath passed away
That wrath of heaven unkind.
No fickle dream is this, to cheat thy mind;
For mark! when thou shalt see, 'neath ilex bough,
Of bulk immense, recumbent on the ground,
With brood of thirty young, a mother sow,
White, with her offspring white her dugs around—
There shall thy city stand, this doubt not thou.
For soon as years twice ten have ta'en their flight,
Illustrious Alba's walls thy son shall found.
Sure truths I bring, brief counsel. Note thou well
How thou mayst bear thee victor in this fight.
For know, on yonder hills Arcadians dwell,
Who whilom with their king Evander came
And built their city, from his grandsire's name
Called Pallanteum: foes implacable
Of Latin tribe: go then, their friendship claim,

And bind them with firm treaty to thy side.
Myself betwixt these banks thy ships will guide
That so my seaward stream thou mayst surmount.
Rise, goddess-born; and when night's watch-fires fade
To Juno make thy prayers, thy vows recount,
Whereby her vengeful threats may be allayed:
To me thy triumph-offerings shall be given.
My stream it is that flows from brimming fount
Cleaving its course through smiling dales and downs;
Tiber, proud river-god, most dear to heaven:
Here dwell I, flanked and crowned with lofty towns."
    So saying, he sank from view where flowed his tide;
Lost in its depths. Then sleep, with night, was gone:
Æneas rose, and as the daybreak shone
In eastern skies, fresh water from the wave
He lifted reverent in his palm, and cried:
"Ye nymphs, Laurentine nymphs, of stream and spring,
Thou, father Tiber, in thy sanctitude,
Receive me now, and from these perils save!
Whether thou sit'st unseen beneath thy flood,
Or leapest forth from earth with wavelets pure,
Since thou hast pitied my long wandering,
Thy name and fame shall evermore endure,
Of fair Hesperia's streams the sceptred king.
Be thou my present aid, my guardian sure!"
    He spoke, and from his fleet two vessels chose,
Fitted with oars, and armed forthwith his crew;
When lo! a sudden marvel met his view:
For there, milk-white beside the greenwood glade,
A sow he saw with milk-white brood repose.
Her, with her young, before thine altar laid,
To thee for solemn sacrifice he slew,
Great Juno, queen of heaven, to none but thee.
That night, how long soe'er its hours might be,
His swiftly surging stream old Tiber stayed;
With waters whist and refluent tide he flowed;
Till, like some placid pool or windless mere,

The yielding surface 'neath the oar was strowed,
And on their course they sped with joyous cheer.
Swift glide the keels; the while, in deep amaze,
The woods, the waves, on that strange pageant gaze—
On painted prows that ride the river's breast,
On shields that flash afar their fitful sheen.
All night, all day, their task those oarsmen ply
Far up the winding stream, 'neath canopy
Of arching trees in various verdure dressed,
And cleave their tranquil way 'twixt forests green.
   High was the sun at burning noontide hour,
When they beheld the walls, the citadel,
The scattered roofs, where now Rome's mighty power
Has piled its gorgeous mansions to the sky:
In lowlier palace did Evander dwell.
Shoreward they steer, and to the town draw nigh.
That day the Arcadian king, as it befell,
Made solemn feast to godlike Hercules,
Fronting the city's gates; and with him stood
Pallas, his son, and all his lords beside
(Nor mickle wealth, though nobly born, had these);
Where incense-laden altars steamed with blood.
But when they saw, beyond the belt of trees,
On noiseless oars the towering galleons glide,
The consecrated tables they forsook,
Risen in sudden fear; till Pallas bade
Quit not those holy rites: a spear he took,
And rushed to front the menace undismayed.
   "Say, warriors, whence and whither voyaging
To sail these ways unknown were ye compelled?
Your home? your race? is't peace or war ye bring?"
Then from the lofty stern answered the king,
With olive-branch, for pledge of peace, forth-held:
"Trojans we are. To champion our right
'Gainst Latium's haughty power the sword we draw.
We seek Evander. This, I charge thee, say:
Troy's chosen chiefs his arméd aid invite."

That mighty name young Pallas heard in awe.
"Come, step thou forth," he cried, "my sire to greet.
Whoe'er thou art, I'll bring thee on thy way,
A welcome guest within our halls to bide."
Then hand with hand in friendly clasp they meet;
So to the grove they pass from river-side.

    There to the king the Trojan chieftain cried:
"Worthiest of Greeks, to thee, by fortune's will,
My prayer I make, and stretch this peaceful bough,
Fearless; albeit a mighty chief art thou
Of Argive race that wrought my country's ill,
And kinsman of the great Atridæ twain.
My own pure faith, thine honour without stain,
God's oracles, our kindred ties of old—
These join us, these my willing steps have led.
For Dardanus, Troy's ancient sire, 'tis said,
Was fair Electra's son, great Atlas' child;
Atlas, whose shoulders strong the heavens uphold.
Thee, too, a god, wise Mercury, begot,
Whom Maia bore on mountain-summit wild;
And Maia, if old tales we question not,
From that same Atlas sprung who props the skies.
Mark, then; from common source our lines descend.
Trusting therein, nor envoys did I send,
Nor tried thee first with wiles and subtleties;
Myself, my life, I risked, and suppliant came.
That Daunian race, relentless foe of thine,
Us too assails, and if Troy's spirit cowers
Doubts not Hesperia 'neath its yoke to tame,
And east and west to lord it o'er the brine.
Then pledge we now our faith. Brave hearts are ours,
And warriors tried in many a daring deed."

    As thus he spake, long time the king gave heed,
Watching his looks, his port, with earnest gaze,
Then answered brief: "With what unfeignéd joy
I hail and greet thee, noblest knight of Troy!
How well the very words, the voice, the face

Of thy great sire Anchises I recall!
For I bethink me how, in bygone days,
King Priam, voyaging to regions Greek,
Made sojourn in his sister's royal hall
At Salamis, and thence, an honoured guest,
To our Arcadian heights his footsteps turned.
To me, a youth—the down upon my cheek—
Most wondrous seemed that courtly Trojan band,
Wondrous the king; but tallest, stateliest,
Thy sire: my mind with boyish ardour burned
The hero to accost and grasp his hand.
Drawn near, I led him home with eager heart
To Pheneus' walls; nor thence did he depart
Ere treasured gifts he gave—a quiver bright
With Lycian shafts, a cloak with gold inwrought,
Two bridles (Pallas hath them now) of gold.
Have then thy wish; hands clasped, our faith we plight;
And soon as earliest dawn is on the wold,
Glad on your homeward way ye shall be brought,
Equipped with whatsoe'er these realms afford.
Meanwhile, since friends ye be, come celebrate
With joy this sacred feast that may not wait,
And share with us, ev'n now, our social board."

Therewith, the feast renewed, the cups restored,
Their warrior guests to grassy couch they guide;
The Trojan chief, on lion's shaggy hide,
Hath place of honour, set on maple throne:
Then do the priests from holy altar-side
Bring roasted flesh and baskets piled with bread,
Kind Ceres' gifts, and serve the flowing wine;
So banquet they, in joyous union,
On savoury meats and sacrificial chine.
But when their thirst was quenched, their hunger fled,
Then king Evander spake: "This solemn feast,
These hallowed rites, this meed of praise and prayer,
Spring from no credulous imagining,
No idle fear of gods. Nay, Trojan guest;

From fearful perils saved, these gifts we bear,
As year on year renews our offering.
Mark yon o'erhanging cliff, with shattered stair
From ruined fortress in the steep rock hewn,
And boulders vast in wild confusion strewn!
A cave there was, in hidden grot profound,
Which once the savage Cacus had for lair,
By the sun's rays untravelled; and the ground
Reeked with fresh blood, and on the frowning door
Hung pallid human heads that dripped with gore.
This ogre, huge of bulk, was Vulcan's son,
And from his jaws breathed Vulcan's smoky flame.
Long prayed we for release; till lo! there came
A god to save us, an avenger strong,
Decked with the spoils of conquered Geryon,
Great Hercules, and drove his herds along
Yon valley where the cooling waters wind.
Then Cacus—so besotted was his mind
That naught of guilt or guile might rest undone—
Four bulls, of beauty rare, stole from the pen;
Four heifers, likewise, of exceeding grace;
And lest their footprints should the theft betray,
Backwards he dragged them to the cave, each trace
Reversing, and so hid them in his den:
Make search who might, naught pointed to the place.
But soon, when lord Alcides went his way,
Driving his sated kine to pastures new,
Ev'n as they parted, loud their lowing grew,
And filled the wooded glades and mountain slope:
Whereat one cow made answer from that hold,
And foiled, though closely pent, her captor's hope:
For straight the hero's wrath burned uncontrolled;
His heavy knotted club he seized, and sped
To the steep summit of that lofty height.
Then first did Cacus show his soul's affright
Through troubled eyes; swifter than wind he fled,
And sought the cave with terror-wingéd feet:

There did he hide him in his dark retreat,
Lowering the ponderous rock that hung for guard
With craft of iron chains learn'd of his sire,
And with that solid mass the gateway barred.
But soon his swift pursuer was at hand,
With roving eyes that all the approaches scanned,
And teeth that gnashed with fury. Thrice, in ire,
Right o'er the ridge of Aventine he pressed;
Those rocky portals thrice in vain he tried;
Thrice, wearied, in the vale took pause and rest.
There rose a peak, with stark precipitous side,
Up-towering high behind that darksome cave,
Fit spot for birds of prey to set their nest:
'Gainst this sharp spire, impending o'er the wave,
He matched his mighty strength, and pushed amain,
Till, from its base uprooted by the strain,
It fell—at that great fall, thundered the heaven,
The banks recoiled, the river shrunk dismayed.
Then were that ogre's halls to sight betrayed,
And pierced the cavernous depths of his domain,
As if by some strange power the earth were riven,
And those deep realms and pits of Death had bared
That the gods loathe, and in the abyss displayed
Trembled the pale ghosts by the daylight scared.
Thus was he caught in sudden glare of day,
Trapped in his den; and wildly now he roared
With unfamiliar sounds of brutish fear:
High o'er him, Hercules his missiles poured—
Tree-trunks, huge boulders, aught that nearest lay.
He, for no path from peril did appear,
Breathed forth a wondrous mass of smoky cloud,
His lair in blinding darkness to enshroud,
And robbed men's eyes of vision—such a wreath
Of vaporous fire came curling through the cave,
This brooked not great Alcides: from the height
He leaps where smoke rolls thickest, wave on wave,
And murky vapours through the cavern seethe:

There Cacus, belch his fire-cloud as he might,
He grasps and strangles, till in death-grip tight
He lies with bloodless throat and starting eyes.
Now is his gloomy den laid bare to sight;
The stolen kine, his vainly hidden prize,
Are seen of all: his hideous corse they fling
Forth by the feet, then gaze with fearful zest
On that inhuman visage, shaggy chest,
And jaws whence nevermore those flames shall spring.
    "Thus saved we were; and now with joyfulness
We greet the day that set our fathers free.
Potitius first its honours did acclaim:
He, with the clan that guards our Hero's fame,
Built us yon woodland altar that we bless;
Greatest 'tis named, and greatest still shall be.
Come, sirs! to praise such valour, doubt not ye
To bind your locks with leaves, your goblets fill,
And this our god invoke with hearty will!"
    So saying, with poplar crown he wreathes his brow;
Part green, part grey, its trailing garlands fall;
The sacred cup is in his hand; then all
Libation pour, and make to heaven their vow.
So day declines, the dusk returns, and now
The priests, Potitius leading, move in line,
Skin-clad, and far their lifted torches flare.
Soon is the feast renewed; gay fruits and wine,
Most grateful gifts of second course, they bear,
Heaping with dish on dish the loaded shrine.
Then round the smoking altars wildly throng
The Salii, all in poplar garlanded;
Here chants the youths', and there the elders' quire,
Lauding the feats of Hercules in song:
How first he foiled his ruthless step-dame's ire,
With infant hand strangling her serpents dread;
How cities, famed in war, his strength o'erthrew,
Œchalia, Troy; how countless labours sore
'Neath king Eurystheus, by the jealous whim

Of Juno, faithful to the end, he bore.
"Thy hand it was, unconquered one, that slew
Those cloud-born Centaurs twain; 'twas thou didst smite
The monstrous bull of Crete, the lion grim
Whose lair was 'neath the crags of Nemean glen.
Thy coming did the Stygian realms affright,
And Hades' watch-dog trembled, as he lay
Crouching o'er half-gnawed bones in gory den;
But thee no shape of terror could dismay;
Not ev'n Typhœus with uplifted sword;
Nor failed thy courage, when in snaky horde
The Hydra's heads rose round thee on thy way.
Hail then, Jove's offspring sure, new pride of heaven,
And be thy grace to us, thy votaries, given!"
    So tells the song of many a deed renowned,
Nor ever of that darksome cavern tires,
And Cacus belching forth his baleful fires:
Loudly the woodland rings, the hills resound.
    Then straightway all, that solemn service done,
The city seek: Evander, bowed with years,
Companioned by Æneas and his son,
The rugged way with friendly converse cheers;
The while his Trojan guest, in glad surprise,
Turns on that novel scene quick-glancing eyes,
Charmed by each noted spot, as one by one
Strange tales of ancient times he asks, and hears.
Then spake the founder of the towers of Rome:
    "Yon forests were the fauns' and wood-nymphs' home;
Men, too, of stubborn hard-grained stock were there,
Lawless, uncultured; nor was tillage known,
Nor wealth they sought, nor hoarded gains would spare;
Fed on wild fruits and hunters' scanty fare.
Then came old Saturn from Olympus' height,
Banished by Jove from his primeval throne:
He first, 'mid pathless mountains, bade unite
Their scattered tribes, and taught them truth and right,
And called that region Latium, since therein

Latent he dwelt in harmless hermitage:
Thence did the storied Years of Gold begin,
When long he reigned in peace and restfulness.
Followed a baser and degenerate age,
Mad warfare, and the passion to possess;
Then rude Ausonians and Sicanians came
('Twas now the mild Saturnian land no more),
And kings—huge Tybris, of gigantic frame;
From whom our native stream was called, more late,
Tiber, that erst had Albula for name.
Myself, an exile on earth's farthest shore,
The whim of fortune and resistless fate
Here set me: 'twas my mother's stern command,
Carmentis, prescient nymph of heavenly lore,
And lord Apollo drove me to this land."
    So spake the king, and passing thence he showed
The sacred altar and Carmental gate
That from old time the nymph commemorate,
Sage prophetess, whose speech did first forebode
Æneas' greatness, Pallanteum's pride:
And next, the grove that sanctuary gave,
By Romulus ordained; and hidden deep
Pan's secret haunt, the chill Lupercal cave,
And veritable spot where Argus died.
Then, where the Capitol uprises steep,
And famed Tarpeian rock, the way he led:
Now gleams the place with gold, where then they saw
But lonely wild, with thickets dense o'erspread;
A spot the simple peasant passed in awe,
Gazing on grove and grot with nameless dread.
    "There haunts those forest-glades, that summit stark,
Some god—his name we know not, but a god.
Men say 'tis Jove himself whose form was seen,
Whene'er he waved aloft his ægis dark,
And drew the gathering storm-clouds at his nod.
Then see those ruined walls, where once have been
Two towns, old monuments of heroes gone;

By Janus one was built, by Saturn one;
Each to its founder thus their names they owe."
    Thus parleying to the lowly gates they go
Of king Evander, and thereby they meet
An herd of straggling kine, and hear them low
Where stands the Forum now and sumptuous street:
Then spake the monarch: "Through this portal strode
Our lord Alcides, fresh from vanquished foe;
In this poor palace was he fain to rest.
Then shrink not, friend, but prove thy worth, and rise
To hero's height, nor scorn our mean abode."
This said, 'neath sloping roof he guides his guest,
And there the stalwart Trojan warrior lies
On couch of leaves, in Libyan bearskin wrapped.
    Soon 'neath night's dusky wings the earth was lapped.
But Venus, anguished for her Trojans' sake—
Nor vain her terrors, since to heaven above
Such threats, such din of war, from Latium rose—
Thus to her wedded lord, great Vulcan, spake,
As stretched on golden couch she took repose,
And breathed in plaintive words immortal love:
    "When Troy by Grecian kings in dust was laid,
And burned were those proud towers foredoomed to fall,
Thou know'st, dear spouse, I sued not for thine aid,
Ev'n for my hapless Trojan friends, nor prayed
That thou wouldst forge me weapons of thy skill,
Nor tasked my Vulcan's strength, since vain was all.
Natheless were Priam's sons to me most dear,
And oft Æneas' woes my thoughts would fill.
Now to Rutulian lands his way is won:
Wherefore with suppliant prayers I draw anear
To thy great deity that I revere:
'Tis arms I ask—a mother for her son.
Such boon to Nereus' daughter thou didst yield;
Thou pitiedst when Aurora shed the tear.
Mark now, what mighty tribes in war combine;
What gated cities deadly weapons wield,

Sharpening the vengeful sword 'gainst me and mine!"
  So saying, she clasps him with her snowy arms,
In soft embrace, still hesitant, till swift
The wonted fire of love his bosom warms,
And thrills his melting limbs with burning tide:
As when Jove's lightnings flash through skyey rift,
And with resistless flame the clouds divide:
This felt she, guileful, conscious of her charms,
As, sunk in deathless love, the god replied:
  "What mean thy far-fetched pleadings? Hast thou lost
Thy faith in me, fair goddess? Grief so great
Had won me, sure, to arm thy Trojan host;
Nor did the almighty Sire forbid, nor fate,
That Priam's tall towers should stand for years twice ten.
Come, trust me now, if war be thy design.
Whate'er my craft can fashion—all is thine:
Thine is the strength of steel; the iron's might;
The blast of fiery furnace. Cease thou, then,
By needless prayers to mock thy wedded right."
  He spake, and gave the coveted caress;
Then tranquil slumber o'er his senses came:
But when the midnight hours had spent their gloom,
And that first sleep had eased his drowsiness,
He rose, what hour might rise a drudging dame
Whose lot it is with distaff and with loom
To earn scant living; then unweariedly
She fans the embers, to her days austere
Night-vigils adding, as, with lamp alit,
Their lengthy tasks her tired handmaidens ply,
That so her husband's home she still may keep
Unsullied, and her infant children rear.
So did the God of Fire, less keen no whit,
From downy couch to craftsman's labour leap.
A rocky island rises stark and steep,
Nigh Lipare, from the broad Sicilian wave,
Its lofty summit capped with trailing smoke;
And, far below it, lies a sunken cave,

By Cyclopean forges hollowed deep,
Thundering with groan of many a sturdy stroke
On anvil dealt, and molten metal's hiss,
Where, shut in roaring furnace, pants the fire:
Vulcania called, great Vulcan's home it is.
Thither from bright Olympus came the Sire.
In that huge cavern the Cyclopes' band—
Brontes, and Steropes, and naked-limbed
Pyracmon—forged a mighty levin-brand,
Whereof the part was polished, part untrimmed;
Such bolt as oft from Jove's high throne is cast;
And round them others all-unfinished lay.
Three shafts of hail they mixed, of vapour three,
With three of ruddy flame, of wingéd blast;
Then hideous glare, and din, and heart's dismay,
They added, and swift wrath that none can flee.
But Mars—a swift-wheeled chariot for him,
Wherewith the tribes of men to war he hales;
For Pallas, roused to wrath, an ægis dread
In haste they framed, with coil of golden scales
And clustering serpents, and her breastplate grim,
Still rolling hateful eyes, the Gorgon's head.
　　Then Vulcan spake: "Put ye those tasks away;
Ay, let them wait, and to my words give heed.
Now must a hero's arms be wrought; now strength,
Now dexterous hand, now master-craft ye need.
Quick, tarry not!" Nor sooner said, than they
Turn to the toil, and share in equal length
Their labours; flows in streams the brass, the gold,
And pools of deathly steel on furnace glow.
A ponderous shield they fashion, that shall stay,
Single, the foemen's darts; 'tis forged seven-fold,
Circle on circle. Some with bellows blow
The fires to fury; some in water dip
The hissing metals; loud their anvils ring,
As stroke by stroke harmonious arms they swing,
Or strive with tongs the molten mass to grip.

While thus the god his zealous aid bestows,
Roused was Evander by the sunrise sweet
And birds that 'neath his eaves their matins sung:
Straightway from humble couch the veteran rose,
And donned his tunic, and with sandalled feet
Forth hastened, girded with Arcadian sword,
And skin of panther o'er his shoulder flung.
Two hounds before him raced, his guardians fleet,
Companioning the footsteps of their lord.
His pledge of yester-night was in his thought,
As now the chamber of his guest he sought;
Nor had the Trojan chieftain lagged behind,
But with Achates, trusty friend, alone,
Went forth to greet the monarch and his son.
Then hands are clasped; in palace court they find
Fit resting-place, and tranquil talk enjoy.
First spake the king: "Most mighty chief—for Troy,
While thou dost live, defeat can never know—
Matched with thy glorious name, small strength is ours
To lend thee succour. Here we have for bound
The Tuscan stream: there, the Rutulian foe
Thunders with din of arms our walls around:
Yet can we league thy force with mightier powers,
Such fortune unforeseen doth chance bestow:
Thou'st come at moment when the fates demand.
Not far remote, on rocky crest up-towers
Agylla's fortress, where a warrior band
From Lydia settled on Etruscan height.
Long years they flourished; then Mezentius reigned,
Prince of o'erweening pride and ruthless might.
Ask not what hideous crimes this wretch had stained:
Heaven send the like on him and his curst race!
For oft the living to the dead he tied,
Fast coupling hands with hands, and face with face,
For torture: so by lingering deaths they died,
With foul gore sprinkled, locked in loathed embrace.
At length, by nameless wrongs exasperate,

His folk took arms, and gathering round his gate
His minions slew, and fired his roof o'erhead:
He, to Rutulian soil an exile fled,
In Turnus' camp found refuge from their hate.
Then, as one man in wrath Etruria rose,
Demanding that their lord just penance pay.
That host, Æneas, none shall lead but thou!
For by the beach is ranged full many a prow,
And thousand warriors clamour for the fray,
Yet pause, withheld by warning words that spring
From lips of aged seer: 'Ye Lydians true,
Brave flower of race that rose from valiant seed!
Just wrath is yours against that traitorous king,
Bitter your wrongs; yet this hath fate decreed:
No native chieftain may such foes subdue:
Look ye for foreign lord your host to lead.'
Wherefore the Tuscans stir not from the field,
Affrighted by divine admonishment:
Yea, Tarcho to myself hath envoys sent
To pray me rule them and the sceptre wield:
But slow chill age begrudges me such throne;
My strength for valorous deeds is long outworn.
Thereto, perchance, I might exhort my son,
Save that his blood, of Sabine mother born,
Were part Italian. Thou, in race, in age,
Favoured by fate—a heaven-sent champion—
Step forth, and link fair Italy with Troy!
With thee shall go our chiefest hope and joy,
My Pallas. Thou shalt train him war to wage,
A warrior's toils to bear: each daily deed
Of thy heroic hand he shall admire:
Himself ten score of chosen knights shall lead,
Ten score beside, assigned him by his sire."
    Scarce had he spoken, and with downcast eyes
Æneas and his faithful comrade stood,
Their minds perchance to sombre thought subdued,
When Venus sent her signal from the skies—

A lightning flash through azure depths revealed,
With din so great the heavens might seem to fall,
And far o'erhead the Tuscan trumpet pealed.
Skyward they gaze: then rolled that thunderous knell
Again and yet again, where not a cloud
Veiled the serene expanse, and high o'er all
Were brandished fiery arms that clashed aloud.
Marvelled the rest; the Trojan chieftain well
That token knew, by goddess mother sent.
"Nay, ask not, friend," he cried, "what strange event
Yon signs foreshadow: me those heavens demand.
'Tis thus my Goddess, should war's darkness grow,
Celestial armour, wrought by Vulcan's hand,
Hath proffered for mine aid.
Alas, what blood of Latin folk shall flow!
What heavy ransom, Turnus, shall be paid!
How many a shield and helm of warrior slain
Shall father Tiber roll, his tide below!
Ay; let them crave the sword, the truce disdain!"
   He spake, and rising from his lofty seat
Kindled to life anew the flame divine
Of yester-eve that slumbered by the shrine:
Next, to the gods that guard Evander's house,
With sacrificial rites and homage meet,
Beside his host the Trojan monarch bows,
Then seeks his comrades waiting by the fleet,
And chooses for his henchmen in the fight
The stoutest hearts; the rest shall turn their prows
Homeward in gentle course down Tiber's tide,
And to the prince his father's greetings bring.
Then steeds are saddled for each Trojan knight,
And chief a noble war-horse for the king,
Caparisoned with tawny lion's hide,
Its front with golden talons gleaming bright.
   Quick rumour through the little city spreads
How to the Tuscan kingdom horsemen start.
Then mothers kneel affrighted; terror treads

On danger's heels, as War's full form appears.
Evander clasps young Pallas to his heart,
As thus he cries, nor stints his flowing tears:
  "Oh, would Jove give me back my bygone years!
That strength I had, when, by Præneste's wall,
I broke the foremost rank of foemen's spears
And burned their bucklers piled upon the plain.
Then did their leader 'neath my weapon fall,
Great Herilus, Feronia's charmèd son,
Who at his birth a triple life had ta'en
(Dread privilege!); for thrice must sword be bared,
Thrice lay him low in death; yet this I dared:
Three times his life was spilled, his trophies won.
Ah, then, my Pallas, from thy loved embrace
Ne'er were I severed; nor with ruthless might
Mezentius, trampling on a neighbour's right,
Had put so oft our subjects to the sword.
Ye heavenly powers, I pray ye, of your grace,
And Jove, of gods and men the peerless lord,
To sad Arcadia be compassionate,
And hear a father's prayers! If kindly fate
Preserve for me my Pallas—if his face
I still shall see, if still our paths shall meet—
Then would I live, nor care what toils impend:
But if stern Fortune nurse some deadly threat,
May life's sad burden now, ev'n now, have end,
While fears are unfulfilled, the future dark—
While still, dear child, my last and sole desire,
I hold thee in mine arms, nor yet must hark
To tidings that would leave me all forlorn."
Thus, at that piteous parting, spake the sire;
Then fainting to his palace-gates was borne.
  Soon passed the mounted troop through portals wide,
Æneas first, Achates at his side,
With train of Trojan chiefs; and 'mid the rest
Young Pallas rode, resplendent from afar
With bright embellished arms and mantle gay:

As when from ocean's bath the morning star,
Of all heaven's fires to Venus loveliest,
Rises to chase the gloom with sacred ray.
Behind them, on the wall, pale women stand,
Watching through swirl of dust the steely flash,
As sheer through brake and briar they cleave their way.
A shout: they close their ranks, and onward dash,
Their horse-hoofs thundering o'er the mellow land.

    Nigh Cære's chilly springs a forest lies,
Revered from olden days, and girdled round
With hollow hills and belt of sable pine:
This dale the folk of old Pelasgian line,
That erst had dwelt on Latium's boundaries,
To kind Silvanus gave for sacred ground,
The god of fields and flocks, with solemn rites.
There Tarcho lay encamped, secure from foes,
With all his Tuscan band; and from the heights
On tented slopes his legions were espied.
Hither in haste the Trojan horsemen ride;
Here rest their weary steeds, and seek repose.

    Then down through cloudy skies fair Venus flew,
Bearing her gifts, and when she saw her son
By that secluded stream in valley lone,
She spake, and stood confessed to mortal view.

    "Behold these gifts, by skill of Vulcan wrought;
Take them; and doubt not, son, therein arrayed,
Thy haughty Latin foemen to pursue,
Nor fear to challenge Turnus to the fight."
So saying, her son's embrace the goddess sought,
And 'gainst an oak the glittering armour laid;
While he, with inexhaustible delight,
Each gift in turn with roaming eye surveyed,
Wondering, and fain 'twixt eager hands to wield
The fateful sword; the crested helmet dire,
That seemed aflame; the mail of metal stark,
Huge, ruddy, gleaming like some storm-cloud dark
By the sun's burning radiance far revealed;

The greaves of polished gold oft purged in fire;
The spear; the unearthly sculpture of the shield.
   Thereon, prophetic of a future age,
Were shown the splendours of triumphant Rome,
And proud Italia's distant heritage,
Graved by the god; thereon, the sons to come
Of Trojan sires, the wars their arms should wage.
   First, pictured by his craft, the She-Wolf lay
In cave of Mars, and hanging at her breast
The lusty twins were seen, at fearless play;
She, bending o'er them, each in turn caressed,
And licked, with loving tongue, their limbs to shape.
Next, Rome's young city, and the lawless rape
Of Sabine women when the cirque was thronged
At festive season; then that strife unblest
With agéd Tatius and his townsmen wronged:
And later, when their wrath had found surcease,
The self-same kings before Jove's altar stood,
With sacrificial rites ensuing peace.
Hard by, false Mettus, doomed in judgment stern,
And torn by parting steeds, his treachery rued
(What ailed thee, Alban, plighted word to spurn?);
Dragged is his mangled body through the wood,
Where brake and brambles drip with traitor's blood.
See, next, Porsenna, bidding the return
Of tyrant Tarquin from just banishment,
With haughty siege the city's walls beset;
While Troy's bold offspring for fair freedom bleed:
There stood he, lifelike—on his lips the threat—
Wroth, that by Cocles' strength the bridge was rent,
And Clœlia swam the wave, from bondage freed.
   High on Tarpeian rock brave Manlius watched,
Unsleeping guardian of Rome's citadel,
Standing by that rude palace roughly thatched,
Where Romulus had not disdained to dwell;
And fluttering fast down gilded galleries
A silver goose proclaimed the Gauls were nigh:

Nigh were the Gauls, and scarce had failed to seize
The Capitol—the boon of night so well
Had darked their forms 'neath sylvan canopy.
Of golden hue their garb is, and their hair;
Gold-striped their mantles; golden chains depend
From milk-white shoulders; each a gleaming pair
Of Alpine spears they brandish dauntlessly,
And with long targe the stroke of foeman fend.
　　The dancing Salii, the Luperci nude,
The mitred priests, the shields that fell from heaven,
These, too, are imaged, and the solemn line
Of matrons pure in cushioned chariots drawn;
And far below them lies the vastitude
Of Death's domain, with gloomy gate deep-riven,
Where sinners rue their deeds—where Catiline
Hangs from a dizzy mountain-summit thrust,
Trembling to see the Fury's form malign:
Afar, in blest abodes, wise laws are given
By Cato, ruling o'er the meek and just.
　　Then leagues of heaving ocean were portrayed,
Golden, with crests that broke in hoary foam;
And all around, gay silvery dolphins played,
Stemming with wavy fins the gentle tide:
Midmost, by Actium's coast, the fleets of Rome
Lay full in sight, and all Leucate seethed
With arms, her waves in golden lustre dyed.
There, leading his Italian host to war,
With guardian gods and Senate at his side,
High on the lofty stern, his temples wreathed
With shimmering flame, Augustus Cæsar stands,
And o'er his head is seen the Julian star.
There, too, Agrippa gazes proudly down
On that embattled host his skill commands,
Favoured by gods and winds, a naval crown,
Symbol of triumph, burning on his brows.
　　'Gainst these, with fleet of wild barbaric prows,
And multifarious arms, Antonius fought.

From far auroral lands, from Red Sea shore,
From Persia's utmost bounds, in pomp he brought
His oriental powers; and in his train
(Ah, shame!) was his Egyptian paramour.
Then ships 'gainst ships are hurled; then foam the seas
Furrowed by blade and beak; 'twould seem the main
Were shook by clash of drifting Cyclades,
Or mass of mountains upon mountains thrown,
So huge the hulls their towering bulk up-raise:
Hurtle the darts, the hempen torches blaze,
And Neptune's realms are red with blood unknown.
    Full in the battle's midst, the swarthy Queen
With clash of cymbals bids her vessels close
(Nor sees those adders twain that lurk behind);
The while her motley gods, in troop obscene—
The dog Anubis and his monstrous kind—
Minerva, Venus, Neptune dare oppose
In impious combat. There the War-God keen
Stands iron-wrought; the Furies flit o'erhead;
Exultant, with rent robes, stalks Discord dread,
And fierce Bellona plies her bloody scourge;
While lord Apollo from o'erhanging verge
Bends his bright bow in battle. Scared thereby,
Dark Egypt's host hath turned its back in flight,
With Indian and Arabian chivalry.
Herself, invoking some fair breeze to save,
Sets sail, flings cables loose distractedly;
And now, while thoughts of death her soul affright,
Her barque is pictured driven by wind and wave,
Where Nile, his shadowy form with grief oppressed,
Unfolds his secret channels to invite
His vanquished children to that sheltering breast.
    Last, Cæsar, borne in triple triumph home,
Pays to his gods that deathless debt he vowed—
An hundred stately temples reared in Rome.
Filled are the streets with glad acclaim and mirth;
In every sacred shrine the matrons crowd,

And many a slaughtered victim strews the earth.
Himself, by Phœbus' snowy steps throned high,
Receives the nations' gifts, affixing each
To those proud portals; while, in pageantry,
The long array of conquered tribes goes by,
Diverse in arms and vesture, as in speech:
Nomads, and Libyans clad in flowing weeds,
And Carians, and fierce Scythians armed with bows;
Euphrates (humbler now his current flows),
And Morini, the North's remotest clan;
And Rhine, and Dahæ famed for doughty deeds,
And swift Araxes that no bridge may span.

   Such wondrous legend did Æneas scan,
Inscribed on Vulcan's shield, his mother's gift;
Those scenes he knew not, yet rejoiced therein,
Right glad on stalwart shoulders to uplift
The fame and fortune of his future kin.

BOOK IX

ARGUMENT

DURING the absence of Æneas at the court of Evander, Turnus besieges the Trojan camp. An attempt made by Nisus and Euryalus to cut their way by night through the Latin lines ends in their discovery and death. The rest of the book is devoted to a description of the feats of Turnus, who forces an entry alone into the beleaguered town, and escapes therefrom by swimming the Tiber.

While thus in distant fields these feats befell,
Came Iris down from heaven (so Juno bade)
To where undaunted Turnus sat in thought
By sire Pilumnus' consecrated dell;
And thus her tidings spake the rose-lipped maid:
"Turnus, the very boon which, hadst thou prayed,
No god had dared to grant thee, time hath brought.
Æneas, from his comrades severed far,
Hath sued for succour at Evander's throne;
Nay, more, to distant Corythus hath gone,
Rousing the Lydian countryfolk to arms.
Why wait'st thou? Tarry not, but mount thy car,
And smite his camp perplexed with wild alarms."
She spake, and skyward soared on graceful wing,
With glittering bow across the storm-cloud trailed.
That sign the warrior knew; then lifting high
His palms in prayer her fleeting form he hailed:
"Fair Iris, pride of heaven, who bade thee bring
This message to mine ear? Why flames the sky
With sudden glory? I see its depths dispart,
And hosts of circling stars. Whoe'er thou art
That call'st me thus to arms, not loth am I
To thine auspicious leadership to bow."
Straight to the stream he stepped, and reverently
Its water lifted, and from prayerful heart
Loaded the vault of heaven with many a vow.

Full soon the open plains in pomp they tread
With wealth of steeds, and purfled cloaks, and gold;
Messapus in the van; the rearguard led
By sons of Tyrrheus; midmost Turnus goes,
And by a head o'ertops his fellows all.
So Ganges rolls his stately stream seven-fold
In silent pomp; so Nile, majestical,
Withdraws his fertilising flood, and flows
Serene, within his wonted banks controlled.
   Sudden the Trojans see the dust uprise
Far o'er the field in dense and murky shroud;
Then from the rampart first Caicus cries:
"What troop is this, that stirs yon sable cloud?
Quick—arm ye, mates, nor leave the walls unmanned!
Haste, for the foe is nigh!" With uproar loud
Shelter they seek and by the bulwarks stand;
For so their lord had charged them, ere he went,
If aught of doubtful fortune should betide,
To shun the field, nor challenge open war,
But rest secure behind the rampart pent:
Wherefore, though stung by martial wrath and pride,
The gates, obedient, 'gainst the foe they bar,
And armed within their hollow turrets bide.
   Then Turnus, spurring swift before the rest
With score of chosen knights, ere men were ware,
Drew nigh the walls: on Thracian steed he sate,
White-mottled; gold his helm, with ruddy crest.
"Who now with me," he cried, "the fight will dare?"
And lo! he flung his spear, precipitate,
For sign of battle, and rode tempestuous on:
Whereat, with lusty shout in unison,
His comrades follow. Wondrous strange they hold
The craven spirit of their foes, that none
Come forth to front the combat on the plain,
But nurse their fortress. Oft, in foray bold,
He skirts the walls, and entry seeks in vain.
As waits a wolf beside some teeming fold

With savage howlings, scourged by storm and rain,
Till midnight hour, while safe beneath their dams
In rage and wrath he hears the bleating lambs,
And craves the prey he wins not; hunger's pain
Long racks him, and his jaws are parched for blood:
So gazed that warrior in embittered mood
On walls and ramparts; deeply chafed was he,
When access none his fury found, nor way
To drag the Trojans from their close retreat
And fling them forth to battle on the lea.
Then marked he where in hidden nook their fleet
'Twixt earthen mound and Tiber's waters lay;
And fire he bids his eager comrades bring;
Himself hath grasped a blazing pine in hand;
Nor lag his henchmen 'neath their chieftain's eyes,
But haste to arm them each with pitchy brand
Snatched from the altars; soon the dark flames spring,
And smoke and fire soar mingled to the skies.
    Say, Muse, what god repelled that perilous flame,
And from such wrong the Trojan keels could keep?
Old is the story, but of deathless fame.
When first, by Phrygian Ida's lonely dale,
Æneas built his ships, and dared the deep,
The Mother of the Gods—so runs the tale—
Thus prayed almighty Jove: "Son, wilt thou grant
This boon, since now in heaven thou'rt dominant?
A wood of pines I had, loved from of yore,
On that high summit where men's gifts were laid,
A grove of solemn pines and maple shade.
These grudged I not, when ships were needed sore,
To him, the Trojan chief; but now dark care
Afflicts me, for their sake my heart is sad.
Calm thou my fears, and grant thy Mother's prayer,
That wind and wave may whelm them nevermore,
Since on my holy hill their growth they had."
    Then spake the ruler of the spheres, her son:
"Mother, wouldst call the fates from out their course?

What ask'st thou for those favoured trees of thine?
Shall fleet by mortals built be held divine?
This Trojan safely sail where safe are none?
Nay, for no god in heaven can wield such force.
Yet this I grant thee: when their voyage is done,
Port gained, those barques that 'scape the waves, and bear
The Dardan chieftain to Laurentian strand,
Their mortal shape abandoned, shall become
Nymphs of the sea, like Galatea fair
And Doto, maidens of the Nereid band,
That cleave with comely breast the salt sea foam."
He spake, and sware it by his brother god
That rules those darksome Stygian realms below,
Whose gulfing streams in fiery surges flow;
Then, nodding, shook Olympus with his nod.
Now came the destined hour, and Fate at last
Had brought that moment when the foe's assault
The goddess roused her darling ships to save.
Then flashed strange radiance in men's eyes, and vast
A storm-cloud sped from eastward o'er the vault,
With din of heavenly hosts, while stern and grave
A voice from heaven o'er camp and city passed:
    "Nay, Trojans, rush not to my ships' defence!
Arms take not. Sooner shall he burn the sea
Than those my sacred pines. But ye—go hence!
Go, sea-nymphs now; the Mother bids!" Then free
They burst their cables from the strand, and each
Plunging her prow, like dolphin, in the tide,
The ocean depths they seek; and rising thence
(Strange sight) so many nymphs the billows ride
As ships before lay banked upon the beach.
Scared were those warriors; ev'n Messapus stood
Aghast, with frighted steeds; a raucous roar
From Tiber rose, as backward surged his flood:
But all unchanged was Turnus' hardihood;
Ev'n more his mates he cheered, and urged the more:
    "'Gainst Troy these marvels point: thus Jove in wrath

Robs them of refuge; ev'n their fleet hath fled
Our conquering fires. Now barred is ocean's path
Nor hope of flight, since half the world is lost,
And ours the solid land—so huge a host
Italia lends us. Not one jot I dread
The fateful oracles these Phrygians boast.
Be it enough for Venus, and for Fate,
That these fair shores they've touched. Fates too have I,
This crafty Trojan race to extirpate
That stole my bride. Not Sparta's kings alone
Are stung to wrath by that indignity,
Nor only Greece hath war of vengeance known.
But 'Troy once fell: let that suffice.' Troy sinned:
Their sin should have sufficed—to make them hate
Thenceforth the very name of womankind;
Cravens, who trust in rampart, sit confined
By trench that scarce divides them from their doom:
Such courage win they! Watched they not Troy's towers,
By Neptune reared, subside in fiery gloom?
But ye, my bravest! yours and mine the task
To scale those bastions, make their stronghold ours.
Not Vulcan's arms, nor thousand ships I ask,
To meet Troy's host, though all Etruria's powers
Be added. Let them fear no stealth by night;
No Horse's belly shall our swords conceal:
Certes, their walls we'll fire in open day,
And teach them that no more with Greeks they fight,
For ten long years by Hector held at bay.
But come! since day is spent, of body's weal
Bethink ye, friends, and let your hearts be light;
So make we ready for the morrow's fray."
    Meanwhile, to block the gates, surround the wall
With ring of fire, Messapus waits on guard.
Twice seven the chieftains chosen that watch to hold,
And each hath hundred sentries at his call,
Gay-helmed, with crests of purple and of gold:
From post to post they saunter on the sward,

And drain from brazen bowls the brimming wine;
And thus the night, while blazing watch-fires shine,
In sport goes sleepless by.
    This saw the Trojans from their ramparts high
Forth-gazing, while with anxious care they test
The gates, from tower to tower the drawbridge fling,
And store of missiles pile. Such the behest
Of Mnestheus and Serestus, whom the king,
If so it chanced that fortune were unkind,
Had named for rulers, and fit power assigned:
And now their band, to that grim work addressed,
Kept vigil, guarding each the portion due.
    The guardian of the gate, brave knight and true,
Was Nisus; from mount Ida had he come,
With hunter's spear and arrows dexterous;
And nigh him was his mate, Euryalus,
Whose beardless cheek was soft with boyhood's bloom:
The fairest he of all the youths that donned
Their Trojan armour in Æneas' train.
Thus fought they, side by side, in friendship's bond,
And now at common station stood the twain.
Then Nisus: "Is't the gods our minds inspire
With burning zeal? or doth blind impulse reign
O'er each man's will, a god within his breast?
Long time my heart for battle is afire
Or some great deed, nor tranquil here can rest.
Thou seest our foes with confidence possessed:
Few gleam their fires; they lie in sleep or wine
Deep-buried; the broad plain is hushed around.
Hear, then, whereto my surging thoughts incline.
One hope hath Troy—to call Æneas back
And send him tidings of our camp siege-bound:
Enough for me, that such bold deed be mine,
If thou the rightful guerdon shalt not lack:
And now, methinks, beside yon lofty mound
A path to Pallanteum can be found."
    Astounded, thrilled with eager lust of fame,

Thus did Euryalus his friend bespeak:
"But I—wouldst bar me from thy bold emprise,
Thyself alone endangering, to my shame?
Not trained was I, nor tutored in this wise
By my brave sire Opheltes, when the Greek
Struck terror into Troy; nor such a friend
Hast found me, since, through many a year of strife.
We serve our lord Æneas to the end:
Here, here, a dauntless heart is, deeming life
Small cost for that great glory thou wouldst seek."
    "Of thee no fears I had," Nisus replied,
"Nor right to fear; 'tis truth: so may great Jove,
Or whosoe'er in heaven this deed approve,
Restore me soon triumphant to thy side!
But if some peril, such as oft betide,
From god or chance, should all my hopes o'erthrow,
Live thou—thine age hath better claim to live.
Let there be one who to the earth shall give
My corse, regained or ransomed from the foe;
Or, if that boon by fate forbidden be,
Last obsequies at cenotaph shall pay.
Nor on thy mother would I bring such woe,
Since among many mothers none but she
Safe in Sicilian city scorned to stay."
But he: "'Tis vain these idle words to weave,
For not one whit my mind canst thou convince.
Then haste we." Straight he calls the sentries; they
Come forth and change the guard. Their post they leave,
Those twain, and seek the presence of the prince.
    All creatures else that lived lay slumbering,
Their hearts from anxious care and labour freed.
Troy's chieftains with their chosen chivalry
Took counsel, pondering on their grievous need,
And who should bear those tidings to their king:
Bucklered, and leaning on long spears, they stand,
In centre of their camp. Then hurriedly
Those eager-hearted youths for audience plead;

Great themes are theirs, nor mickle time demand:
Whereat Iulus bids their tale be told;
And Nisus: "Hear, nor deem us overbold!
Youths are we; but by years adjudge ye not
Our project. Silent, sunk in wine and sleep,
The Latins lie; ourselves have spied a spot
Whereby to sally forth in stealthy raid
'Twixt branching paths from gate that fronts the deep.
Few are their watch-fires; naught but smoky pall
Drifts skyward. If this feat may be assayed—
To seek our lord at Pallanteum's wall—
Full soon, with ample spoil and gory blade,
Shall we return. Nor doubt we of the way;
For oft, when hunting in some leafy dell,
We saw where precincts of the city lay,
And Tiber's banks our feet have conned full well."
    Then spake Aletes, old in years and wise:
"Gods of our fathers, in whose power is Troy,
Not wholly can ye purpose to destroy
Folk in whose sons such dauntless hearts ye breed!"
So saying, he fondly clasped them, and his eyes
With streaming tears his agéd visage wet:
"What thanks, what guerdons worthy of such deed,
Can hand of man bestow? The noblest prize
Shall come from heaven and your own hearts; nor yet
Can aught deprive ye of your honours won
From lord Æneas and the prince his son,
Who ne'er such wondrous merit can forget."
    "Yea," cried Ascanius, "since no hope have I,
Save in my sire's return, this vow I make—
By Troy's great gods, by that dread deity
Our fathers worshipped, by hoar Vesta's shrine—
What faith soe'er, what joy in life be mine,
All, all on your high courage will I stake.
Recall my sire: no ills but can be faced
If he return our fortunes to uplift:
Then will I give two goblets richly chased,

Which prize he captured when Arisba fell;
Two tripods; talents twain of solid gold;
And ancient Tyrian tankard, Dido's gift:
But if it so be destined that we hold
Italia's sceptre and the spoil divide—
Saw'st thou on mettled charger Turnus ride,
Arrayed in glittering arms? That very steed,
That shield, that flaming helm with ruddy crest,
Await thee, Nisus, and none else, for meed.
Nay, more; my sire shall give the comeliest
Of captives for thy recompense, and add
Rich lands that king Latinus counts his own.
But thee, whose tale of years, heroic lad,
Scarce outstrips mine—I take thee to my breast
For comrade, be my fortunes dark or glad:
Henceforth no glory will I seek alone:
Or peace, or war, whate'er my thoughts pursue,
With thee I'll share it." And Euryalus
Made answer: "Never will I prove untrue
To this bold venture that we dare to-day,
So fortune frown not, but still smile on us.
But for one boon above all else I pray.
I have a mother: Trojan born is she,
Who broke the sad sweet ties of native land,
Left safe Sicilian home, to sail with me:
Her now I leave, nor have farewells been said,
Nor knows she of these risks whate'er they be.
Be Night my witness, and thine own right-hand,
A mother's tears I could not bear to see!
I pray thee help her, left uncomforted.
If this thou promise, free from doubt or dread
I face all perils." Much his pleadings move
The Trojan chieftains; most, Æneas' son,
Who, smit by thought of his own filial love,
Cries: "Doubt not, all things worthy shall be done
To match this valorous deed; assured be thou
Thy mother shall be mine, Creusa's name

Alone be lacking: long shall live her fame
Who bore a child so brave. Fail thou or win,
By my own life, my father's life, I vow,
What gifts await thee, safe returned, the same
Shall still await thy mother and thy kin."
In tears he spake, and doffed his princely blade,
By wondrous skill of Cretan craftsman made,
Golden, in ivory scabbard deftly set;
To Nisus, Mnestheus gave the shaggy skin
From lion torn; his helm Aletes lent.
So started they, full armed; and as they went,
By old and young beside the gate were met,
Pursuing them with prayers—Iulus most,
Mature beyond his age in thoughtful mind,
With many a message to his sire: the wind
Caught them, and fruitless to the welkin tossed.

   So sallying forth they cross the trench, and steal
Within the foemen's camp 'neath gloom of night,
Destined, ere all be ended, death to deal
On many a warrior. Round them they descry
Men sunk in slumber, chariots poised upright
Along the shore, and stretched 'twixt reins and wheel,
Swordsmen and armour mixed confusedly,
And flasks of wine withal. Spake Nisus low:
"Now must the deed be dared with instant hand.
Here pass we: keep thou watch upon the foe,
Lest force be raised against us from the rear,
While I will smite, and ample pathway clear."
This said, his lips he closed, and drew his brand
On lordly Rhamnes, who, couched high on heap
Of rugs outspread, breathed heavy in his sleep;
A king, by Turnus loved, nor less a seer;
Yet could his seership parry not death's blow.
Three henchmen, lying by their arms a-row,
He slew, with Remus' squire and charioteer,
Beneath their horses found, and with sharp sword
Slashed through their drooping necks; then from their lord

The head he shore, and cast the corse away
Bubbling with jets of blood, as the dark tide
O'er sodden bed and steaming soil was poured.
Nor long ere Lamyrus and Lamus died,
And young Serranus, with much sport outworn,
Fond reveller; fair his features, as he lay
By wine-god mastered—happier, had his play
Been long as night nor slackened till the morn!
   So Nisus raged, as lion ravenous,
Maddened by hunger, leaps upon the pen
'Mid mute and cowering flock, and rends and mauls
With dripping fangs. Nor less Euryalus
His fury gluts with blood of nameless men:
On Fadus, Abaris, the death-stroke falls,
Stretched heedless; Rhœtus, that dread blow foreseen,
Watchful, had sought a ponderous cask for screen,
Whence as he rose, the sword was in his breast,
Then quick withdrawn; and straight in purple flood
With wine commingled gushed his heart's best blood:
Still, stealthy, on grim task his murderer pressed.
   Soon come they to Messapus' camp, and see
The watch-fires low, and tethered steeds hard by,
Cropping the grass; then Nisus whispers brief:
Of lust for blood, o'ermuch indulged, aware;
"Desist we now; the accusing dawn draws nigh:
Vengeance enough, a clear-cut path, have we."
There leave they scattered spoils of many a chief;
Steel armour, rugs embroidered, flagons bright:
Euryalus, in Rhamnes' trappings dight,
Bears off the belt adorned with studs of gold,
Which Cædicus, from treasures manifold,
Erstwhile had sent, his friendship's faith to plight,
To Remulus of Tibur: he, at death,
That gift, long cherished, to his grandson gave,
Since by Rutulian conquerors possessed.
This belt the youth upon his shoulders brave
Fits proud (but naught alas! it profiteth),

Then dons Messapus' helm with gaudy crest.
So pass they forward, drawing easier breath.
   It chanced a troop of horsemen, sent ahead,
Had spurred from Latium's royal capital
Where lay their host embattled on the plain,
Bearing to Turnus tidings from the king—
Three hundred, bucklered all, by Volscens led—
When, as they rode by the beleaguered wall,
Skulking to left they spied those Trojans twain;
And in the starlight faintly shimmering
His vaunted helm the unwary youth betrayed.
One glimpse sufficed; then quick came Volscens' cry:
"Stand, sirs! Your purpose, that thus armed ye go?
Say, whither speed ye?" Résponse none they made,
But to the forest 'neath night's shadows fly:
Then rush the horsemen to the paths they know,
Till egress all with ring of steel is stayed.
   Dark was the wood with shrubs and ilex shade,
A savage spot, with brambles dense o'ergrown,
And scarce a track to guide through thickets lone.
Trammelled by boughs, and with his spoils down-weighed,
Euryalus roamed in fear, where all was strange:
But Nisus fled, nor knew his mate was gone;
Then, as he passed the grove, now Alban hight,
That lay within the royal forest's range,
He stopped, and missed his comrade lost to sight:
"Alas! where did I leave thee, luckless friend?
Or where shall find thee?" Back through tangled maze,
Each dubious step retracing, must he wend,
As silent through the silent brake he strays:
Then tramp of horse is heard, pursuing loud;
And lo! the boy, whom those dim woodlands daze,
Is captive dragged by that o'ermastering crowd,
Nor 'vail his struggles aught, how bold soe'er.
Ah, how should Nisus bring deliverance?
Rush headlong on those ranks, to perish there,
And, falling, die the death of warrior proud?

In haste his arm he bent, poising the lance,
And to the Moon o'erhead thus breathed a prayer:
"Thou, goddess, be mine aid at this dark hour,
Night's peerless queen, that guard'st the greenwood bower!
If e'er thy shrines were honoured for my sake
By Hyrtacus, my sire—if I did make
Fresh offerings from my hunting-grounds, and come
To hang my gifts upon thy sacred dome:
Grant me to scatter now yon foemen's force,
And guide my flying javelin on its course!"
So saying, he hurled with strength his steel-tipped dart,
Which, cleaving swift the shadows of the night,
Smote heedless Sulmo, as averse he stood,
And, breaking, bore its splinters to his heart:
Sore stricken he lay, while ebbed his life's warm blood,
With long-drawn sobs and heaving side, death-white.
Turning, they gazed around. Quickened thereby,
A second shaft the Trojan brandished high;
And 'mid their uproar, whizzing on its way
Through Tagus' brows it lodged within his brain.
Maddened was Volscens, yet could naught discern
Whence came the shaft, nor where his wrath to turn:
"Thou in default," he cried, "the price shalt pay
For both." With naked sword he rushed amain
On young Euryalus. Then in wild dismay
Shrieked Nisus, for no longer might he bear
To lurk unseen while such dread grief befell:
"Me, me—the deed was mine—turn swords on me,
Rutulians! Mine the guilt: no part had he,
Nor could not; by yon conscious stars I swear,
He only loved his luckless friend too well."
So cried he; but the sword, with fury sped,
Pierces the side, and rends that breast so white;
Euryalus falls and dies, his shapely limbs
Blood-crimsoned; on his shoulder droops his head.
So, by the ploughshare cleft, some blossom bright
Fades gently to its death; so languor dims

The poppies' beauty by the rainstorm bent.
But Nisus in their midst dashes apace—
On Volscens, Volscens, and none else intent;
Though all around in thronging crowd they close,
To thwart him—on he springs, with lightning sweep
Of sword, till full in the Rutulian's face,
Ev'n while he cries for aid, he plunges deep
His steel, and sells his own life for his foe's:
Then flings himself upon his comrade's corse,
Stabbed through, and so at length wins death's repose.

   Blest pair! If aught avail these songs of mine
Your names shall never fade from glory's scroll,
How long soe'er the unshaken Capitol
Be held by warriors of Æneas' line,
And Earth still own the Roman sire's control.

   Now, with lost trophies gotten back, the foe
To camp their lifeless leader weeping bear;
Nor less the grief where Rhamnes was laid low,
Numa, Serranus, and full many a lord
In that same carnage slain. Huge crowd was there,
To view where Trojan brands had busy been,
The stream of blood still trickling on the sward:
Oft point they to the spoils—that helmet sheen,
That far-famed belt with mighty toil restored.

   Soon, showering earliest lustre on the land,
Upsprings from saffron couch the dawning Day,
And all things shine new-spangled in the sun:
His armour Turnus dons, then gives command
To rouse the host—his chieftains, one by one,
Urging their steel-clad swordsmen to the fray
With tales of midnight deeds that whet their hate:
Then spears are lifted and, grim sight, thereon
The heads, by shouting foemen followed hard,
Of Nisus and his mate.
Sternly their landward flank the Trojans guard,
Girt by the sheltering river on the right,
And man the trenches, and on turrets tall

Stand firm, though moved to sadness by the sight
Of comrades' features, known full well to all,
Now stark in death and wet with gory dew.
Soon through the startled city Rumour flew
On sounding plumes, and bore its mournful tale
To that unhappy mother. Chill she grew,
And sudden from her grasp the shuttle fell,
Its threads unwound, as with loud woman's wail
Forth from her door she sprang, her tresses rent,
And rushed in frenzy uncontrollable
Where raged the fight by trench and battlement;
Reckless of men, of darts, of perils near,
As thus she filled the heavens with piteous moan:

"Is't thus I see thy face? Couldst thou, the stay
And solace of mine age, thus leave me lone?
Cruel—on such dark hazard to have gone,
Nor let thy mother speak one last goodbye!
Alas, on foreign soil thou'rt left, a prey
To dogs and birds; nor can a mother's love
Bring thee sad funeral gifts where thou dost lie,
Nor close thy lids, nor wash the blood away,
Nor wrap thee in the robe that, night and day,
To soothe mine old heart's weariness I wove!
Where shall I seek thee? On what shores are flung
Thy mangled limbs? Is this poor remnant thou?
Was it for this I shared thine exile long?
On me, Rutulians, be your javelins shed;
Yea, of your mercy, slay me with the sword!
Great Father of the Gods, in pity now
With thine own bolt strike down this hated head,
That else can 'scape not from a life abhorred!"

Smit were men's hearts with sorrow as she 'plained;
They sighed; their martial zeal grew numb and slack;
Till, when the weeping prince had willed it so,
By Actor and Idæus' care constrained—
Still kindling grief to feed her burning woe—
Safe to her dwelling was she guided back.

Then pealed the brazen trumpets' dreadful din,
Followed by shouts, and roar of echoing sky.
'Neath shelter of locked shield the Volscians press
To fill the trench and rend the ramparts high;
Some, fain to mount the walls, would vantage win,
Where, through the ring of sentries, sparser grown,
Clear interspace appears. Their shafts no less
In showers the Trojans hurl, and poles they ply
With sturdy strokes to shove the foremost down,
Long taught to fend the assailant from their wall:
Nor spare they stones to fling of bulk immense,
To break that serried penthouse where the foe
Hath sworn to bide all buffets that befall:
Yea, vain his onset; for on phalanx dense
A mighty mass the Trojans thrust and throw,
Which strews his ranks and bursts his steely fence.
Nor now for that blind battle doth he care,
But fights with bolts far-flung.
Hard by, Mezentius wields, in savage might,
A huge Etruscan pine with smoky glare;
Messapus, lord of steeds, from Neptune sprung,
For ladder calls, to scale the bulwark's height.

I pray thee, Muse, inspire me to recite
The deeds of Turnus' sword—what heroes bold
Fell on that field, and by whose stroke they fell;
So shall the war's great records be unrolled:
For, goddess, this thou mindest and canst tell.

A dizzy tower there was, with bridge that hung
High o'er the battle: this the Latins strove
With utmost stress to batter and o'erthrow—
Met with dense hail of boulders from above
And volleying darts through deep embrasures flung.
Then Turnus, leading, hurled a fiery brand
That clave to the side, and by the breezes fanned
Held fast, and set the smouldering beams aglow.
Scared were the guards, and from their evil plight
Vain refuge sought; for backward as they crowd,

To shun that fiery plague, the turrets fall
O'erweighted, and the welkin thunders loud.
Lifeless 'neath that huge bulk on earth they light,
By their own weapons stabbed, and pierced withal
By wooden splinters. Save Helenor none,
And Lycus, 'scaped alive: a beardless boy
Helenor was, the Lydian monarch's son,
By secret handmaid reared and sent to wield
Forbidden arms—so raw his age—at Troy,
A bloodless sword and yet unblazoned shield.
He, 'mid that host of Latin warriors thrown,
When rank on rank about him they arose—
Like savage beast by hunters ringed around
That chafes with rage and courts the doom foreknown,
And springs across their spear-heads at a bound—
So rushed the youth to perish 'mid his foes,
Yea, where the darts fell thickest, there he sped.
But Lycus, fleeter far, 'mid foemen fled,
'Mid arms, and reached the rampart, fain to clasp
Its summit and his comrades' hands outspread;
When Turnus, following fast upon his track:
"Didst hope, poor fool," in mocking tones he 'gan,
"To 'scape me thus?" Therewith in ruthless grasp,
Hanging, with half the wall, he plucked him back:
As when a fleet-foot hare, or snowy swan,
By Jove's sharp-taloned bird is haled aloft;
Or lamb, by bleating mother summoned oft,
Is seized by ravening wolf. From every throat
Cries rose. By some the fosse with earth was filled;
Some hurled their flaming torches high and higher:
Ilioneus with massy boulder smote
Lucetius creeping toward the gate with fire;
Asylas, Liger—one with javelin skilled,
One with the feathered shaft that flies remote—
Slew Corinæus and Emathion:
Cæneus Ortygius vanquished, but anon
Was slain by Turnus' hand; and thus, I wis,

Fell Clonius, Promulus, and Sagaris,
And Idas, guardian of the topmost tower;
Nor 'scaped Privernus, whom Temilla's steel
Had grazed but lightly: he, at evil hour,
Flung down his targe and stretched his hand to feel
The wound, when Capys' arrow, winged with death,
Pinned palm to side, and deep, where naught could heal,
Pierced to the inmost haunts of life and breath.

Stood Arcens' son, conspicuous 'mid the throng,
His cloak red-broidered, dark with dyes of Spain;
His aspect noble: him his sire had sent,
Reared in his mother's sacred grove along
Simæthus' banks, by rich Palicus' fane
(Kind, gracious god, e'er ready to relent):
But see! Mezentius, naught but sling in hand,
Thrice o'er his head whirled high the sounding thong;
Then swift the bullet through his temples went,
And stretched him at his length upon the sand.

Then first Ascanius drew, in war, the bow
That oft the flying deer had terrified,
And brought, 'tis said, a valiant leader low,
Numanus, Remulus surnamed, who late
Had won him Turnus' sister for his bride.
He, in the newness of his high estate,
Strode forth before the host with clamorous pride,
Shouting he recked not what, of false and true:
"Feel ye no shame, that thus besieged anew,
Twice-vanquished Phrygians, from your fate ye hide?
(Lo, they who with the sword our brides demand!)
What god, what madness, drove ye to this land?
No sons of Atreus here for foes ye have;
No crafty-tongued Ulysses; but a race
Sprung from a sturdier stock. Early we lead
Our children to the river-bank, to brave
With hardened limbs the chill of wintry wave;
Our boys unsleeping ply the woodland chase—
Their sport to bend the bow, to rein the steed;

Frugal our youths and never-wearied are
To tame the soil in peace, the foe in war.
In arms we live and labour; with the lance,
Reversed, we goad our oxen; nor can age
Weaken our will, our manly vigour mar.
Grey hairs 'neath helmet hidden—as may chance,
We heap the spoil, and live the wild free life.
But ye—'tis saffron robes your thoughts engage,
And gleaming purple dyes; ye love not strife,
But sloth, and ease, and pleasures of the dance,
Sleeved tunics, and the coif with ribands sleek.
O Phrygian women, sure, not men! go seek
Your Dindymus, where shrills the wonted fife!
Hark how the Mother's flutes and timbrels call!
Leave arms to men, and let the broadsword fall."

Such windy boasts and threats Æneas' son
Brooked not, but faced around, and on the string
An arrow set, and stood with bow tight bent
Before high Jove, and breathed an orison:
"Almighty Sire, help Thou my bold intent!
So to thy courts due tribute will I bring.
With gilded horns beside thy shrine shall stand
A young white bull, his mother rivalling
Ev'n now—he bears his lusty head so high,
With horns that butt, and hoofs that spurn the sand."
This heard the Father, and from cloudless sky
Thundered to left. One twang the bowstring gave,
As forth the droning shaft sped fatefully,
And bore its sharp steel through Numanus' brow.
"Go, with thy braggart words insult the brave!
Twice-vanquished Phrygians send thee this reply."
No more Ascanius spake. Exulting now
The Trojans shout applause with rapturous cry.

It chanced the comely-haired Apollo sate
High on aerial cloud, and gazing down
Beheld the Latin host, the 'leaguered town,
And deigned the conquering prince to gratulate:

"Grow thou in valour, boy! Thus heaven is gained.
Of gods the son, of gods the sire to be!
Rightly the Dardan race that nurtured thee
Shall rule a world wherein all wars shall cease,
Nor in Troy's narrow bounds could be contained."
Then, gliding down, he clove the whispering breeze,
And sought Ascanius; mortal shape he wore,
As aged Butes, once Anchises' squire,
And long the trusty guardian of his door,
Now young Iulus' henchman. His attire,
His countenance, his voice he chose to take,
His hoary head, the clanging arms he bore;
And, thus arrayed, the fervent child bespake:
"Suffice it that yon lord thou hast o'erthrown,
Scatheless: 'tis Phœbus grants this earliest prize,
Unenvious of the craft that is his own.
Now quit thee, boy, from battle." This he said,
But ere he finished, fading from men's eyes,
In unsubstantial air was lost to view.
Yet to the Trojan chiefs the god was known
By shafts divine that rattled as he fled:
Wherefore, at Phœbus' bidding, they withdrew
The lad, still yearning for the fray: the rest
Back to the field with reckless valour pressed:
From battlemented walls the clamour grew;
Tireless the bow they bend, the javelin fling
Till earth with darts is strewn; loud clash and ring
Bucklers and hollow helms in frantic fight.
So, 'neath the rainy Kids, a western squall
Lashes the land; so hailstones countless fall
On smitten waters, when with stormful might
Rages the South and rends heaven's cloudy pall.
    Then Pandarus and Bitias, stalwart pair—
Alcanor's sons, whom in Jove's sacred wood
Hiera reared 'neath Ida's solitude—
Youths tall as pines upon their native hill—
Flung wide the gate entrusted them for care

(Their strength in arms had bred such hardihood),
And bade the foeman enter at his will;
To right, to left, before the towers they stood,
Steel-clad, their haughty heads with crests ablaze:
So, high above the crystal-flowing flood,
By Padus' bank, or Athesis' fair tide,
Twin oaks in concert to the heaven up-raise
Their heads unshorn, and nod in lofty pride.
In rushed the foe where ample room they spied—
Bold Quercens, and Aquicolus, fair knight,
Hot-headed Tmarus, Hæmon sword in hand—
But soon with all their host were turned in flight,
Or at the very portals fell and died:
Then were the flames of wrath to fury fanned;
For now the Trojans, massed in solid band,
Made bold to charge, to close, to sally wide.

    To Turnus, as in other parts he warred
With fury none could face, were tidings brought
How Trojans, flushed with slaughter, oped their gate.
His task he left, and spurred by vengeful hate
Rushed where those dauntless brothers stood on guard:
And first Antiphates, who foremost fought—
Sarpedon's son, from Spartan mother bred—
His javelin smote: on airy pinion flew
The native cornel shaft, and in his breast
Sank deep; from gaping wound the blood-stream red
Forth bubbled; in warm lungs the steel found rest.
Then Meropes and Erymas he slew,
And Bitias fiery-eyed and fierce of heart;
No dart it was—he ne'er had died by dart—
But ponderous brandished spike that hurtling came,
Like thunder-bolt: not bull-hides twain could hold,
Nor stout cuirass with golden scales two-fold,
Such deadly stroke; down sank his giant frame;
Rumbled the earth; loud clashed his shield above.
Thus oft on Baiæ's shore there falls o'erthrown
A rocky mass, which men have piled in heap

For basement 'neath the waves; in ruin prone
It plunges down to lodge within the deep:
Then boil the seas, as dusky sand-clouds rise,
And Prochyta is shaken to its steep,
With stark Inarime, that couch of stone,
Whereon by Jove's command Typhœus lies.
   Then to new strength and thoughts of high emprise
The Latin ranks were spurred by mighty Mars
(On Troy fell craven Flight and dark Dismay):
Naught hindering now, they gathered to the fray,
Cheered by the god of wars.
But Pandarus, when he saw his brother slain,
And in what grievous plight their fortunes lay,
Swung back the gate and bolted it amain,
By his wide shoulders shoved, and shut without
Full many a comrade struggling on the plain,
But entry gave to some, nor, 'mid the rout,
Madman! was ware of the Rutulian king
Rushing unchecked within the city's bound,
Like ravening tiger 'mong defenceless sheep:
Strange light gleams from his eyes; his armour's sound
Strikes terror; o'er his helm tall crests upspring
Blood-red, and from his shield live lightnings leap.
   Sudden those mighty limbs, that visage dread,
The startled Trojans knew, and Pandarus
Sprang forth with cry of rage for brother dead:
"Not here is that queen's palace thou wouldst wed,
Nor Ardea's native walls enclose thee thus:
Thy foemen's camp thou seest; way forth is none."
But he, with smile, no whit disquieted:
"Strike then, if fight thou cravest—come thou on!
Thy Priam shall learn thou'st found Achilles here."
So said he; and the Trojan hurled a spear
Massy with rugged knots and bark untanned;
But in the wind 'twas caught, for Juno stayed
The coming shaft and fixed it on the gate:
"Think not this stroke of mine thou shalt evade:

For mark! no weakling he that wields the brand."
So saying, he lifted high his sword, and straight
The Trojan's forehead 'twixt the temples cleft
And both his beardless cheeks with ghastly rent:
Trembled the earth 'neath crash of ponderous weight,
As with lax limbs and armour blood-besprent
Dying he fell; the while to right, to left,
His splintered skull on either shoulder lay.
Then fled his fellows in wild disarray;
And if quick thought had spurred the victor's mind,
To burst the gate and call his comrades through,
The war had ceased, Troy's race had died, that day:
But driven by burning wrath and blood-lust blind
He spared not to pursue.
First Gyges hamstrung fell; then Phaleris
He caught and killed, and snatched their spears to fling
On them that fled (his heart by Juno steeled);
Then Halys; Phegeus, smitten through the shield;
Alcander, Halius, and Prytanis,
Ta'en unawares, for battle rallying;
But Lynceus, craving aid in open fight,
He smote from rampart, lunging to the right
With brandished sword—one stroke, and downward rolled
Shorn head with helmet; next, that hunter bold,
Great Amycus, deep skilled all men above
The javelin's barb with poisoned drugs to smear;
Clytius, and Cretheus to the Muses dear,
Cretheus, the Muses' comrade, famed for love
Of song and harp, the voice wed to the string;
Who oft of steeds and dauntless knights would sing.
   But now the Trojan chiefs, that carnage known,
Mnestheus and brave Serestus, meeting see
The foe within, their comrades' valour spent:
Then Mnestheus: "Friends, what seek ye? whither flee?
What homes, what walls are yours, save these alone?
Shall this one man—yea, in your stronghold pent—
Thus stab and slay your ranks in murderous war,

Scatheless, and strike so many a champion down?
Bethink ye of your gods, your leader's fame,
Your hapless country—cravens that ye are,
Have ye for these no pity and no shame?"
   Stung by such taunts, their broken ranks they close,
Firm-set; then Turnus slowly from the fray
Makes for that foreland where the river flows;
Whereat they press more keen with clamour loud,
In denser troop; as when a lion at bay
Is mobbed with shower of darts; he, grim, tho' cowed,
Retreats with glaring eyes; his reckless wrath
Scorns flight; yet, lusting much, no power he hath
To win his desperate way through spears and crowd:
So did great Turnus hesitant retire
With slow deliberate steps and heart of fire.
Ev'n then he twice rushed furious on the foe,
Twice hurled their ranks along the walls in flight;
But ever from the camp they reunite;
Nor Juno's self dares greater strength inspire,
For Jove from heights of heaven bids Iris go
To bear his consort warning of his ire
If Turnus pass not from the Trojan walls.
Wherefore less potent must his buckler grow,
Falters his strong right-hand—so whelming falls
The storm of shafts; still round his temples ring
The strokes on helmet; stones have riven his mail;
Shorn are his plumes; nor shield can now avail
'Gainst shower on shower of spears the Trojans fling,
And Mnestheus' thunderous strength. Then thickly poured
The sweat in torrents—breath he seemed to crave
In vain—sick pantings shook his weary side:
Till in the river, girt with shield and sword,
Headlong he leapt, and lo! the yellow tide
Received and rescued him on gentle wave,
And, cleansed of blood, to friends and joy restored.

BOOK X

ARGUMENT

JUPITER calls a council of the gods, and after hearing the rival claims of Venus and Juno decides that the issue of the war must be left to the Fates. Æneas returns with Tuscan reinforcements to the rescue of his camp, and the battle is renewed. Turnus slays Pallas, and Æneas in revenge deals havoc among the Latin chieftains; but by a device of Juno's Turnus is withdrawn from the field. Lausus son of Mezentius, and then Mezentius himself, are killed by Æneas.

Meanwhile Olympus throws its portals wide,
And Jove, the almighty Sire, his council calls
In starry mansions, whence, on earth below,
Troy's camp and Latium's armies are espied:
Eastward and westward ope those heavenly halls,
Where to the seated gods thus spake their king:
"Great deities, why shifts your purpose so?
Why strive ye thus, your hearts embittering?
This was forbidden—race 'gainst race to fling:
Yet still ye breed new terrors that impel
Now these, now those, the sword in wrath to draw.
War's destined time shall come—speed not that hour—
When angered Carthage 'gainst Rome's citadel
Shall launch the cloven Alps with deadliest power;
Then hate, then rapine, shall be quit of law:
Rest now, and keep fate's truce inviolable."
   Thus briefly Jove: less brief was the reply
Of golden Venus: "Sire, who dost preside
O'er men and all their works, eternal Lord,
To what save to thy godhead can we cry?
Seest how Rutulians vaunt exultingly,
With Turnus gaily charioted, in pride
Of prosperous battle? Close-fenced walls afford
Scant safety to Troy's folk; within their gate,

Yea, on their bastioned ramparts they contend,
And with their blood the trenches inundate.
Naught knows their absent chief. Wilt never end
This weary siege? Shall foemen still impend
O'er Troy reborn, fresh armies congregate,
And Diomede rise from Arpi's fields anew?
Myself, methinks, must bleed in battle still;
For me, Jove's daughter, mortal weapons wait.
How then? If Trojans sought against thy will
Italia's shores, their rashness let them rue,
And be thine help denied them; but if led
By counsel given again and yet again
From heaven and hell—who thus is warranted
To mar thy mandates and fresh fates ordain?
What of their fleet burned on Sicilian strand?
The storm-king, and that furious tempest bred
In his Æolian isle? Or Iris sent
To bear from heaven thy haughty Queen's command?
Ev'n Hades now is to her purpose bent
(Naught else was left), and loosed in upper air
The fiend Alecto roves the Italian land.
Empire we seek not; once we deemed it fair,
While fortune smiled; but to thy will we bow.
If refuge none her hatred will allow,
Then, by Troy's smoking ruins, this I pray,
That young Ascanius from the sword thou spare,
Albeit o'er trackless seas his father roam,
And ev'n where fortune beckons seek his way;
Fain would I save my grandson from this strife.
In Paphos, in Cythera, have I home,
And Amathus; there let him live his life,
Heedless of glory's call: 'neath world-wide sway
Let Carthage rule Ausonia—'gainst her might
Our folk shall strive not. Hath it brought them joy
To 'scape war's fury, the Greek foeman's spite,
Toiling o'er shores and seas in fruitless quest
For Latium and resurgent towers of Troy?

To have tarried where their city sank were best,
On soil where Troy once stood. Thou, of thy grace,
Restore them to those rivers that they loved,
There to repeat the sorrows of their race!"
    Then queenly Juno, by fierce anger moved:
"Why must I break deep silence, and betray
In words the keenness of my stifled pain?
Did man, did god, thy Trojan chief constrain,
When 'gainst the Latin king war's fires he lit?
Fate led him to Italian kingdoms? Yea;
Cassandra's ravings! Did we bid him quit
His stronghold? to the winds his life commit?
Trust to a boy his camp, his armament,
Scheming the loyal Tuscan tribes to win?
Was it some god, some cruel craft of ours,
Drove him to those dark deeds? Dost find herein
Juno, or Iris from the clouds down sent?
A crime it is, if Latium's banded powers
Besiege Troy's rising walls, or Turnus dare
Set foot on land for which his fathers died,
Land of that nymph divine from whom he sprung:
How, when the sons of Troy their firebrands flung
On Latium—stole its fields and stripped them bare—
From bridegroom's bosom reft the plighted bride—
Poising the javelin while for peace they cried?
Thou from the Grecian swords couldst save thy son,
And in his stead thin clouds and vapours strow,
Transform his burning ships to nymphs o' the sea:
'Tis treason, if like deeds by us be done.
Absent he is, naught knowing? Be it so.
Paphos and high Cythera wait for thee:
Why, then, dost vex this realm by battle scared,
This passionate-hearted folk? Was't we that dared
Thy Trojans' tottering empire to o'erthrow?
We? or that wretch who hurled them 'gainst the Greek?
What caused two races to take arms and wreck
Through treacherous theft their friendship? Did we lead

Troy's amorous prince to Sparta's ruining?
Arms lent we, or bade Cupid kindle war?
'Twas then thou shouldst have trembled for Troy's deed:
Too late thy plaints and void of reason are,
And vain these wild reproaches thou wouldst fling."
    So Juno pleaded, and the great gods all
Made varying résponse, as the rising wind,
Pent in the forest, murmurs low and deep
To warn the mariner of gathering squall.
Then spake the Sire, sole ruler of mankind;
And, at his voice, stilled was that heavenly hall,
The welkin stilled, earth's deep foundations shook;
Down sank the Zephyrs, sank the seas unstirred:
    "Now hark ye, and give heed to this my word.
Since peace betwixt these hosts ye will not brook,
But still must nurse your discord without end,
As either race to-day fair hopes hath won—
Trojan or Latin—favour show I none;
Whether the Fates for Italy have fought,
Or Troy's ill-omened counsels bear the blame.
Nor less is Latium bound. As each hath wrought,
So fare they: Jove to all is still the same.
The Fates shall guide us." By the Stygian god,
Those fiery streams, that dark abyss, He swore;
Then, nodding, shook Olympus with his nod.
Closed was their conclave. From his golden seat
Jove rises, and with ceremony meet
The gods attend their monarch to the door.
    By now the foemen round the portals press
To gird the camp with fire, to smite, to slay;
Troy's 'leaguered host the ramparts still confine;
Escape they know not; in forlorn array
The towers they man, albeit in hopelessness,
Guarding the walls with thin and thinner line.
Asius, Thymœtes—these the foremost are—
The Assaraci, with Thymbris, veteran knight,
And Castor; nigh them stand, a valiant pair,

Sarpedon's brothers twain, from Lycian height.
Acmon with ponderous strength heaves to the wall
A rock in girth like mountain—warrior tall,
And stateliest son of Clytius, stately sire;
With stones, with javelins, some sustain the fight,
Some bend the bow, some hurl the flaming fire.
Midmost is Venus' joy and just delight,
The young Iulus, bare his comely head;
Like some pure jewel framed in tawny gold
For coronet or necklace, or the gleam
Of ivory set in box: o'er shoulders white
Downward from golden hoop his fair locks stream.
Thee, too, brave Ismarus, the clans behold,
Thy deadly strokes, thy darts in venom dyed,
Scion of ancient race whose fruitful soil
Pactolus waters with his golden tide.
Nor is great Mnestheus absent; proud his fame,
Whose strength ev'n haughty Turnus' self could foil;
Nor Capys—Capua hath from him her name.
   While thus they strove, in grip of battle dread
Close-locked, the midnight seas Æneas ploughed:
For when, in Tuscan camp, he held debate
With Tarcho, and his name, his race avowed—
And what the help he craved, the powers he led—
He spared not of Mezentius' schemes to speak,
And bade beware of Turnus' furious hate,
Since human hopes full oft are vain and weak.
So warned he, and so prayed; and Tarcho straight
Joined force in friendly league. Fulfilled is fate;
Embarked with foreign king, the Tuscans fear
No wrath of gods. Æneas leads the van,
With Phrygian lions carved beneath his prow,
And Ida's crest above—glad sight to cheer
With thoughts of home the Trojans' exiled clan.
There sits Troy's mighty chief, with thoughtful brow,
Pondering war's countless hazards; at his side
Young Pallas, asking now of stars that guide

Their passage o'er the dusky depths, or now
Of many a risk on sea or shore defied.
  Ope, Muses, now your Helicon, and sing
What Tuscan tribesmen, ranged with Trojan king,
In arméd galleons o'er the deep seas go.
First Massicus, on Tiger, rides the wave,
From Clusium's walls, from Cosæ's town, to bring
His thousand carles: with feathered shafts they fight,
Shouldering smooth quiver and death-dealing bow.
Stern Abas next—gay arms his henchmen have,
And on his poop a Phœbus glimmers bright:
Six hundred youths by Populonia lent,
Skilled soldiers; Ilva, too, her sons hath sent,
Isle rich in iron's unexhausted mine.
Third sails Asylas, heaven's interpreter,
In starlight learn'd, in flesh of slaughtered kine,
In lightning's bodeful fire, in wild bird's cry;
Dense band he leads, bristling with many a spear,
From Pisa's city, Greek in ancestry,
Tuscan in site. Then Astur, fair to view—
Astur, bold horseman, clad in shimmering mail—
Leads thrice an hundred loyal hearts and true
From Cære, from fair Minio's fruitful vale,
Old Pyrgi, and Graviscæ's sickly coast.
Nor shall the leader of Ligurian host,
Brave Cinyras, lack praise in this my tale;
Nor thou, Cupavo, though small troop was thine;
Swan's feathers in thy crest, thy father's sign:
For Cycnus, racked by love (thy kinsmen's bane),
Long mourned, 'tis said, for his lost Phaëthon,
Within his sisters' poplar shades immured;
Till, while he sang to soothe love's bitter pain—
Lo! white he was, with downy plumes o'ergrown,
Then, rising high o'er earth, still sang and soared.
But now, with comrades of the fleet, his son
Propels his ponderous Centaur; o'er the main,
Up-towering from the prow, the monster heaves

(Ev'n as in act to fling) a massy stone,
High-poised, and with long keel the water cleaves.
   Next Ocnus with his fellows rides the waves,
Child whom wise Manto to Dan Tiber bore:
To Mantua's walls he gave his mother's name;
Mantua, of proud descent, but diverse blood:
Triple her tribes, and clans in each were four;
Herself the head; of·Tuscan race was she.
Thence, too, for hatred of Mezentius came
Five hundred warriors from Benacus' flood,
Whom Mincius, crowned with sedge, by reedy shores,
Brought down in stately war-ship to the sea.
Followed Aulestes, with an hundred oars,
Strong-plied, that scourged the glassy waves to foam;
Onward with monstrous shell his Triton pressed,
Scaring the deep: that shaggy countenance
Was man's; below, the belly of sea-beast;
Loud wailed the water 'neath its wolfish breast.
So to Troy's succour did those chieftains come,
In ships twice ten that ploughed the salt expanse.
   Now had the daylight died; in chariot pale
The Moon's mild presence scales Olympus' height.
Æneas, for his cares endure not sleep,
Himself the rudder rules or trims the sail:
When lo! in midmost voyage there meets his sight
A friendly quire, his ships—now mermaids fair,
Made goddesses and guardians of the deep.
In ordered line they swim, nor fewer are
Than brazen prows once banked along the beach.
Their lord they spy, and troop in sportive band;
And one, Cymodoce, most skilled of speech,
Close following, on the stern laid strong right-hand,
Uplifting neck and shoulders o'er the tide,
While still her left, submerged, she softly plied;
Then hailed him, ere he knew: "Dost watch, great king
Ay, wake and watch, and free the canvas fling.
Thy pines are we, from sacred Ida's side;

Now sea-nymphs, once thy fleet. When that false foe
With sword and fire rushed on us ravaging,
Sadly our bonds we burst, yet still were fain
To find thee. Then, in pity for our woe,
The Mother changed our form, and bade us dwell
Immortal 'neath the bosom of the main.
But young Ascanius in the camp is pent,
Where darts fly densest and fierce war-cries swell.
What though Arcadian, joined with Tuscan band,
Ride true to tryst—'tis Turnus' firm intent
To meet and bar them from the Trojan wall.
Haste, then; with earliest dawn thy comrades call
To arms, and grasp thy shield, by Fire-god's hand
Made matchless and with gold emblazoned round!
To-morrow's sun, if faith in me be found,
Shall see thy foemen in full harvest fall."
She spoke; then, parting, shoved the ship ahead
With force unerring: through the waves it sped
Swifter than arrow that outstrips the wind;
So haste they all. That portent in amaze
The Trojan sees, yet lifts, inspirited,
His eyes to heaven's high vault, and briefly prays:
"Great Mother of the gods, Thou who dost find
In Dindymus, in tower-girt towns, thy joy;
In harnessed lions twain that draw the car:
Be Thou my guide and leader in this war;
Fulfil thine omen, and give aid to Troy!"
  Ev'n as he spake the circling orb of day
Was waxing, and had pierced night's darkness through.
Forthwith he bade his folk those signs obey
And steel their courage for fresh battlefield:
And now his camp, his comrades are in view,
As high he stands and holds aloft his shield
Blazing with lustre. Joyous shouts arise
From Trojans on the wall; hope springs anew,
And darts fly thicker. So, 'neath scowling skies,
Strymonian cranes give signal, as they pass

High on the boisterous South with gleeful cries.
Then on Rutulian chiefs great wonder was,
Till, as they gazed around, lo! shoreward turned,
A sea of ships draws near, a mighty fleet.
They saw the hero's helm, with crest that burned;
They saw the flames from golden shield shot forth:
As when on cloudless night some comet's ire
Casts dismal beams blood-red; or Sirius' heat,
That brings to weary mortals drought and dearth,
Rises to blast the heavens with baleful fire.

But Turnus' dauntless spirit naught can quell:
Eager, the vantage seized, to guard the shore,
His mates ev'n more he cheers, ev'n chides the more:
"Heaven grants your prayer, to fight this battle out.
The war—'tis in your hands. Bethink ye well
Each of his wife, his home, and how of yore
Your fathers flinched not! Haste we to the strand,
While yet they plant their faltering steps in doubt;
'Tis Fortune aids the bold."
So saying, he ponders who with him shall stand,
Who still the 'leaguered camp in durance hold.

Now from the lofty ships stout planks they fling,
To gain the land. Some, watching for recoil
Of the spent waves, amid the shallows spring;
Some grasping oars. But Tarcho, for he spied
A creek wherein no broken surges boil,
But all unhindered rolls the swelling tide,
Steered shoreward straight, his oarsmen challenging:
"Row, now, ye best of boatmen, tug and toil!
Make your ships leap and bound: 'tis foemen's soil;
Then cleave it—let your keels deep furrows trace!
Nay, for such port my vessel would I break,
So land at last were won." Such words he spake;
Then one and all they plied their blades apace,
The spray-drenched barques on Latin land to hurl;
Till prows strike earth, and all find resting-place
Unscathed, save one—ah, Tarcho, whose but thine?

For dashed on perilous reef, 'mid eddying swirl,
Long time it hangs and battles with the brine,
Then, parting, spills its crew where drifting spar
And shattered oar the swimmers' efforts mar,
And refluent waves their struggling feet impede.
  Nor tarried Turnus, but with hottest speed
To seaward flung his host to front the foe.
The trumpet's signal pealed. Æneas, first,
Leapt forth to lay the Latin tribesmen low,
For omen of the fight. There Theron died;
No goodlier knight-at-arms than he, who durst
Invite such combat; yet the rapier burst
Through steel, through gold cuirass, and gashed his side.
Slain, too, was Lycas, who at dawn of life,
Cut from his mother's corse, was consecrate,
Phœbus, to thee, a child that 'scaped the knife.
Hard by, stout Cisseus and huge Gyas fought
With massy bludgeons dealing death around;
Yet were they smitten both, nor 'gainst their fate
Could arms of Hercules avail them aught,
Nor that their sire had been the Hero's mate
What time on earth those grievous Tasks he found.
Next Pharus fell—the sharp steel in his throat,
Ev'n as he uttered boastful words and vain:
Thou likewise, Cydon, who didst blindly doat
On Clytius, thy latest heart's-delight,
Whose fair young cheek with earliest down was flushed,
Hadst surely felt the Dardan sword, and lain
To all thy many loves oblivious quite,
Had not thy brothers in close phalanx rushed;
Seven were they—Phorcus' sons—and javelins seven
They hurled; but some from helm and shield unriven
Glanced harmless; some, by kindly Venus' might,
Scarce grazed the Trojan's body as they passed;
Then to Achates did the chieftain speak:
"Hand me those shafts, so none be vainly cast,
That pierced in bygone battles many a Greek

On plains of Troy." A mighty spear he grasped
And flung: through Mæon's shield it sped with force,
And tore its way through breastplate to his heart.
Alcanor, next, his stricken brother clasped
With hand outstretched, but through his arm a dart
Flew swift, nor lingered on its bloody course
Till nerveless hung his hand, its sinews rent.
Last, with a lance from brother's body torn,
Came Numitor, his heart on vengeance bent:
Balked was his blow, and grazed Achates' thigh.

See, Clausus, fired with youthful strength and scorn,
Strikes Dryops down with sturdy spear far flung:
Deep in his throat it lights; he, robbed thereby
Of voice and life, falls headlong on earth's breast,
And from his lips the clotted blood-drops run.
Three Thracians, too, from ancient Boreas sprung,
And three from Ismara sent—Idas their sire—
He spared not. To the front Halesus pressed,
With his Auruncan troop, and Neptune's son,
Messapus, glorying in his steeds: none tire,
None halt; for at Italia's very gate
The fight is. As when winds 'gainst winds contest,
With equal fury striving, nor abate
Their wrath, nor clouds nor waves withdraw one span—
Earth's forces all in stubborn conflict set—
Ev'n so the Trojan host with Latin met,
Close-matched, foot locked with foot, man hurled on man.
Elsewhere, on rugged slope, by torrent side
With rolling rocks and shattered tree-trunks strewed,
Arcadia's sons, to novel fight constrained
(Nor mounted now, where room was none to ride),
Fled panic-struck by Latin foe pursued.
The which when Pallas saw—naught else remained—
With prayers and taunts he strove to sting their pride:
"Where fly ye, comrades? By your bold deeds done,
By sire Evander's realm that proudly rose—
By mine own hope an equal fame to earn—

Retreat not! By our good swords must be won
A way where yonder ranks around us close:
Thus loyal to our land must we return.
No gods oppress us; mortal are our foes,
We mortal, framed like them, or strong or weak.
Mark well what hindering seas your flight oppose,
What leagues of land! Is't Troy's far shores ye seek?"
So saying, where thickest fell the spears, he sped.

   First on his path, by luckless fortune led,
Came Lagus; him, ere ponderous stone he threw,
He pierced with brandished javelin, where the spine
Divides the ribs; then back the shaft he drew,
Deep-sunk. In vain did Hisbo, with design
To smite him as he stooped, in anger hot
Rush on him, crazed by comrade's cruel lot;
For swift his lungs were gashed by Pallas' blade.
Fell Sthenelus, of Rhœtus' ancient line;
Fell he who dared his step-dame's bed invade,
Anchemolus; fell those twin sons begot
By Daucus, who so like of feature were
Not ev'n their kin might judge betwixt the pair,
And pleasing doubt on parents' eyes was laid:
But Pallas now a stern distinction wrought;
For Thymber's head his sharp steel shore away,
Larides' hand—there, ownerless, it lay,
With twitching fingers that the dagger sought.

   Thus chid, their captain's deeds before their eyes,
The Arcadians stay their rout, remorseful, shamed.
Then Rhœteus in light car, as past he flies,
Falls pierced, such respite brief did Ilus gain:
Ilus, 'gainst whom was Pallas' javelin aimed,
When Rhœteus intervened—by brothers twain,
Teuthras and Tyres, harried—and so smit
Rolled dying from his chariot on the plain.
And as, when welcome winds arise, some swain
A surging fire in summer woods hath lit;
And straight the flames, embattled in one blaze,

With furious front the wooded wold o'errun;
He, seated high, their conquering march surveys:
So were those valiant hearts all massed in one,
To help thee, Pallas. Comes in headlong charge
Halesus, covered with his trusty targe;
Demodocus and Ladon low he lays—
Severs with gleaming sword Strymonius' hand
Uplifted at his throat—then Thoas slays
With stone that crashes blood-stained through the skull.
Halesus, by prophetic sire's command
(His end foreseen), had lurked in forest lair;
But when his father's eyes in death were dull,
Fate claimed him—victim of Arcadian dart;
And this, ere yet he struck, was Pallas' prayer:
"Grant, father Tiber, to this lance of mine
Fair flight, and passage to Halesus' heart:
So shall his trophies deck thy leafy shrine."
Heard was his vow: Halesus, in his care
To shield Imaon's breast, his own laid bare.
  Not ev'n this blow the Latin valour broke;
Such chief they had in Lausus. Abas straight
He met and slew, opponent tough as oak:
Arcadians, Tuscans, 'neath his onset fell,
With Trojans who had 'scaped Troy's hapless fate.
So meet the hosts well balanced, captained well:
Forward the rearguard press, and none can move
Or hand or hilt. Here Pallas chides and cheers;
There Lausus—valiant champions, like in years,
In form most beauteous—yet shall neither know
The joys of home return: nor doth great Jove
Permit them, youth 'gainst youth, to hurl their spears:
Ev'n now there waits for each a mightier foe.
  To Turnus then, as swiftly charioted
He clove the ranks, the Nymph his sister cried
To face the Arcadian prince in Lausus' stead:
So to his friends he spake: "Stand ye aside:
Pallas is mine; be Pallas left to me,

My due: I would his sire were here to see."
He spake, nor they his royal right denied,
But left the field. Young Pallas in amaze
That haughty bidding heard, and fixed his gaze
On Turnus' giant frame unflinchingly;
Then dauntless to the chieftain's threat replied:
  "Proud trophies now, great glory, shall I gain,
Or honoured death: whate'er my lot bestows,
My sire shall shrink not: leave thy boasts unsaid."
So saying, he strode upon the open plain,
The while his kinsmen's hearts were chilled with dread:
And Turnus from his chariot leapt, to close
In mortal combat: his the lion's spring,
When from some rocky lair he sees afar
A bull stand on the plain and challenge war:
So rushed to battle the Rutulian king.
But Pallas, when he deemed his javelin's fling
Might reach the mark, stepped forward, and assayed,
O'ermatched in strength, what succour chance might bring;
And first to heaven for help he looked, and prayed:
"Hear me, Alcides, once my father's guest!
Aid thou, for friendship's sake, this bold emprise,
And grant that Turnus see with dying eyes
My conquering hand his gory trophies take!"
Alcides heard the youth, and in his breast
Stifled a groan, and wept for vain love's sake,
Till Jove in gracious speech his son addressed:
  "To each his day is portioned: past recall
Is man's short lifetime: but in glory's quest
Doth Valour find its task. 'Neath Troy's high wall
Full many a god-begotten warrior died
(There did mine own beloved Sarpedon fall):
Ev'n Turnus to the will of fate must yield,
And nears the appointed limit of his pride."
Jove spake, and turned his eyes from that fierce field.
    Then Pallas with strong arm his javelin flung,
And from its scabbard plucked his gleaming blade:

Straight to its mark the flying dart sped true,
And lit, and passed the targe's rim, nor stayed,
Till Turnus' mighty shoulder it had grazed.
But he his deadlier steel-tipped lance up-raised,
And poised it long, and shouted ere it flew:
"Look thou! This spear of mine can pierce more deep."
And lo! through folds of brass and iron, and through
The tough bull-hide that wrapped the shield around,
Failed not that quivering shaft its course to keep,
Till sheer through breastplate to his breast it passed.
Vainly he strove to draw it from the wound
Whence blood and life alike were fleeting fast:
He fell; his armour clanged with doleful sound,
As, biting foreign dust, he breathed his last.
Then o'er him Turnus spake:
  "Arcadians, mark ye well: this message take
To king Evander. Thus his son I send,
And justly; but if aught it ease his pain
With honour due the dead in earth to lay,
I freely grant it. Dearly must he pay
Who took my foe Æneas for his friend."
So saying, with foot firm planted on the slain,
The huge and heavy belt he tore away,
Whereon that tale of love and guilt was told—
The bridegrooms foully stabbed on bridal night,
All graved by craftsman's hand in purest gold:
Full proud went Turnus in those trophies dight.

  Blind hearts of men, that ponder not, nor guess,
How fortune changeth with the changing year,
Nor shrink in prosperous season from excess!
Turnus shall yet repent that blood-stained prize
And curse the triumph doomed to cost him dear.
But now by weeping friends that loved him well
Homeward is Pallas borne, with shield for bier,
Great pride, great sorrow, to his parent's eyes.
Brave youth! on that one day he fought, he fell,
Yet left full many a foeman ne'er to rise.

No fearful rumour now, but message sure
Flies to Æneas—barriers thin divide
His folk from death, nor long can they endure.
With sweep of sword that lays the nearest low
Hotly he cleaves a passage through the foe:
Eager to face thee, Turnus, in thy pride
Of fresh-won triumph. To his vision came
Pallas, Evander—how their guest they led,
An homeless exile, to that festal board,
Hands clasped in friendship. Then his anger claims
Sulmo's four sons, and four by Ufens bred,
To die, for funeral offering, by the sword,
Drenching with captive blood the sacred flames.
    'Gainst Mago next his vengeful spear was drawn:
He, deftly stooping, saw the shaft speed o'er,
Then clasped with suppliant hand the chieftain's knee:
"Now by thy buried sire, thy son's fair dawn—
I too have son and sire, then spare thou me!
A mansion proud is mine, with deep-delved store
Of polished silver, gold inestimable;
Not by my death will Troy victorious be,
Nor wilt thou reck one victim, less or more."
Whereto the warrior answered vehement:
"Thy gold and silver, that thou guard'st so well,
Keep for thy sons. 'Twas Turnus first forbade
Such bloodless barter, when young Pallas fell.
Take this from sire and son for answer sent."
As thus he spake, his helm, while still he prayed,
He grasped with strong left-hand; then, backward bent,
Hilt-deep within the throat buried the blade.
    Hard by, conspicuous in Rutulian line,
Stands Hæmon's son, the priest of Phœbus' shrine:
With sacred fillets is his forehead bound;
Raiment all white and gleaming arms he wears:
But soon, o'ermatched, along the plain he flies,
Then, stumbling, 'neath the Trojan's rapier dies
By sacrificial stroke that wraps him round

In death's great darkness. Back Serestus bears
His choicest trophies for the War-God's prize.
   Forth strode bold Cæculus, of Vulcan's seed,
And with him Umbro, Marsian hillsman rude,
To face the Dardan chief; he furiously
Both shield and hand at once from Anxur hewed.
Vain boasts had Anxur flung, and deemed the deed
Would match the word; his thoughts perchance soared high,
Long life he hoped and many a placid year.
Next Tarquitus, in shining armour drest,
Of wandering Faunus and fair wood-nymph sprung,
Rushed to the combat; but his brandished spear
Æneas drove through buckler and through breast;
Then, heeding not his prayers or subtle tongue,
Smote off his head, and heaved the trunk away,
Still warm, and o'er him spake in bitter mood:
"There lie, dread warrior! Thee no mother's care
In proud ancestral tomb shall fondly lay.
Thy limbs wild birds shall rend, or waters bear
Where hungry fish shall lick thy clotted blood."
   Antæus next, and Lucas, he pursued,
Knights of the van, and hard on Numa pressed,
And gold-haired Camers, son of generous sire,
Silent Amyclæ's ruler, who possessed
Large wealth unrivalled of Ausonian lands.
And as, with hundred arms, with hundred hands,
With fifty mouths that belched the fabled fire,
'Gainst Jove's own bolts Ægæon dared aspire,
Clashed fifty shields, and waved as many brands—
So raged Æneas on his conquering path,
His sword once warmed with blood. Behold him meet
Niphæus drawn by harnessed horses four:
They, when they saw him charging in his wrath,
Turned, terror-smitten, and in wild retreat
Flung forth their lord and galloped to the shore.
   Then Lucagus, by two white coursers borne,
Rode forth, his brother Liger ruled the rein;

He, waving naked sword, made brave display.
Such frenzied vaunts so stirred the chieftain's scorn,
Huge shape, with lifted spear, he barred their way.
Then Liger: "Look not now for Phrygian plain,
Nor Diomede's horses, nor Achilles' car;
For here shall end thy lifetime and this war—
Here, on this ground we tread." Wild words and vain
He flung abroad; not so the Trojan king;
No words, but javelin keen for speech he sent;
And Lucagus, as o'er his team he leant,
With spear for goad, his fullest strength to bring—
Left foot advanced—saw sudden, 'neath his shield,
The deadly spear emerge and pierce his side,
And dying from his chariot fell to field.
Then grimly spake his victor: "Lucagus,
No slackness of thy steeds betrayed thee thus,
Nor fled they by vain shadows terrified:
Thyself didst leap to leave them." At the word,
He stayed the chargers. Then for mercy cried
The brother, hands outstretched, and sank to earth:
"Now by thy grace—by them that gave thee birth—
I pray thee, Trojan, be thy pity stirred!"
And more; but he: "Not such, of late, methought,
Thy speech was. Die: so kin shall quit not kin."
Then pierced he with sharp rapier through and through
His breast, and loosed the life that lurked therein.
Such havoc wide the Dardan chieftain wrought;
Like surging torrent or dark hurricane
Resistless, till the prince, with comrades true,
Came forth from camp beleaguered long in vain.
    To Juno then great Jove his speech addressed:
"Thou who both sister art, and spouse adored,
Thou saidst it. Mark the wisdom of thy word!
'Tis Venus, and none other, doth uphold
Troy's craven ranks that lack the warrior's zest,
Lack strength in peril and endurance bold."
But she, submissive: "Nay, most gracious Lord,

Why must thou gall me with thy bitter jest?
If of thy love, as once, I were possessed
(As right it were), this would'st thou not deny,
Omnipotent, that Turnus be restored
Scatheless from battle to his aged sire:
But now, to glut Troy's vengeance, let him die.
Yet from our own celestial blood he springs,
The seed of great Pilumnus, nor doth tire
To load thy shrines with bounteous offerings."
Whereto the Lord of Heaven made brief reply:
"If time thou cravest, and delay from death
(Since die he must), and seest my fixed design,
Go, snatch him from this doom that threateneth:
Thus far thy wish I grant; but if thy plea
Conceal some deeper respite—that this strife
May change its whole event—vain hope is thine."
Then Juno, tearful: "Would thy thoughts were free
To grant what lips refuse, my Turnus' life!
Now, guiltless, must he face the woful end,
If true my fears: ah, joy, if false they be,
And thou, who hast the power, this doom amend!"
    She spake, and straightway wrapped in robe of storm,
Down gliding earthward from the heavenly realm,
To Trojan ranks and Latin army came;
And there of mist and shadows did she frame
A wondrous image of Æneas' form,
In Dardan armour decked—with shield, with helm
To match majestic brow; vain speech she gave,
Speech void of thought, and semblance of his gait;
Like shapes that flit, 'tis whispered, from the grave,
Or dreams that mock men's slumbering sense in sleep.
There, in the van, this spectre stalked elate,
With shafts and taunts for challenge to the brave:
Then forth, with brandished spear, see Turnus leap,
And hurl; whereat the wraith to rearward fled.
He, for he deemed his foe had shunned the fray—
His throbbing heart with idle fancies fed—

Cried: "Flee not, lord Æneas, nor betray
The nuptials thou didst plight. From this my hand
Shalt thou receive for gift thy long-sought land."
Shouting, he charged, and waved his steel o'erhead,
Nor guessed the winds had whirled his hopes away.
   It chanced 'neath verge of rocky cliff there lay
A barque with gangways ready, ropes out hung,
That from the Clusian coast Osinius brought:
There did that false Æneas refuge find
In the dark hold; and Turnus, hard behind,
With frantic haste o'er lofty ladders sprung.
Scarce had he touched the prow, when Juno's thought
Cut loose the ship and back to ocean bore:
Whereat the phantom form, concealed no more,
Flew high, and vanished in the vapours dun.
Thus while Æneas claimed his absent foe,
And many a valiant lord in death laid low,
Was Turnus hurled in tempest from the shore,
Back gazing, heedless of the respite won;
Then, hands and voice upheld, to heaven he prayed:
"Almighty Sire, didst deem me to have earned
Such shame that this great forfeit must be paid?
Whence, whither, is my flight? and how, returned,
On Latium's city can I gaze again?
What of the troop that followed in my train,
Now left to perish by remorseless fate?
Scattered I see them, hear them groaning fall.
What do I? Can Earth's nethermost abyss
Hide me? Ye winds, be more compassionate!
Fling me on rocks ('tis Turnus begs ye this),
Or 'mid some sandy shoal my ship enthrall
Far from my fellows and accusing fame!"
He spake, by doubts distraught, nor knew at all
Whether, in fierce resentment of such shame,
Upon his sword-point fallen to die outright,
Or leaping 'mid the waves to strike for land,
And so rejoin his fellows in the fight.

Thrice tried he either course: thrice Juno's hand
Withheld him, though her heart was filled with ruth:
Wafted by prosperous tides and breezes light,
Thus to his father's kingdom sailed the youth.
  Anon, at Jove's behest, with heart of flame,
'Gainst Troy's exulting host Mezentius came;
On rushed the Tuscan legion, all, as one,
Hurling their hate, their spears, on him alone:
Like rock he stood, that juts into the sea,
Fronting the winds, and by the wild waves lashed,
Nor wrath of heaven, nor ocean's threats can tame
Its all-enduring strength. To earth he dashed
First Latagus, then Palmus fain to flee;
The one with massy rock from hillside reft
Full in the face he struck; Palmus he left
Stretched hamstrung on the field; his armour bright
To Lausus gave, with plumes his helm to grace.
Evanthes next, and Mimas did he smite,
The friend of Paris—born the self-same night
When Hecuba her fateful firebrand bore,
The Trojan prince; but now in Troy's embrace
Lies Paris, Mimas on far western shore.
  As when, by hounds disturbed, a boar has fled
From mountain lair, long housed in piney glen
Of Vesulus, and long in Latium's fen,
On forest herbage and lush sedges fed;
Now in his captors' toils undauntedly
He stands and foams, bristling infuriate,
Nor of those huntsmen bold dares one draw nigh;
They hurl from distance safe, with loud debate:
So, of those Tuscans fired with righteous hate,
Close combat, sword with sword, not one but fears;
With clamorous din they fight and distant dart:
He, fearless, slowly turns toward every part,
Gnashing, and from his shoulders shakes the spears.
  From ancient Corythus had Acron come;
A Greek, from sundered nuptials torn away.

Mezentius marked him as he stemmed the fray,
Flaunting the purple pennon of his bride:
As when a lion, wont the woods to roam,
Perchance, by hunger maddened, hath espied
Fleet goat, or stag with antlers high upreared—
Instant, with lifted mane, mouth gaping wide,
He lights upon his quarry at a bound,
His jaws with blood besmeared:
So leapt Mezentius where his foeman stood;
Ill-fated Acron falls, and beats the ground,
Reddening the broken spear-head with his blood.
    Natheless, when fled Orodes, he disdained
With wingéd shaft to deal a privy blow;
Man matched with man, and front to front, they met;
'Twas force of arms, not craft, the conquest gained:
Then foot and spear on prostrate form he set:
"See, friends," he cried; "a mighty lord brought low":
And loud their cry of triumph rose long while.
He, with last breath: "Not unavenged I die;
Brief joy is thine; like doom awaits thee yet:
Soon vanquished on the self-same field thou'lt lie."
Then spake the chief, with anger in his smile:
"Die, then. For me—let Heaven's great lord dispose
My fate." Then back he drew the steel; and now
Death's iron sleep is on Orodes' brow,
In everlasting night his eyelids close.
    There likewise was Alcathous struck to earth;
Parthenius died the death by Rapo's hand,
And stalwart Orses; then Messapus' brand
Both Clonius and Ericetes slew;
One by his restive charger flung on ground,
One foot to foot engaged. Stepped Agis forth,
But soon his victor in bold Valerus knew.
'Twas Salius aimed the blow when Thronius bled;
And him Nealces smote, for spear renowned,
Or viewless arrow from far distance sped.
    Thus freely were War's wounds and death-blows shed,

As long they strove, now slaying and now slain,
Victors or vanquished, thought was none of flight.
The high gods grieved to see that fury vain,
And all those weary toils by mortals braved:
Here Venus, there great Juno watched the fight;
Midmost the ranks the pale-faced Fury raved.
　　See, shaking massy spear, Mezentius stride
Tempestuous o'er the field, a giant form,
Huge as Orion when he walks enorm
Through deep mid-ocean, and o'ertops the tide,
Or homeward bears from some high mountain-side
An ancient ash, and plants on earth his feet,
And heavenward lifts his brow above the storm:
So stalked Mezentius in vast arms arrayed.
Then moved the Trojan chief his foe to meet,
Seen from afar. He, standing undismayed,
Waited in all his ponderous strength complete,
Measuring his javelin's compass ere he threw:
"Now be my guardian gods mine own right-hand
And this far-reaching weapon that I wield!
I vow that soon, my Lausus, for thy due,
Decked in yon bandit's trophies thou shalt stand."
So said he; and his sounding shaft forth flew
At distant range, then shaken from the shield
Swerved far, and pierced the brave Antores' side,
Alcides' friend, who to Italian land
From Argos in Evander's train had passed:
Slain in another's stead, one glance he cast
Skyward, and dreamed of Argos as he died.
Then sped the Trojan javelin; sheer it went
Through triple orb of brass, through linen fold,
Through bull-hides three, and sank, its strength far spent,
Deep in Mezentius' groin. With swift intent
The Trojan drew, and gladdened to behold
His foeman's blood, leapt hotly forth to smite.
　　But Lausus, when he saw his father's plight,
Groaned deeply, and down his cheek the tear-drops rolled.

Brave boy! thy piteous death, thy glorious deed—
If aught a future age such valour heed—
In this my poem shall not pass untold.
For when his crippled sire drew backward slow,
Sore stricken, and in his shield the Trojan spear,
Forth sprang the youth and mingled in the fray;
Ay, as the hand was lifted for the blow,
He crossed the sword, nor feared not to delay
And thwart the Trojan's stroke. With lusty cheer,
Till sire, by son protected, creeps away,
His folk in baffling shower their javelins ply:
Æneas, wroth, behind his buckler bides;
As oft, when hailstorm bursts from clouded sky,
From open ploughland hinds and peasants run,
And 'neath some sheltering arch the traveller hides
Or river-bank, or cleft of lofty rock,
While falls the rain; then with returning sun
Each seeks his daylong task: so, whelmed with darts,
Æneas bore that war-cloud, till its shock
Was spent, as thunder from the sky departs.
Lausus he chides, Lausus he threateneth:
"Too venturous boy, why speed'st thou to thy death?
Thy filial love betrays thee." He, no less,
Joys in his peril, till the chieftain's wrath
Swells high and higher, and the dark Fates spin
Last threads of Lausus' life: with fiery stress
Deep to the hilt the sword its way must win
Through targe—defence too slight for heart so bold—
Through tunic, by his mother woven in gold,
And filled with blood his bosom: to the dead,
Quitting his corse, the soul in sadness fled.

But when Anchises' son beheld that face,
That dying face so wondrous pallid grown,
He sighed, with hand outstretched, and saw in ruth
The likeness of the lad that was his own:
"How shall Æneas show thee worthy grace?
How honour thy true heart, ill-fated youth?

Keep thou thy cherished arms: if aught allays
Thy grief, thou shalt be buried with thy sires:
And let this thought console thee for death's pain:
Thou diedst by hero's hand." His lingering squires
He chides, and hastes that prostrate form to raise,
Its fair young tresses smirched with gory stain.

His sire the while, where Tiber's water ran,
Was fain to rest his limbs, his wound to stanch,
'Gainst tree-trunk propped; upon a neighbouring branch
His helmet hung; his armour lay below.
Around him stood his chiefs; he, breathless, wan,
Chafes neck, his beard dishevelled flowing down,
And oft of Lausus asks, or message sends,
Bidding him come to swage his father's woe.
He came—on buckler borne by wailing friends,
A mighty prince by mighty stroke o'erthrown.
That cry with prescient mind the father heard;
Then soiled in dust his hoary head, and flung
His hands to heaven, and to the pale corse clung,
And cried: "Were joys of life by me so craved
That for my sake I let thee face the sword,
My son? Yea, by thy sufferings was I saved,
And by thy death I live! Ah, now, at last,
I perish; now soul-deep the wound has gone!
'Twas I, none else, whose lawless deeds abhorred
With guilty taint thy youthful fame could blast,
From sceptre banished and ancestral throne;
And for such treason justly to atone
I had not feared an hundred deaths to die;
But here I live, nor quit the realms of light:
Yet will I quit them." Then on wounded thigh
He rallied, and despite his deep wound's ache
Bade them lead forth his war-horse. He, his pride,
His joy, his partner in victorious fight,
Stood waiting, mournful, while his master spake:

"Rhæbus, long have we lived, if aught on earth
Lives long. To-day thou shalt bring back, elate,

Those blood-stained trophies and Æneas' head,
And 'venge with me my Lausus' cruel fate;
Or, if my strength of arm be nothing worth,
Beside me die. For certes, gallant steed,
Thou ne'er wilt deign a Trojan lord to bear."
He mounted, and in wonted posture sate,
Grasping in hand full many a steel-tipped dart:
Brazen his helm, his crest of long horse-hair;
So rushed he straight to combat—in his heart
Fierce shame, and madness mingled with despair.
   Then thrice with ringing voice he hailed his foe.
Æneas heard, and paused in joy to pray:
"Now Jove and lord Apollo will it so,
That thou to fight come on!"
And strode with threatening lance athwart the way.
But he: "Nay think not to affright me now,
Savage, since thou hast robbed me of my son;
For thus, thus only, was my strength undone:
Death mock I, nor to aught divine will bow.
Then cease: I come to die; but first I bring
These gifts." So saying, a dart he hurled—anon,
Another and another—galloping
Far round; but scatheless stood that golden shield.
Thrice round his firm-set foe leftward he wheeled,
Showering his shafts; and thrice the Trojan king,
With javelins bristling on his buckler, turned;
Till, of unequal combat wearying,
As dart chased dart nor yet the end was near,
Biding his chance he bounded forth, and deep
Within the charger's forehead drove his spear.
High reared the war-horse, as the air he spurned,
And on his fallen rider, in one heap,
Himself with broken shoulder headlong fell;
Then, as with rival shouts the welkin burned,
Æneas from his scabbard drew the blade.
"Where now is that grim chief implacable,
Mezentius?" But the Tuscan, as deep breath

He drew, and felt his wandering sense returned:
"Why, bitter foe, dost menace and upbraid?
Slay me: no truce I ask, nor fight I so;
Nor thus my Lausus bargained 'gainst my death.
Yet for one favour may the vanquished crave,
Grant that my corse have burial. Well I know
My Tuscans' hatred. Be their wrath withstood,
And let me lie with Lausus in the grave!"
So saying, his throat he proffered for the blow,
And yielded life with copious stream of blood.

BOOK XI

THE funeral of Pallas is described. Overtures for peace having been made by the Latins, a truce is concluded for twelve days. A discussion in king Latinus' council, in which Drances advocates peace, Turnus war, is interrupted by an advance of the Trojan army, which causes a renewal of the fighting. The feats and death of Camilla occupy the last portion of the book.

Now was Aurora risen from the main.
Æneas, though with careworn heart and sad—
Intent on burial of his comrades slain—
Fulfilled at earliest dawn a victor's vows.
A massive oaken trunk, shorn of its boughs,
Was hoisted high, in glittering armour clad,
The War-God's trophies, from Mezentius ta'en:
Thereon were fixed his helmet blood-besprent,
His shattered spears, his corslet riven and rent
With blows twice six; to left, his brazen targe,
And strapped on arm his ivory-hilted sword.
Then did Æneas, as his comrades pressed
Exulting round, thus give them joyful charge:
    "Great deeds have been accomplished: for the rest
Fear naught. Behold the spoils of that proud lord,
Our first-fruits: once Mezentius—this is he!
Now march we 'gainst Laurentum and its king.
Arm, then, and let your hopes unbounded be;
That when the gods have willed it, and we spring
From camp, and forth our host to battle lead,
No chilling doubts your courage may impede,
Nor coward purpose keep you faltering.
Now lay we our dead comrades in the tomb

(Sole honour left on Acheron's dark strand):
Go, give those dauntless hearts their latest meed,
Whose blood hath earned us this new fatherland;
And bear ye first to his grief-stricken home
Young Pallas, lacking naught of valorous deed,
But whelmed untimely by the day of doom."

In tears he spoke, then turned toward the door
Where lay the corse of Pallas, and thereby
Watched old Accœtes, who had been of yore
Evander's squire; but now, by fate less fair,
Guarded the child he loved so loyally:
There all his mourning folk were gathered round,
And Trojan women with dishevelled hair.
But when Æneas passed those portals high,
Their bosoms they beat, and raised a dolorous cry,
Till wide the palace echoed to the sound:
He, when he saw that pillowed face death-white,
And on the marble breast the gaping wound
Made by Ausonian lance, thus weeping spake:

"Alas, that Fortune, when she smiled more bright,
Grudged me thy presence, nor would let thee take
Joy in my new-gained kingdom, nor return
Acclaimed victorious in thy father's sight!
Not such my parting promise to the king,
What time with fond embrace he bade me go
On conquering course, yet warning gave how stern
Must be the combat with remorseless foe.
And now, perchance, by hollow hopes misled,
Vain vows he breathes, with gifts to altar brought;
While we with unavailing honours tend
This lifeless youth whom heaven hath holpen naught!
Unhappy sire, thou'lt see thy Pallas dead.
Is this our triumph? this, the wished-for end?
For this didst trust me? Yet be comforted,
Evander; by those wounds was glory won,
Nor need'st thou crave for death, like sire whose son
Lives, but hath purchased life at honour's cost.

Lament, Ausonia, for thy saviour gone!
And thou, Iulus, for such guardian lost!"
   Therewith he bade them lift their burden sad,
And sent a thousand warriors, tried and true,
To pay last honours to the hero lad,
And greet the weeping father—solace small
For grief so great, yet to lorn parent due.
Some weave for wicker bier a pliant pall
Of arbutus, or oaken foliage strew,
Shading his cushioned couch 'neath leafy bower;
There raised, the youth on rustic litter lies.
So, plucked by maiden's finger, fades a flower
Of drooping hyacinth or soft violet,
Still beauteous, nor hath lost its lustre yet,
Though mother earth no kindly strength supplies.
   Then broidered mantles twain Æneas brought
Of gold and purple, which in bygone days
With her own hand Phœnician Dido wrought—
Labour of love wherein she had delight—
Parting the warp with slender golden thread.
One on the youth for latest gift he lays,
And shrouds those locks that soon the fire shall feel.
There ranged he many a trophy of the fight,
And bade the spoils in long array be led,
With pageantry of captured steed and steel—
Bound prisoners, doomed, for offering to the dead,
To drench with blood the sacred altar-flame—
And trunks, whereon was foeman's armour hung,
Borne in procession, graven each with name:
There walked Accœtes, sad, with years oppressed;
And now his cheeks he tore, or smote his breast,
Now on the earth his limbs dejected flung:
Nor lacked there chariots splashed with Latin blood:
The war-horse, Æthon, stripped of trappings gay,
Went weeping, and big drops his face bedewed:
Next, Pallas' spear and helmet—but the rest
Proud Turnus held. Last marched, in slow array,

Trojans, and Tuscans, and Arcadians all,
With arms reversed; but ere they went their way,
Æneas stopped, and deeply groaning cried:
"Me now war's harsh necessities recall
To other scenes of death. But thou, our pride,
Hail, Pallas, and for evermore adieu!"
Few words; then back toward battlemented wall
He turned, and to the Trojan camp withdrew.

Now from the Latin town came envoys forth,
With olive garlands, and entreaty made:
The bodies that lay scattered o'er the plain
They begged for burial in the lap of earth,
Since none may wrong the vanquished and the slain;
His host, his sire once called, such favour prayed.
Nor doth the kindly chief their plea disdain,
But hastes in gracious words assent to give:

"Latins, what evil chance your race could drive
To war 'gainst us who fain your friends would be?
Ask ye a truce for warriors fallen in fight?
Nay, I would grant it ev'n to them that live.
I came not hither save by Fate's decree:
Count me not foeman. 'Twas your king held light
Our friendship, and in Turnus' sword put faith.
'Twere fairer Turnus' self should face the death
That these have died, and if his purpose stand
To crown the war with Trojan host in flight,
Meet me in combat. He his life would save,
Whom heaven should prosper or his own right-hand.
Go, give your hapless dead the rites ye crave."

So spake Æneas; they in silence heard,
Astonied, turning each on each his gaze:
Then aged Drances, ever moved by hate
Of youthful Turnus to malignant word,
Thus made reply: "O great in fame, more great
In deeds, I know not which the first to praise,
Thy justice, or thy valour with the sword.
Now will we take these tidings back with joy,

And to our king unite thee, whensoe'er
Chance offers; new allies let Turnus find.
Thy fated walls with gladness would we rear,
And lend our strength to lift the stones of Troy."
He spake; and all applaud with single mind.
Twelve days the truce protects them; fearless now,
Latins, with Trojans mingling, range in peace
The woodland glades; with ringing axe o'erthrow
Tall ash, and pines that soar to heaven's domain,
Or cleave the fragrant cedar without cease,
And with stout rowans load the creaking wain.

  Now Rumour, wingéd harbinger of woe,
Had thrilled Evander's city—Pallas slain!
Pallas, whose glorious deeds but now she told!
Then to the gates men haste, by usage old,
With funeral torches; down the roadways glow
Long lines of fire that light the dusky wold.
Soon, when the Trojan mourners drew anear,
The city burned with wailing women's cries.
Then naught Evander's anguish could withhold;
But forth he rushed, and bending o'er the bier
Clung to his lifeless child with sobs and sighs,
And scarce could speak for sorrow uncontrolled:

  "Pallas, was this thy promise to thy sire—
To court not peril too precipitate?
I knew how potent is war's earliest prize,
That sweetest fame whereto young hearts aspire.
Unhappy first-fruits! Sad novitiate
Was thine in battle! Vain my prayers, my vows,
Unheard in heaven! And thou, most saintly spouse,
Blest in thy death, and spared this grievous wrong!
But I, his sire, have cheated fate, too long
Surviving. Ah, that I myself had fought
In Trojan ranks, and fallen 'neath Latin spear!
Would that myself were slain, my corse it were,
Not Pallas', that this dolorous pageant brought!
Yet you I blame not, Trojans, nor repent

The league we pledged in friendship. Fate hath sent
This sorrow on my age; and since 'twas willed
My son should early die, some solacement
It yields me that he fell not till his brand
Its tale of slaughtered Volscians had fulfilled,
And oped your glorious path to Latin land.
Nor prouder tribute can I wish my son
Than this which Troy's high chivalry has given—
And Tuscan chiefs, and all Etruria's band—
This pomp of trophies by his prowess won:
Ev'n Turnus' image, too, with these would stand,
If but with equal age and strength he'd striven.
But let not grief of mine your swords delay!
Go, tell your king, nor this my charge forget:
If still I live this life, of joy bereft,
'Tis that I trust his strong right-hand to pay
To son and sire that one remaining debt,
The life of Turnus. Naught but that is left
To crown his honours nobly merited:
Myself, I crave not joys of living; nay;
I wait to take those tidings to the dead."
    Now did the Dawn her kindly beams display
And woe-worn men to tasks and toils recall.
The Trojan chief with Tarcho piles the pyres
High on the shore; thereon the dead they lay,
With native customs each; then flash the fires
And heaven's great dome is hid in murky pall.
Thrice round the flames they march in armed array,
Resplendent; thrice beneath that sombre glare
They circle on their steeds with woful wail:
Tears wet the ground, tears wet their glancing mail;
Loud ring the shouts of men, the trumpets' blare.
Some on the furnace cast the trophies torn
From dying foemen—helmets, swords of pride,
Bridles and wheels that glow; some, gifts more rare,
The shields and luckless shafts of chiefs that died.
Many the victims to Death's altars borne

From the near pastures, oxen, swine, and sheep,
And slaughtered o'er the flames. Then steadfastly
Men watch their comrades burn, nor cease to keep
Watch o'er the smouldering pyres till dewy night
Once more inverts the solemn arch of sky
Studded with gleaming constellations bright.

Elsewhere the Latins, with like grief oppressed,
Unnumbered pyres upbuild; but first their dead
Some 'neath the lap of earth they lay to rest,
Some back to neighbouring croft or city send:
All else, from heaps of carnage harvested,
They burn unclassed, unhonoured. Far away
Those rival fires their gloomy lustre blend:
Not till night's shade hath yielded thrice to day,
On pile of bones and ashes, wide outspread,
A last sad shroud of smoking soil they fling.

But most, within the walls of Latium's king,
Is unremitting grief and uproar wild:
Mothers, and brides, and many a tender heart
Of sorrowing sister, many an orphan child,
The war and Turnus' courtship execrate.
Himself, they cried, should play the champion's part,
Himself decide that combat with his sword,
Who to the throne aspired and high estate.
Then Drances loosed his rancorous tongue, with claim
That Turnus meet the challenge, he alone:
Natheless in Turnus' praise were voices heard;
Still was the queen's high favour o'er him thrown;
On valorous deeds he leant and well-earned fame.

As thus they raged, in angry feuds aflame,
Their envoys answer brought—a dolorous band,
From Diomede's mighty realm—with empty hand
They came, their labour lost: nor gifts, nor gold,
Nor prayers had aught availed them: new allies
Must Latium seek, or Trojan peace demand.
Then sank the king in deep despair, and knew
Æneas fate-appointed, for behold

God's wrath, and those fresh graves before their eyes!
Wherefore his chiefs and councillors he drew
By royal summons to his lofty hall:
There met they, surging through the crowded street.
Midmost he sate, in age majestical,
High-sceptred, yet of woful brow and wan,
As those his legates new-returned he bade
Their message tell, and word by word repeat
In order due: thereat was silence made,
And Venulus, so charged, his tale began:
    "Friends, we have seen great Diomede's Argive town.
All perils past, we journeyed on our way,
And touched the hand that struck proud Ilium down.
There, in the fields below Garganus' crest,
His city, named from native Argos, lay:
Entering, and bid to speak before his face,
Our gifts we proffered, told our name, our race,
Who warred on us, whereof we came in quest;
And he in placid speech thus made reply:
    "'O sons of ancient land by Saturn blest!
What change hath shattered your tranquillity,
That ye would brave the plague of wars unknown?
How prospered we, who wrong to Troy had done?
(Let pass that siege, and all our toils therein;
Our dead by Simois' wave rolled to the sea.)
Such penalties we suffered, tempest-tost
In fearful expiation of our sin,
As Priam's self might pity. Witness be
Minerva's baleful star, Eubœa's coast
Crag-bound, and dark Caphareus' vengeful steep!
Far scattered from Troy's battlefields were we:
To utmost Egypt Menelaus passed,
Exiled; Ulysses saw those ogres dread
That have their haunt in Ætna's caverns deep.
What need to speak of Pyrrhus' realms o'ercast?
Idomeneus, his country desolated?
Or Locri shipwrecked on lone Libyan strand?

Himself, great Agamemnon, at his door,
Died by his faithless consort's murderous hand;
Asia's rich spoils waylaid by paramour!
I too—for heaven hath grudged my heart's desire
To greet my spouse in Calydon's fair land—
Am long beset by fearful prodigies:
Lost friends, to birds transfigured, skyward soar,
Or roam by desert streams (ah, penance dire!),
Or fill the rocky wold with wailing cries.
How dared I hope aught else, from that wild day
When 'gainst the heavenly gods, infatuate, crazed,
I fought, and wounded Venus with my steel?
Nay, press not me to mingle in such fray!
No feud have I with Troy, since Troy was razed,
Nor joy in those ill memories can feel.
Wherefore these gifts, from your far country brought,
Hand to the Trojan chieftain. I have faced
His deadly shafts, and in close combat fought.
Trust one who knows: his shield he can upheave
Immense; with whirlwind force his spear is flung.
If Troy had bred two other knights as strong,
Herself had dared our Argive shores invade,
And for reverse of fortune Greece would grieve!
Ay, for if aught the Grecian host delayed,
'Twas Hector, 'twas Æneas' hand, that stayed
Their onset till the bygone years were ten:
Most valorous both, both famed beyond compare;
Æneas first in piety. Go, then,
While yet ye may, join hands, and treaty make;
But lest in battle-shock ye meet, beware!'
Great king, how Diomede in answer spake,
Thou'st heard, and how on war he laid his ban."
    Scarce was he silent, ere dim murmurs ran
Along their troubled ranks, like muttering sound
Of rushing stream in rocky channel pent,
When roars the flood and cliffs re-echo round:
But when their lips were hushed, their passion spent,

First to the gods appealing reverent,
From his high throne the monarch thus began:
   "Sirs, had we pondered this high theme ere now,
More prudent had it been: time waxes late
For counsel, when the foe is at the gate.
A luckless war we wage, 'gainst godlike race,
Heroes unvanquished—to no strength they bow,
Nor ev'n when beaten back their swords unbrace.
If faith ye cherished in Ætolia's might,
'Tis fled: be each man his own hope; but this—
How frail, how false it was—forget not, you!
Yea, all whereon we leant hath perished quite,
In naked ruin that no eye can miss.
None blame I: all that valour's self could do
Was done; with Latium's utmost force we fought.
But now through wavering doubts there comes a thought,
Which list ye, and in brief will I declare.
Anigh my Tuscan stream a land there is,
Stretched westward to the far Sicanian bound:
Rutulian tillers plough its uplands bare,
Or graze their herds along the rugged ground.
This mountain tract, where lofty pine-woods wave,
Grant we to Trojan friendship, with fair bond
Of peace, and bid them in our empire share.
Here shall they found the city that they crave;
Or, if they fain would pass to lands beyond,
'Mid alien tribes, and quit our Latin soil,
Let ships be built of native oak a score,
Or whatsoe'er they need; close by the shore
The timber ready lies: of bulk and mode
'Tis theirs to tell; give we the tools, the toil.
This, too: to bid them deem us foes no more,
An hundred envoys of pure Latin blood,
Shall journey, laden with fair olive-sprays,
With ivory, and with gold in goodly weight,
My curule chair and royal robe of state.
Give counsel, sirs, in these our darkest days."

Then Drances, ever hostile, whom the praise
Of Turnus' deeds to bitter envy stirred
(Large wealth he had, of eloquence no dearth;
Listless in war, but high in council famed;
In faction mighty, for his mother's birth
Was noble; of his sire was dubious word),
Uprose, and still the more men's hearts inflamed:
  "Obscure to none, nor needing words from me,
Good king, is this whereon thou wouldst confer.
What ails our commonweal, all men profess
They know, and fain would speak if speech were free:
Let him unlock their lips, his wrath repress,
Whose ill-starred pride, ambition sinister
(Say it I will, albeit he threaten death),
Have darked so many lives, and sunk in grief
Our land beyond repair; while he, bold chief,
Would storm the Trojan camp, and puts his faith
In flight, and scares with clash of arms the skies.
One gift to those most gracious courtesies
Which thou designest for the lord of Troy,
I pray thee add, and let no force withstand:
To noble suitor give thy daughter's hand
In worthy wedlock, for our lasting joy.
But if men's hearts and minds such terror sway,
Then to himself for grace we cry, we plead:
Let him submit to king, to fatherland!
Why wilt thou thrust our folk in peril's way,
O thou, of Latium's woes the source, the head?
In war no safety lies; for peace we pray,
Turnus, for peace that shall be shattered not!
I most, thy fancied foe (nor aught I care
If foe I be), entreat thee that thou spare
Thy friends, and beaten as thou art, retire!
Too long have death and panic been our lot,
Our country's fields too long left desolate.
If glory lure thee, and thy heart be great
For combat, and thy courtship hath such fire,

Then doubt not, but to battle dauntless go!
Must we—so Turnus win his royal bride—
We worthless wights, unburied and unwept,
Lie strewn along the plain? Nay, if thou'st kept
One atom of thy fathers' martial pride,
Go forth, and face the foe!"
   Thereat with fiery wrath was Turnus thrilled.
He groaned, and from his breast this answer wrung:
"Drances, of speech thou hast unfailing store,
When deeds are needed most. At council door
Thou'rt foremost; but it boots not to have filled
The Senate with vainglorious words, forth flung
By one in safety, while the rampart's fence
Still guards us, and the trench is dyed not red.
Ay, Drances, thunder in thine eloquence,
As wont, and prove me craven—thou, whose hand
Has struck to earth such piles of Trojan dead,
And decked our fields with trophies! Wouldst thou try
Thy valour's worth, thou hast not far to stray
Seeking the foe—around our walls they stand.
Come, shall we charge? Why shrink'st thou from the fray?
Is it with windy words, with feet that fly,
That thou must fight alway?
I beaten? Who, thou wretch, would speak such lie,
Since Tiber's stream with Trojan blood was swelled,
Evander's house made childless utterly,
And trophied armour from Arcadians ta'en?
Not such by giant Bitias was I found,
And all his lusty comrades that I felled,
When shut within their walls by hostile mound.
'No safety lies in war.' Sing that mad strain
To Trojan chief and thine own dupes! Since vain
It were to pray thee cease these wild alarms,
Vaunt thou twice-vanquished Troy's exceeding might,
And dim the prowess of our Latin arms!
No more, forsooth, can Greeks 'gainst Phrygians fight;
Achilles, Diomede, like terrors have:

Ay, and perchance swift Aufidus in fright
Flows backward from the Adriatic wave.
Mark how he meets my taunts, that subtle knave,
Pretending fear—to make his charge more fell!
Of life I ne'er will rob thee (fear thou naught!):
Keep it; 'tis worthy in such breast to dwell.
Now to thy speech, great Sire, returns my thought.
If all thy faith in Turnus' strength hath fled—
If so forlorn we be that, once undone,
We sink in ruin irretrievable—
Sue we for peace with suppliant hands outspread!
Yet, oh! if all our courage be not gone,
Him would I deem our happiest champion,
And noblest, who, to look not on such hour,
Hath bit the dust in death and made an end.
But if we lack not wealth, nor manhood's power,
If kindred tribes our banner still befriend,
If Troy hath bought her gains with mickle blood,
And war's fierce storm alike o'er friends and foes
Hath swept—why shrink we in decrepitude,
Scared at the outset, ere the trumpet blows?
Full oft doth time, with toil of chequered years,
Turn ill to better; fortune's varying mood
Oft mocks us, then restores to solid ground.
What though we lack Ætolia's friendly spears?
Messapus, wise Tolumnius, aid us still,
And lords from many lands; nor less renowned
Shall Latium's chosen youths our ranks refill;
And she, Camilla, noble Volscian maid,
Leading her troop in shimmering steel arrayed.
But if to single combat called I be,
Think'st thou I would withstand thy people's will?
Not yet so lost is victory's smile to me
That, in such cause, worst peril would I shun.
Full glad will I confront him, though he wield
Achilles' might and Vulcan's armour don.
Latins, to you, and to my sire the king,

I vow this life—I Turnus—nor will yield
In valour to no knight of olden days.
Æneas calls: I meet him, nothing loth:
Myself, not Drances, if the gods be wroth,
The death will die: but if the issue bring
The glory valour seeks—not his the praise."
    While thus in dubious strife they held debate,
Perplexed, the Trojan camp was moved more nigh:
Anon a courier rushed to palace-gate,
And shook the town with tidings of dismay:
How from the Tiber's banks, in war's array,
Advanced the hosts of Troy and Tuscany.
Then were men terror-smitten—desperate
Their hearts, to fury spurred by stings of fear.
For arms they clamour, arms the youths demand,
While greybeards moan and mutter; far and near
The shouts of men in tones discordant rise:
So swell through forest depths the countless cries
Of thronging birds, or by Padusa's strand
The din of swans along some sounding mere.
    Then Turnus seized the moment: "Friends, 'tis well!
Sit ye in conclave, praise of peace to sing,
While foes o'errun our kingdom!" Silence fell,
As from the lofty hall he strode amain.
"Volusus, thou must bid the Volscians arm,
Thou the Rutulians call; Messapus fling,
With Coras, all his horsemen o'er the plain;
Some guard the ports, the turrets, 'gainst alarm;
The rest await their leader's beckoning."
    Then "To the ramparts" was in all men's thought.
His royal counsel, his august design,
The sire abandoned, foiled by chance malign,
And cursed his blindness that had welcomed not
The Dardan lord, Æneas, for his son.
Some at the trenches toil, or stone and stake
Heave upward: hark the raucous bugle blown
For battle! boys and women on the wall

In many a wondering group their station take,
As for the final task that summons all.
    Next, with attendant ladies in her train,
The queen to Pallas' lofty temple passed:
Gifts bore she: by her side Lavinia went,
Sweet cause of strife, her beauteous eyes downcast.
Then incense pure is burned within the fane,
As by the threshold in sad voice they chant:
"Hear us, O warrior maid armipotent!
Break thou this Phrygian robber's spear, and grant
That 'neath our gates he perish on the plain!"
    Soon Turnus, arming eager for the fight,
Had donned his stout Rutulian cuirass,
Rigid and rough with gleaming scales of brass,
And girt his legs in gold—bareheaded yet—
And to his side his trusty falchion set.
So stepped he, golden, down from castle height,
Exultant, and his foe in fancy met,
Ev'n as a stallion, from the stables fled,
Breaks bonds, and scours the prairie in delight;
Straight to the herd of pasturing mares he goes,
Or plunging in the pool that well he knows,
Leaps forth, and neighs, and tosses high his head,
With streaming mane that o'er his shoulder flows.
    Then, with her Volscians, did Camilla ride
To greet him: straight from saddle at a bound
She glided, and her mounted troop to ground
Leapt likewise, ere the queen to Turnus cried:
"Turnus, if valiant heart its strength may trust,
This deed I dare, and vow it shall be done—
The charge of Trojan horse to wait and ward,
And front the Tuscan chivalry alone.
Let me be first to foil the foeman's thrust:
Thou by the rampart stand, the walls to guard."
    He, gazing on that maid so stern, so fair:
"Thou who thy country's pride and wonder art!
How can I speak the thanks that are thy due?

How make return? But since thy dauntless heart
Transcends all words, my labour shalt thou share.
'Tis rumoured, if our scouts bring tidings true,
Æneas, wily foe, hath sent light horse
To range the plains; himself will now pursue
By desolate highland track his secret way.
An ambush, there, in hollow glen we lay,
Blocking the narrow gorge with arméd force.
Check thou the Tuscan troop ere it draw near.
With thee Messapus, warrior keen, shall go;
The Latin squadron and Tibertus' host—
Be leader thou—shall thy commands obey."
He spake, and with like hardihood bade cheer
Those other chiefs, then sallied 'gainst the foe.
　A branching dale there is, for wiles of war
Most apt; dense-foliaged cliffs o'erhang its sides
Precipitous, and slender pathway guides
Through deep ravine and stark forbidding cleft.
Above, where topmost ridge gives prospect far,
Lies level space that stranger may not spy,
Wherefrom can foeman strike to right, to left,
Or stand and roll big boulders down the steep.
In that familiar spot did Turnus lie,
And in those perilous woods his station keep.
　Meanwhile in heavenly regions far above,
To Opis, nymph and comrade of her train,
Diana spake, and mournful words addressed:
"To yon dread combat hath Camilla gone,
With Dian's weapons armed, but armed in vain:
Dearest to me she is, nor new my love,
Nor sudden sprang such fondness in my breast.
When Metabus, an outcast from his throne,
Banished through hate of his o'ermastering might,
From old Privernum fled, 'mid war's alarms,
His infant child he took to share his flight:
Casmilla was the queen, her mother, hight,
Whence as Camilla was the maiden known.

Himself he gently clasped her in his arms,
Seeking the woods that skirt the mountains lone,
While, all around, the foes their javelins fling,
And Volscian horsemen roam the region wide.
Then lo! across his path with foamy tide
Rolled Amasenus, by the rainstorm swelled,
And he, a swimmer strong, stood pondering,
Fearful for that loved burden that he held,
Till sudden in his thoughts a way he found.
It chanced a spear of mighty bulk he bore
For battle, stout with knots and seasoned core;
Thereto her lissome limbs he deftly bound,
Close-wrapped in bark of supple cork around,
And poised it in his strong right-hand, and prayed:
    'Fair Dian, virgin goddess of the glade,
To thee this child of mine for life I vow.
Thine is the shaft she clasps for earliest aid,
A suppliant, from the foeman 'scaped—thy maid,
Borne on the fickle gales—accept her thou!'
    "So saying, with arm drawn back, his strength to brace,
He flung her. Loudly roared those waters wild,
While far she flew, poor waif, on sounding spear:
But Metabus, for now the foe drew near,
Leapt in the flood, and by my godhead's grace
Plucked from the bank his javelin and his child.
Thenceforth nor town nor roof e'er gave him rest;
By no constraint was his stern heart beguiled,
But on far pastoral heights his life he led:
There, where dense thickets hid the desolate land,
With milk of strong brood-mare the babe was fed,
As to her tender lips the dugs he pressed.
And when on tottering feet she learned to tread,
Forthwith he set a spear in her young hand,
And from her shoulder hung the hunter's bow:
No gold she wore, no robe with sinuous flow,
But skin of tiger from her neck was tied.
Soon from her childish hand sharp darts she sped,

And with the sling whirled high above her head
The crane and snowy swan would lay alow.
In vain fond mothers hoped her for a bride:
Desiring none but Dian, 'twas her will
To live an huntress and a virgin still.
I would this pitiless war had left her free,
Nor 'gainst the Trojan host her hand were steeled;
So cherished 'mid my sisterhood were she!
But come: since bitter fate she must fulfil,
Glide earthward, nymph, and seek the fatal field
Where soon will rage that inauspicious fray.
Take from this quiver one avenging shaft,
That whosoe'er shall deal my queen her doom—
Trojan, Italian—shall the blood-price pay:
Then in a shroud of vapour will I waft
Her piteous corse, her armour, to the tomb,
And in her native soil inviolate lay."
She spake, and Opis winged her glancing way,
Mantled from vision in tempestuous gloom.

Now do the Trojan cavaliers advance,
And Tuscan knights with all their mounted men
In ordered squadrons: neighing coursers prance
With din of hoofs, and tug the tightened rein,
Straining for battle. Soon with lifted lance
Bristles the field and burns with brazen glow.
'Gainst these, Messapus and the Latin horse,
And Coras, with Camilla's flying force,
Ride forward with couched spears: more furious grow
The rider's haste, the rush of panting steed.
But when they stood within a javelin's throw,
A yell they raised, and spurred to frantic speed
Their chargers; dense as hail the darts flew fast,
As though with cloud the welkin were o'ercast.
Then first Tyrrhenus and Aconteus meet
In ruinous shock of combat, spear 'gainst spear
Resounding; and their steeds, together flung,
Dash chest on chest. Aconteus from his seat,

Like thunder-bolt, or stone from engine slung,
Falls headlong, and his life is spilled in air:
Whereat the Latin knights, in sudden fear,
Shield covering back, toward the city fly:
Follows the Trojan troop, Asilas first;
And now they near the gateways; now, in turn,
Rutulians wheel and charge with savage cry,
And Trojans with loose rein are backward borne:
So, when successive waves on foreland burst,
Now o'er the rocks they hurl their waters high,
Foaming, and swamp the furthest fringe of sand;
Now refluent sink, and suck the shingle down,
In rapid flight retreating from the strand.
Twice rode the Tuscans on the Latin town;
Twice, flying, backward gazed, the foe to scan:
But when the third encounter locked them tight—
Rank flung on rank, and grappling man with man—
Then were the groans of dying warriors heard;
And there, in pools of blood, promiscuous,
Lay shattered spears, and many a fallen knight
And war-horse nigh to death: so fierce the fight.
Orsilochus, since close assault he feared,
Poised lance, and smote the steed of Remulus;
Deep 'neath the charger's ear was lodged the dart:
Whereat, with clattering hoof-beats, high he reared,
Nor brooked that cruel wound, but plunged and threw
His rider prone to earth. Catillus slew
Herminius, great of stature, great of heart;
Bare-headed was he; yellow locks o'erflowed
His shoulders bare; of wounds he recked not aught,
So scant his armour: through his side the steel
Stood quivering, ere he fell in anguish bowed.
Thus widely blood they shed and death-blows deal,
Raging, and crave for death with glory fraught.
  Exulting through the fray Camilla pressed—
Bare for the fight, like Amazon's, her breast—
And now her shafts in blinding shower she threw,

Now plied her dreaded axe with tireless hand:
Down from her shoulder hung the bow of gold,
Diana's weapon; and if flight she planned,
Ev'n as she fled, the sounding string she drew.
Around her rode her chosen virgin band,
Larina, Tulla, and Tarpeia bold
With battle-axe—Italian maidens they,
Her guard of honour, rendering homage meet
In peace or war, with faithful ministry:
So Thracian Amazons in wild array
Ride thundering by Thermodon's frozen fields,
Guarding Hippolyte, or their queen to greet,
Penthesilea, and with frenzied cry
Those warrior women wave their moonéd shields.
    Whom first, stern maiden, of thy foes, whom last,
Didst smite? of chiefs how many dash to ground?
Eunæus, first, thine onset would withstand,
Till through his heart the shaft of pinewood passed;
Bleeding he fell, and wallowed in his wound.
Then Liris from his stricken steed downcast,
Gathering the reins—and Pagasus whose hand
Unarmed was stretched his falling friend to save—
One ruin whelmed them both. Amastrus fell;
And still her shafts she rained, implacable,
On Tereus, Chromis, and Demophoon;
Yea, by each dart her maiden arm could wave,
A Phrygian warrior fell. Forth rode anon
The hunter Ornitus—uncouth his guise;
Borne on Apulian steed, he wore for cape
An ox-hide broad, and gleaming o'er his eyes
Huge jaws of wolf with grinning teeth agape;
In hand a rustic spear: so came he on,
And by a head o'ertopped his fellows all.
Him (for his scattered followers fled apace)
She pierced, and o'er him spake in words of gall:
"Didst think this war was but a woodland chase?
Behold the day when by a woman's spear,

Tuscan, thy boasts are silenced! Yet in pride
To thy dead sires these tidings canst thou bear,
That by Camilla's weapon thou hast died."
   Then fell the giant forms of Trojans twain:
Its mark in Butes' back her arrow found,
Where, 'twixt cuirass and helm, is sighted plain
A rider's neck, his arm with buckler bound:
Orsilochus designedly she fled,
As in a spacious orb she circled round
On inner course, pursuing and pursued;
Then grasped her axe, and rising to the stroke
Remorseless, as full oft for life he pled,
With shower of blows through casque and skull she broke,
And from the gaping wound streamed brains and blood.
   Stumbling on that grim sight, in terror stood
The son of Aunus, bred in highland vale
Of Apennine; no sluggish tribesman he,
If fate some scope for stratagem would leave:
But when he saw no fleetness could avail,
Nor how her instant onset he might flee,
With cunning speed he 'gan his wiles to weave:
"Is this so wondrous—that a trusty steed
May lend a woman strength? Such flight forgo,
And gird thee for close combat on the lea,
Dismounted; thus full early shalt thou know
To whom capricious fame will give her meed."
Then she, enraged, as keen her anger burned,
To comrade tossed the reins, and stood for fight,
Fearless, with naught but sword and 'scutcheon bared:
He, for he deemed his craft triumphant, turned,
And urged his courser to precipitate flight,
Nor with sharp iron-shod heel the rowels spared.
   "Thou fool, with empty pride infatuate!
Vainly thy native arts wouldst thou assay,
Nor shall they bring thee to thy faithless sire."
So spake she; and afoot, with speed of fire,
Outstripped his horse, and grasped the reins, and straight

Compelled his hated heart the price to pay:
So swoops a falcon from her eyry high,
Majestic bird, on dove that soars elate,
And grips with crooked claws and rends her prey:
Then blood and scattered plumes drift from the sky.
   Not unobserved of Jove these deeds befell,
Where high upon Olympus he abode.
Then did the Sire to that fierce fight impel
The Tuscan chief with stings of burning shame;
So 'mid the rout and carnage Tarcho rode,
And much he strove his scattered knights to cheer,
As each he chid and each recalled by name:
"O lost to pride and honour's cry! what fear,
What coward slackness hath your hearts enthralled?
Doth woman chase you thus around the plain?
Whereto those swords? those spears ye wield in vain?
No courage lacked ye, when 'twas love that called
To midnight battles, and the loud flute shrilled
Tidings of dance, of feast, of wine-cup filled!
Then is your heart content, your purpose sure,
When smiling augurs prosperous omens deign,
And fatted victims to the groves allure."
   He spake, and rushing reckless on the foes
'Gainst Venulus his eager onslaught made,
Then gripped him in strong arm, and plucked from horse,
In sudden flight on saddlebow conveyed.
Turned were the Latins' eyes, as shouts arose
From earth to heaven. But Tarcho, in swift course,
Bearing that armoured knight, the spear-point broke
From javelin, fain to deal a mortal wound,
Groping for access; he, his throat to cloak,
Shrunk from the thrust, and parried force with force.
As when a tawny eagle skyward hales
A snake in unrelaxing talons bound,
The wounded reptile writhes in sinuous coil,
And, hissing, lifts in wrath his bristly scales,
Up-towering; yet her crooked beak no less

Constrains him, and her pinions lash the air:
So Tarcho bore away his living spoil
In triumph; and their chieftain's feats to share,
Rallied his Tuscan troop. Then Fate's stern stress
Brought Arruns, on insidious errand bent,
Camilla's flying footsteps to waylay,
If lucky chance should aid his watchfulness:
Where'er she broke infuriate through the fray
He followed, silent, on her tracks intent;
When back victorious rode she from the rout,
Furtive he wheeled aside—now there, now here
Seeking approach, now circling far about,
And grasped with dark design his fated spear.
   It chanced that Chloreus, consecrated priest
Of Cybele, in gorgeous armour dressed,
Bestrode a foaming steed, caparisoned
In plume-like cloth of bronze with clasp of gold;
Purple of deep-dyed splendour had he donned;
His Cretan bolts were sped from Lycian bow,
A bow of gold; of gold the casque he wore;
Saffron his cloak, with rustling linen fold
Trained through a tawny golden hoop to flow;
His Phrygian leggings rich embroidery bore.
Him, chief of all the field, the warrior maid,
Haply with hope to fix on temple-door
His Trojan arms, or in his gold arrayed
To ply the chase, pursued with ravished eyes,
And followed far in rash precipitance,
Afire with woman's love of glittering prize.
'Twas then, from ambush, Arruns sped his lance
At fateful moment, and the high gods prayed:
"Phœbus, who o'er Soracte's height dost reign,
God whom we reverence most; for whom is fed
The pine-logs' blaze, when, in our faith secure,
We walk the flames and burning embers tread!
Grant, Sire, that from our nation's arms this stain
Be blotted! Me no spoils, no trophies lure,

Of conquered maiden; other fame I have:
So by mine hand this pest be stricken dead,
Homeward content I go, nor glory crave."
   This Phœbus heard, and half his suppliant's prayer
Conceded, half to wasting winds he threw.
To strike Camilla down with stealthy hand
He granted, but return to native land
Vouchsafed not; and that hope was lost in air.
So when the dart was hurled and droning flew,
All thoughts, all eyes of Volscian chivalry
Were turned upon their queen. She, unaware
Of sounding shaft that hurtled through the sky,
Knew naught, till deep below her bosom bare
It lodged and, sinking, drained her maiden blood.
Then rushed her girl companions tremulously
To stay their falling queen. But Arruns, most,
Fled crazed 'twixt joy and fear: small hardihood
He had to face with spear her darts again.
So slinks a wolf, ere yet by foes pursued,
To mountain fastness where his tracks are lost:
Conscious of deed o'erbold—some shepherd slain,
Or goodly steer—he crawls to sombre wood,
With tail 'neath belly curled, and seeks his den.
Thus Arruns slunk dismayed from sight of men,
Content to lurk where thickest battle rolled.
She, dying, strove in vain to pluck from breast
That sunken shaft whose steel was in the bone:
Fainting she fell; her eyes were wan and cold,
And from her cheek the flush of life was gone.
Yet called she of her friends the trustiest,
Chief partner of her cares above the rest,
Acca, and charged her thus with failing breath:
"Sister, I can no more: this bitter wound
Ends all, and round me falls the dusk of death.
Flee thou, and this last word to Turnus take,
That to the city's succour speed he make.
So fare thee well!" Reluctant to the ground

She sank, and dropped the reins, as chill and slow
Her life ebbed from her limbs; her heavy head
Drooped earthward; from her grasp was loosed the bow;
And with a sigh the rueful spirit fled.
Then on the golden stars men's clamours smite,
And bloodier grows the fray, Camilla dead;
Still charge Troy's hosts impetuous on the foe,
With Tuscans and Arcadian squadron light.
    Long time, as Dian's sentry, from the height
Had Opis with calm eye that scene surveyed;
But when, where loudest din of battle broke,
She saw Camilla die on fated field,
She groaned, and from her heart in sorrow spoke:
    "Alas, too bitter was the price thou'st paid,
Maiden, whose hand 'gainst Trojan ranks was steeled,
Nor 'vailed it aught that in wild forest glade
Thou'st served our Dian, and her livery worn.
Yet will thy goddess leave thee not forlorn
In death's extreme; nor void of fame shall be
Thy fall, nor unavenged thy suffering:
For whoso dared thy sacred blood to spill
The deed shall rue." There stood by lofty hill
An earthen mound 'neath shade of ilex tree,
Tomb of Dercennus, once Laurentum's king:
Thereby the nymph alit with nimble wing,
And Arruns from that eminence espied,
Flaunting his sheen of arms with boastful glee.
"Where wanderest? Turn thou hitherward," she cried;
"Come hither to thy doom, and take from me
Due guerdon for the death Camilla died.
Know'st not thou too shalt fall by Dian's dart?"
So saying, an arrow on the string she set,
From golden quiver drawn, and bending tight
Her bow of vengeance till its curved tips met,
One instant stood with level hands apart,
Touching with left the barb, her breast with right.
Then hissed the arrow, and hummed the air with sound,

Which Arruns heard not ere he felt the smart.
Him, as with dolorous groans he breathed his last,
His heedless comrades left on dusty ground:
Opis on airy pinion heavenward passed.
    Their mistress slain, Camilla's troop fled fast,
Fast fled Atinas, fled the Latin band;
Leaders and men, deserted and distraught,
Swift to the city spurred, and refuge sought:
None now the conquering Trojan might withstand,
Nor spearman stem that charge with havoc fraught:
Weary they turned in flight, with bows unstrung,
Their horse-hoofs thundering on the mellow land.
Then was dense dust-cloud to the ramparts flung,
Where women beat their breasts, and gazing out
Lifted to heaven the cry of wild despair.
But when through open gateways rushed the rout,
Beset by foemen mingled in the throng,
They 'scaped not cruel death; for stricken there,
Ev'n by their native walls, their trusted home,
They fell and died. In selfish terror some
All entry barred, reckless of comrades' prayer,
For passage through the gates; then piteous plight
Was theirs who stood without and faced the foe;
For shelterless, in weeping parents' sight,
Headlong in trench they rolled, a helpless herd,
Or blindly to the walls in panic spurred,
Battering the barred and bolted ports in vain.
Yet, when Camilla's glorious deeds were viewed,
Ev'n those sad women on the walls were fain
(Taught by true patriot love) with weapons rude—
Charred stake and oaken pale for steel-tipped lance—
To hold the ramparts 'gainst the foes' advance
With tremulous hands, and fear of death disdain.
    The while to secret glen where Turnus lay
Had Acca borne that news calamitous—
The Volscian troop o'erthrown; Camilla dead;
The foe, in irresistible array,

Master of all; the city smit with dread.
Enraged (but Jove's stern will ordained it thus),
His mountain ambuscade he left full loth,
And scarce to level plain had won his way,
When lo! Æneas dared the dark ravine,
And topped the ridge, and from the forest broke:
So to the self-same goal they hurried both,
With all their hosts, nor mickle space between.
And when Æneas saw the lowlands smoke
With surging dust, where marched the Latin force,
And Turnus marked his mortal enemy,
And heard the tramp of feet, the snort of horse,
That instant had they rushed to close in war;
But Phœbus' way-worn steeds were plunging down
In ruddy western waves, and night was nigh:
So camped they there, entrenched, before the town.

BOOK XII

ARGUMENT

TURNUS having decided to meet Æneas in single combat, a second
truce is proclaimed; but Juno, with the help of the nymph
Juturna, causes the war to be renewed. Æneas, struck by an arrow,
retires from the battle, until by the intervention of Venus the wound is
healed. Then Juturna, acting as the charioteer of Turnus, keeps him
from crossing the path of Æneas, and so postpones for a time the
end that has been decreed by fate. At length, when the city itself is
attacked by the Trojans in his absence, Turnus insists on facing his
rival, and is slain.

But Turnus, when he sees the Latin band,
Dejected, broken by war's adverse blows,
Fulfilment of his promised deeds demand,
And how men mark him with accusing eye—
He brooks it not, but all impatient glows
With rising passion. As on Punic plain
Some lion, sore wounded by the hunter's hand,
Is spurred at last to fling him on his foes,
Tossing his mane in savage revelry,
And snaps with bleeding jaws their shaft in twain;
So did the fire of Turnus' wrath burn high,
As thus he hailed the king impetuously:
  "Hold back who will; not Turnus. Theirs the shame;
Our craven foes, who would their faith betray,
And break the word of honour that they plight.
Your champion here I stand. Thou, sire, proclaim
The truce, and sanction it with sacred rite.
Myself this Dardan chief will meet and slay—
This outcast, fled from Asia's shores—while they,
Your Latins sit and watch what may betide.

My sword alone shall vindicate our fame;
Or he, victorious, all our realm shall sway,
And take the fair Lavinia for his bride."
    To him the king, sedate and calm, replied:
"Most dauntless youth, the more thy heart is bent
On valorous acts, to me the stronger need
To weigh with anxious mind each dread event.
Thou hast thy father's kingdom, and thy meed
Of captured towns; I, wealth, and bounteous will.
Then, since our land hath other maidens still
Of noble lineage, let me speak my thought,
Harsh-sounding words, yet void of guile at core;
And thou, I pray thee, to my words give heed.
To none that sought my daughter's hand afore
Might I betroth her—so the gods decreed,
So seers and sages warned me; yet subdued
By love of thee, by claims of kindred blood,
And by my queen's distress, I broke all laws,
Made null the marriage contract, nor forbore
To wield unrighteous arms in blameful cause.
Thenceforth what ills our banners have pursued
Full well know'st thou, on whom such blows first fall:
Twice vanquished in the field, we scarce maintain
Our fainting hopes within the city wall;
Still reeks the Tiber with our blood, and far
Our warriors' bones lie bleaching on the plain.
Why, then, do maddening doubts my purpose mar?
Were Turnus dead, this Trojan were my friend:
Why not, while Turnus lives, and so make end
Of all our bitter rivalry and war?
What were thy kinsmen's, what Italia's, ire,
If haply thou shouldst fall (which heaven forfend!),
Fighting for me and mine, with love afire?
Then pause; bethink thee of our shattered state,
Ravaged by war, and of thine agéd sire
In distant Ardea left disconsolate."
    But Turnus' wrath no counsel could assuage;

Soft healing speech ev'n further fired his rage,
And soon as words were found he hotly spake:
"Since 'tis for me thou fear'st this single fight,
Prithee for me, good sire, dismiss thy fear,
And let me barter life for glory's sake.
The shafts that scatter death I, too, can wield;
Not bloodless is the blade wherewith I smite;
Nor will his goddess mother now be near,
With soft effeminate cloud to cloak his flight,
Herself through baffling vapour scarce revealed."

But now Amata, weeping in her awe
Of that new combat (her own death foreseen),
Would fain her ardent champion withdraw:

"Turnus, by these my tears, if aught the queen
Thou hold'st in reverence still—since thou alone
Canst soothe mine age and make its burdens light—
On thee the glory of our Latin throne,
Our tottering house, on none but thee, doth lean—
One thing I pray thee: trust not thus the sword.
What lot soe'er awaits thee in such fight,
Me too awaits. To quit this life abhorred
Were sweeter than to dwell in captive plight,
And take Æneas for my daughter's lord."

With tearful eyes and crimson cheeks aflush,
Her mother's speech the young Lavinia heard,
And o'er her visage ran the burning blush:
Like ivory white with purple pigment dyed,
Like lilies pale that glow 'mid roses red,
So was her face by that rich hue o'erspread.
He on the girl long gazed, by passion stirred;
Then, for the combat fiercelier yearning, cried:

"Thy tears and ominous plaints, I pray thee, spare,
Kind mother, since withdrawal now is none,
For Turnus may not shrink, though death be nigh.
Thou, Idmon, to Troy's haughty chieftain bear
These words that scarce shall please him. When the sun
First mounts on rosy car the morning sky,

No more his Phrygian ranks let him array:
Yon rival hosts may put their weapons by;
We twain will meet; our blood shall end the fray:
So shall Lavinia's hand be lost and won."
   He spake, and straightway to his palace hied;
Then for his horses called, and saw with pride
Those lusty steeds, that team without a stain,
By Orithyia to his grandsire given—
Whiter than snow, more swift than winds of heaven—
And round them bustling grooms, whose hands caressed
Each glossy flank and combed each flowing mane.
Therewith he donned with ease his strong cuirass,
All stark with rigid gold and gleaming brass,
Sword, shield, and towering helm with ruddy crest;
That sword which Vulcan for his sire had made,
Tempering in Stygian stream its molten blade;
And next he grasped with mickle might his spear
That propped 'gainst lofty pillar stood anear,
From Actor won, and brandished it amain:
"Good spear, whose aid I ne'er invoked in vain,
As Actor bore thee once, so now I bear:
The hour has come; then fail not, nor forget
To cleave thy way through breastplate, rent and torn,
Of my degenerate foeman, Phrygian-born;
O'erthrow him, soil in dust his soft-kempt hair,
With heated irons curled, with unguents wet!"
   Thus frenzied, from his face an angry light
Broke outward, and his eyes flashed keen with fire;
As when a bull loud bellowing for the fight,
On tree-trunk fain would test his horns in ire,
Or fling defiance to the passing wind,
Or, for fierce prelude, sandy pasture spurn.
Nor less, in heaven-wrought armour, vengeful, stern,
Æneas nerved for fight his martial mind,
Glad that a mutual end of strife might be.
To careworn friends and anxious child he lent
Calm courage, as he taught, for solacement,

What hopes were theirs, what faith in fate's decree:
So to the royal truce he gave assent.

    Ere the first rays the mountain-summits gild,
When Phœbus' steeds, upheaving from the brine,
With quivering nostrils snuff the lucent air,
Those rival hosts the listed field prepare,
Hard by the city's walls, and midmost build,
For gods whom all adore, a rustic shrine;
Others, rich-girdled, wreathed with sacred boughs,
The holy lymph convey, the flame divine.
Forth from the gates the Latin legions fare;
Here streams the Trojan, here the Tuscan line,
Full armed, as though at battle's call they rouse;
While to and fro, athwart that mighty host,
Flit leaders, proud in purple and in gold—
Mnestheus, of Trojan race; Asylas bold;
Messapus, lord of steeds, from Neptune sprung—
Till all, at signal given, have ta'en their post,
And plunged their spears in earth, their shields down flung:
Then women eager-eyed, with greybeards weak,
And folk unarmed, the towers and housetops throng,
Or at the lofty gates their station seek.

    But when great Juno, from the Alban height
(Then but a nameless hill that lacked renown),
Saw that embattled field by Latium's town,
As goddess unto goddess, thus she spake
To Turnus' sister, famed as guardian sprite
Of many a sounding stream and placid lake;
For such the gift wherewith high Jove made glad
The damsel of whose love he had delight:

    "Nymph of the rushing rivers, fair and good!
Thou know'st, Juturna, I have held thee dear
O'er all the maids ungrateful Jove hath wooed,
And glad I set thee in the starry sphere:
Then blame me not for these calamities.
Protectress of thy brother's house I stood
Till Latium from the smiles of fortune fell;

But now I see him matched in fight unfair;
Now dawns the day of doom inevitable.
Such combat will I watch not with these eyes.
But thou, if aught to save him thou wouldst dare,
Go forth: that aid befits a sister well:
Ev'n yet, maybe, shall joy from grief arise."
Scarce uttered were the words, when sore distressed
Juturna wept, and beat her comely breast.
"Nay," Juno cried, "no time is this for tears.
If way there be, go snatch him from that death;
Or break the truce that binds them, and with guile
Rekindle war. 'Tis Juno counselleth."
No more she spake: the sorrowing nymph, the while,
Wavers in thought, beset by darkening fears.

Now ride the monarchs forth; Latinus leads,
Mighty of bulk, in four-horse chariot borne;
Twelve rays of dazzling gold his brows adorn,
Sign of his grandsire Sol: two snowy steeds
Draw Turnus; in his grasp are javelins twain:
And lo! the founder of the Roman line,
Star-bright with fiery shield and arms divine,
Steps forth from Trojan camp upon the plain,
With Rome's next hope, Ascanius. To the shrine
By white-robed priests for sacrifice are led
A ram of shaggy fleece, a bristly boar;
Then turn the princes toward the dawning day,
Sprinkle the salted grain, from victim's head
Shear with sharp steel the topmost hairs away,
And from the goblets due libations pour.

Then gravely prayed Æneas, sword in hand:
"Be thou my witness, Sun; thou, long-sought Land,
For which through grievous labours I have striven!
Thou, mighty Jove; thou, Juno, queen of heaven,
More gracious now, I pray; and thou, dread Mars,
Who reign'st the eternal arbiter of wars!
Ye gods o' the springs and streams, and whoso be
Worshipped in azure sky, in steely sea!

I vow, if I be vanquished on this field,
All claim to this broad realm my son shall yield;
Our host to Pallanteum shall retire,
Nor e'er raid Latin lands with sword and fire.
But if on us sweet victory's smile shall rest,
(As 'twill, methinks: so may our prayers be blessed!)
No true Italian folk will I enslave,
Nor for myself a royal sceptre crave;
'Neath equal laws united evermore,
Latin and Trojan shall Troy's gods adore;
But still in sire Latinus' hand shall wait
The sword, the imperial power and pomp of state:
New-built shall be the city of my throne,
By fair Lavinia's name for ages known."
    He spake; and thus Latinus in reply,
With eyes and hand raised reverent to the sky:
"We too this oath, by Earth and Sea and Air,
By Leto's holy twins, by Janus, swear,
And on the dreaded powers of Hades call:
So hear us, Jove, whose lightnings hallow all!
I touch these altars where the flame burns pure,
And all their listening deities adjure.
Our folk shall nevermore this truce betray;
No force shall warp my will, betide what may;
Not though wild deluge earth in sea should drown,
Or drag high heaven itself to Tartarus down:
Ev'n as this staff, this sceptre that I hold,
Can nevermore in bud and leaf unfold,
Since from its root 'twas shorn in greenwood glade,
Left parentless and leafless by the blade—
A live bough once, but now by craftsman's hand
In fine gold framed, for symbol of command."
Thus is the treaty sealed; their faith they plight
In presence of consenting chiefs, then slay
The victims o'er the flames with solemn rite,
And with their flesh the loaded shrines o'erlay.
    But now the Rutuli that combat deem

Wrongful, unfair; their troubled hearts beat fast;
The more, when Turnus' powers unequal seem;
And as in silence he steps forth to bow
Submissive at the shrine, with eye downcast,
They note his wasted cheek, his pallid brow.
But when Juturna heard these mutterings rise,
And knew the people's heart by passion swayed,
Forthwith she hastens, clad in Camers' guise—
Knight of proud parentage and high descent,
Himself renowned in warfare—thus arrayed,
She speeds her to that camp with shrewd intent,
And there dark rumours flings abroad, and cries:
    "Now shame, Rutulians, that one life should stand
To shelter all our warriors! Lack we might,
Or numbers? Count our foes how few they be—
Trojans, Arcadians, and that Tuscan band
By fate impelled and Turnus' enmity—
Worth naught, if half our host would front the fight!
Brave Turnus, self-devoted at their shrine,
Will join the gods in heaven, himself divine,
And live on lips of men, a glorious name;
But we, our country lost—the coward's fate—
Shall cringe to haughty lords in abject shame:
Yet here, like sluggards, still we watch and wait."
    Thus by her stirring words their wrath is fired,
And through the ranks slow-swelling murmurs run,
Till ev'n the Latin host those doubts invade,
And they who late but peace and rest desired
Now cry for arms, and wish the truce unmade,
Remorseful for the wrong to Turnus done.
'Twas then, the more their witless minds to stun,
A portent strange and wild from heaven she drew,
False augury sent to startle and beguile:
Down blood-red skies a tawny eagle flew,
And flocks of scattered waterfowl, the while,
Fled fast on clanging pinions. Swooping low,
A stately swan he clutched in claws of steel.

'Twas viewed of all the host. Then back they wheel,
That cloud of clamorous birds, their mate to save,
And in resistless mass beset the foe,
Darkening the air with wings; till, wondrous sight,
He, vanquished and o'erburdened, on the wave
His captive drops and seeks the clouds in flight.

Joy to Rutulian hearts that omen brought.
Their hands are stirred for action. First the seer
Tolumnius cries: "The sign, the sign long sought!
Heaven's will I know, I welcome! Let our host
Follow me now, and grasp, with me, the spear:
Poor comrades, whom this brigand from o'ersea
Scares like yon peaceful fowl, and wastes your coast.
Soon shall he sail the ocean waves and flee,
If now your ranks ye close, and scorning fear
Bring succour to your chief ere he be lost."

He spake, and striding forth his javelin flung
Full at the foe. The sounding shaft sped true,
Cleaving the air; then loud the clamour grew,
Their swaying ranks by wrath and tumult torn:
On sped the spear, nor swerved not, till among
A beauteous band of brothers nine it flew;
By Tuscan mother to Gylippus born;
And one it struck, who stood in youthful pride
With shining armour girt, and pierced his side,
Nigh where the buckled belt on waist is worn,
And stretched him lifeless on the yellow sand.
Then some with brandished spear, some sword in hand,
His brethren mad with grief rush to the fray—
Blind shock of battle—there the Latins charge;
Here Trojans, Tuscans, and in dense array
Arcadians bright with painted helm and targe.

Thus did one wild desire for war prevail;
Wrecked were those altars, and o'erhead let loose
A storm of hurtling darts and iron hail:
Vanished the sacred chalices; the king
Fled with his flouted gods, his broken truce.

Some yoke their chargers, some on chariots spring,
Or stand with flashing steel to guard the ground.
Hater of peace, Messapus heads his steed
'Gainst Tuscan prince, with princely diadem crowned,
Aulestes; he, driven backward, by mischance
On altar falls entangled; then, with speed,
Messapus, poising high his giant lance,
Bends o'er him, deaf to prayers, and smites amain,
And as he smites: "Thou hast it now," he cries;
"Thus to the gods a fitter victim dies!"
Then forth his comrades rush, and spoil the slain.

   Next Corinæus hurled a burning brand,
Snatched from the shrine, to balk the threatened blow,
Full in Ebusus' face, its fiery glow
Singeing his bushy beard—then, with left hand,
Firm grasped the long locks of his wildered foe,
And pressed him with his knees, and backward bore,
And stabbed him through the side. In Alsus' tracks,
As through the ranks he hurried to the fore,
Runs Podalirius with impending blade,
Then, cloven from crown to chin by whirling axe,
Falls low, and dyes his victor's mail with gore:
Soon on his eyes the sleep of death is laid,
That iron sleep that endeth nevermore.

   Unarmed, bareheaded, with right-hand out held,
Æneas to his followers made appeal:
"Where rush ye? Let this sudden strife be quelled!
Oh, curb your wrath, for now our plighted word
Is given; 'tis I alone may draw the sword.
Then trust me, fearing naught. My hand shall seal
This treaty firm: to me is Turnus due."
Ev'n as those words he spake, an arrow flew
With droning sound, and on the hero came.
What hand had launched, what whirlwind lent it speed,
What chance, or god, such glory gave, none knew:
Hid was the honour of that signal deed,
And from Æneas' wound had no man fame.

But Turnus, when the Trojan king retired,
And left his chieftains awestruck on the field,
Cried for his steeds, his arms; then flushed and fired
With sudden lust of battle, at a bound
Into his chariot leapt, the reins to wield.
Full many a warrior bold to death he gave,
Or flung to lie half-lifeless on the ground,
Trampling their broken ranks; or lance on lance
Snatched up and hurled upon them as they fled;
As when, beside frore Hebrus' wintry wave,
With clang of shield and gory countenance,
The War-God spurs his chargers o'er the plain,
The wildest winds outstripping; 'neath his tread
From end to end Thrace thunders; in mad dance
Go Fear and Wrath and Treason in his train.
Thus Turnus lashed his horses to the fray
Reeking with sweat, and o'er his foemen slain
Rides ruthless; from those hoofs flies sanguine spray,
And all the trampled turf blood-sprinkled is.
There smote he Pholus, and brave Thamyris
In combat close, but Sthenelus from far;
From far, those warriors twain of Lycian race,
Glaucus and Lades, whom one sire had sent
Equipped for aught that might befall in war—
To mix in clash of serried armament,
Or fleetest winds on horseback to outpace.
    Then forth stepped Dolon's son, for prowess famed,
Eumedes from his father's father named,
But heart and hand the likeness of his sire
Who erst, when bidden on Greek camp to spy,
Dared claim Achilles' chariot for his hire;
And hire he had—by Diomede's sword to die,
Nor now to those swift steeds doth he aspire.
This daring champion on that field of blood
When Turnus saw, with javelin light he smote,
Then stayed his wheels, and leapt to ground, and stood
Bent o'er his fallen foe, with heel down-pressed

On neck, and spared not from his grasp to wrest
The gleaming blade, and deep within his throat
Plunge it, and speak these words of bitter jest:
"Go, Trojan, stretch thee on the Hesperian plain
That thou in war wouldst win! Such spoil is theirs
Who brave me with the sword; such walls they gain.
And soon the self-same fate Asbutes shares,
By javelin pierced; soon Sybaris must bleed;
Soon Chloreus, Dares, and Thersilochus;
Soon dies Thymœtes, thrown from stumbling steed;
And as, when Boreas' blasts rush clamorous,
To chase the breakers on Ægean seas,
Where'er they scour the heavens the cloud-rack flees;
So before Turnus, as he clove his way,
The routed ranks receded in dismay,
And on he swept, by his own impulse borne,
His crest far-streaming as he stemmed the breeze.
Then Phegeus, brooking not the foeman's scorn,
Athwart his chariot sprung, and grasped with force
The foam-flecked bridle, and with hands up-raised
Turned those impetuous chargers from their course.
Thus dragged along, and in the harness tied,
The broad-barbed spear-head found his fenceless side,
And through the corslet driven, his body grazed;
Natheless with shield opposed the foe he faced,
And drew his steel for aid in combat grim;
Till, struck by flying wheel, as on it raced,
Headlong to earth he fell, and Turnus' brand
Shore deep 'twixt helmet's edge and breastplate's rim,
And left his headless trunk upon the sand.

So rode he victor, dealing death around;
But now Æneas in the camp was laid
By Mnestheus and Achates' faithful aid,
And young Ascanius. Grievous was the wound,
And on long spear he leant, his steps to rest,
Angered, and pulling with impatient hand
The broken dart, nor ceasing to demand

What aid soe'er might cure the speediest.
Let them cut deep, and probe with sharpest steel
Where lurked the barb, nor care how wide the rent,
So back that hour to battle he were sent.
Then came the leech Iapis, skilled to heal;
Endeared to Phœbus with a love so great
The god would fain his sacred gifts impart,
His mystic lore, his lute, his arrows keen:
But he, to stay a dying father's fate,
Rather of healing herbs had curious been,
And humbly plied his unambitious art.
There stood the chieftain, propped on sturdy spear,
Embittered, chafing, while his warrior train
And weeping child stood by; but prayer nor tear
Could move him. So the sage, his cloak thrown back,
Leech-wise, of potent herbs brought forth no lack
In bootless ministrations, and in vain
Assayed with hand or steel to gripe the shaft:
Nor fortune showed the way, nor Phœbus' craft
Availed not; loud and louder rose the yell
From stricken field, the danger drew more nigh;
Dust veiled the heaven, as horsemen thundered past,
And in the very camp the spears rained fast,
The while from struggling youths who fought and fell
In pitiless battle rose one anguished cry.
  Then Venus, filled with sore anxiety,
Culled with maternal care in Cretan dell
The sweet and virtuous plant of dittany,
Mature with purple bloom and downy leaf:
Fair flower, to mountain goats 'tis known full well,
What time from hunter's dart they crave relief.
This brought she, robed in cloud invisible;
Then steeped in water poured from gleaming jar
With healing hand occult, and deftly blent
Ambrosial juices that most gracious are,
And panacea with its heavenly scent.
Therewith the leech Iapis bathed the sore,

Nor knew, till sudden he had put to rout
The bodily pain, and stanched the streaming gore;
And lo! all force abandoned, of its will,
Obedient to the hand, the barb fell out,
And whole he stood, and stalwart as of yore.
"Fetch ye the hero's arms! Why stand ye still?"
Iapis cried, to spur them to the field:
"No surgeon's craft was here, no human skill;
The hand that saved thee, chieftain, was not mine:
A mightier power, a god, thy wound hath healed,
And sends thee back to work his great design."
    But he, ere now, had donned his greaves of gold,
Nor brooked delay, but waved his spear o'erhead,
Yet paused awhile, bucklered and corsleted,
With close embrace Iulus to enfold,
And lightly kissed him through his helm, and spake:
    "Boy, learn from me to strive for valour's sake;
Fortune from others learn. My sword it is
That brings thee safety, and to greatness leads.
Do thou, to manhood grown, forget not this;
But let the glory that thy sires could win
Inspire thy heart to emulate their deeds—
Child of Æneas and great Hector's kin."
    This said, from forth the gates he strode immense,
Wielding his ponderous weapons; at his side
Antheus and Mnestheus rushed, and all their band
Poured from the camp; the field with dust grew dense,
And 'neath the tramp of feet trembled the land.
Such sight from distant rampart Turnus spied;
Such sight his followers saw, and chilly dread
Smote them; Juturna first that onset heard,
And knew the sound, and terror-stricken fled.
Thus he, with sombre troop, swept o'er the plain;
As when a storm-cloud, bursting on the main,
Sweeps shoreward, and men's hearts with fear are stirred,
Foreseeing what deadly deluge it shall spill
On fields and fruits in boundless ruin lost;

And soon the winds they hear, its heralds shrill.
So did the Trojan monarch lead his host,
Compact in phalanx dense, to meet the foe.
'Twas then Thymbræus laid Osiris low,
With sword-stroke; Mnestheus great Archetius slew,
Achates Ufens, Gyas Epulo:
Nor 'scaped like fate Tolumnius the seer,
Who first on Trojan ranks his javelin threw.
Then loud the din rose skyward, as in fear
Rutulians routed fled the battle's brunt:
But not on these the chief his vengeance wreaks,
Nor deigns such craven stragglers to pursue,
Nor slays the brave that meet him front to front:
Turnus alone through the dense gloom he seeks,
Him only claims in combat for his due.
  This peril seen, Juturna, warlike maid,
Her brother's teamster flings upon the field,
Fall'n from the shaft, and leaves him there out-thrown;
Herself succeeds, the sinuous reins to wield:
Naught lacks she, in Metiscus' form arrayed;
Her voice, her looks, her armour, seem his own.
As when through lordly mansion on dark wing
A swallow skims, and thrids some spacious hall,
Her light prey gathering at her nestlings' call,
And now down empty courts flies twittering,
Now by some fountain's brink; so 'midst her foes
Juturna went and came in fleeting car—
Now here, now there, her brother hurrying,
Triumphant—yet whene'er he fain would close,
Stayed not, but swerved aside, and bore him far.
Nor in less tortuous course the Trojan king
Follows his foe, and through the broken crowd
Still tracks his path, and calls his name aloud;
But if perchance his rival's form he spies,
And hastes to cross those wingéd coursers' flight,
So oft Juturna's wheels recede from sight.
Perplexed he stands, as wavering thoughts arise,

Toward diverse ends conflicting in his breast.
Then swiftly to the front Messapus pressed;
Two supple lances in his left he bore,
Steel-tipped, and one he launched with flawless aim:
Whereat the chief, his broad shield held before,
Sank to his knee; yet from his helm the crest
By that impetuous dart was shred and shorn.
Then by such dastard stroke to fiercer flame
His ire was kindled, as from view were borne
Chariot and fleet-foot steeds long tracked in vain:
Wherefore, with Jove for witness, and the rite
Of desecrated treaty turned to scorn,
Spurr'd by the war-god's fury, to the fight
He rushed, and slew, naught recking of the slain,
Nor cared thenceforth his passionate wrath to rein.
   Ah, would some god now prompt me to record
What ruthless deeds were wrought, what true blood shed,
Now by Æneas', now by Turnus' sword,
On that fierce field where many a hero fell!
Great Jove, didst thou ordain that conflict dread
'Twixt races destined in deep peace to dwell?
   'Twas Sucro first the Trojan onset stayed;
Yet brief the fight, for soon Æneas found
His side unfenced where deadliest is the wound,
And drove through ribs and breast the reeking blade.
With Amycus, unhorsed, Diores died;
Kinsmen, whom Turnus, leaping swift to ground,
One with long javelin, one with broadsword slew,
Then bore suspended from his chariot-side
Their severed heads that dripped with gory dew.
Next Talon, Tanais, 'gainst Æneas stood,
With bold Cethegus in one conflict slain;
And to like doom was sad Onytes sent;
While Turnus spared not Lycian brothers twain,
And young Menœtes, of Arcadian blood,
Who loathed the works of war, yet loathed in vain:
By Lerna's stream he loved to roam, intent

On fisher's craft, the son of lowly sire
Who to the great and rich small court did pay,
Tilling a soil he owned not save by hire.
And as from diverse sides two flames of fire
Rush through a withered copse of crackling bay;
Or rival torrents leap from mountain brow,
Roaring and foaming as the sea they seek,
Each cleaving its wild course—in like array
Those warriors stem the battle; now, ev'n now,
With unremitting strength their wrath they wreak,
In one fierce task absorbed, to smite and slay.
    Murranus next, for all his boastful pride
In age-long line of princes whence he sprung,
The Trojan felled with rock like whirlwind flung,
'Neath reins and pole dragged headlong o'er the sward;
There, trampled by his chargers' hoofs, he died,
So little recked they of their fallen lord.
Turnus, anon, as Hyllus forward sped
With frantic daring, hurled the ready spear
At gilded casque that on his temples shone:
There lodged the shaft, transfixing helm and head.
Nor saved was Cretheus, knight that knew not fear,
From Turnus' fury; nor Cupencus won
Grace from his gods to stand Æneas' charge;
Ill-fated, forth he went to front the foe,
Nor respite long could gain by brazen targe.
Here, too, was valiant Æolus laid low,
Huge form outstretched on strange Laurentian land;
Here fell he, who had 'scaped the serried row
Of Argive spears and great Achilles' hand
That wrecked old Priam's glory; such his doom:
'Neath Ida was his home—Lyrnessus town
His home was—in Laurentian soil his tomb.
Thus meet those hosts in shock of desperate deeds,
Latins 'gainst Trojans, warriors of renown;
There Mnestheus battles, bold Serestus there;
Asylas; and Messapus lord of steeds;

The Tuscan ranks, Evander's squadron light;
Matched dauntless, man with man, no strength they spare,
Nor pause, nor rest, so furious is the fight.
   Then come new thoughts from Venus, that incite
Her son the city's bulwarks to attack,
And so by sudden stroke his foes confound;
For as he circled oft on Turnus' track,
Now here, now there, and cast his gaze around,
He saw the city scatheless lie and still:
So did a larger hope his vision thrill;
Mnestheus, with fellow-chiefs, he called anear,
Taking high station on a central mound,
Whereto in crowded ranks his followers pressed,
Full armed, nor cast on earth or shield or spear;
Then from the height his comrades he addressed:
   "Hark, and bestir ye, friends! Jove's will is ours:
Nor halt because my thoughts have forward flown.
Yon town that bred the war, yon royal seat,
Shall yield ere sets the sun, and own defeat;
Else will I dash to earth its smoking towers.
Wait I, forsooth, till Turnus, bolder grown,
Dare cross my path, and that lost fight renew?
Mark yonder city: 'tis the cause, the crown,
Of this curst strife: then haste ye, comrades true,
With fire and sword the broken truce reclaim!"
   Thus cheered, in solid mass they march, and frame
Their onset 'gainst the walls in dense array.
Full soon are ladders planted, torches flame;
Some, at the gates detached, the sentries slay;
Some through the darkened air their javelins fling.
Æneas, foremost, lifts accusing hand,
Upbraiding in loud voice the Latin king:
'Fore heaven, no choice was his, but force to bring
'Gainst foes who twice the flames of war had fanned,
And faithless twice, a solemn league had broke.
Then rose wild discord 'mid their startled folk;
Some fain would fling the city's portals wide,

And hale their lord in person to the walls;
Some don their arms to fend the assailant's stroke.
So, when in crannied cliff a swain has spied
A swarm of bees, and filled their camp with smoke,
Frighted, they run distraught through waxen halls
With buzzings loud that whet their anger keen;
Within, the sharp fumes drift through court and cell,
And in the hollow rock low murmurs swell;
Without, is naught but curling vapour seen.
    Then on the Latins fell a new mischance
Which shook their woe-worn city to its core.
For when the queen beheld the foe's advance,
The rampart scaled, the fire o'er roof-tops rolled,
Nor help was nigh, nor Turnus at the fore;
She deemed the battle lost, their bravest lance
O'erthrown, and crazed with anguish uncontrolled
All on herself the grief, the blood-guilt threw,
Then many a wild word spake in her despair,
And rending purple robes, on death intent,
The fatal noose from lofty rafter drew.
But when her trembling womenfolk were ware
Of that dread deed, Lavinia foremost rent
In frantic filial grief her golden hair,
And smote her damask cheeks; with like lament
All followed, till the palace echoed loud.
Soon through the city those dark tidings spread.
Then sank men's hearts. With speechless sorrow bowed
For consort's fate, for Latium's glory gone,
Wandered the king, arrayed in weeds of woe,
Nor spared to soil with dust his hoary head;
And ofttimes cursed the folly that was slow
To take the Trojan chieftain for his son.
    Meanwhile o'er fields far distant Turnus speeds
In chase of straggling foes—now wearier grown,
Now less and less exulting in his steeds.
Fraught with dim terror down the wind there blows
A mingled din; with listening ear he knows

That bodeful sound, his stricken comrades' moan.
"Alas, why seethes the city in such pain?
What dolorous clamour greets me from afar?"
As thus he paused perplexed, with tightened rein,
His sister, still disguised as charioteer,
Still driving far aloof his steeds and car,
Cried: "Hither turn we now: the readiest path
That glory points thee for pursuit is here!
Others there be the stricken town to cheer.
What if the Latins feel Æneas' wrath?
Let us, too, strike full many a Trojan down,
Nor fewer fall the victims of thy spear;
So shalt thou quit thee with as high renown."
    But he: "Nay, sister, long,
Long have I known thee, since thou first didst weave
These wiles, and break the truce, and join the fight;
Nor, goddess though thou art, canst now deceive.
But who hath willed thee thus to suffer wrong,
Sent down to earth from that Olympian height?
Was it to see thy hapless brother die?
What do I here? What refuge is in sight?
Myself have seen Murranus slain; full well
I loved him; on my name I heard him cry:
Mighty in strength, by mighty stroke he fell.
Ufens is slain: he died, scorning to gaze
On my defeat; the Trojans spoil his corse.
And now there lacks but one indignity:
Shall I stand idle while our walls they raze,
And Drances' words by coward flight endorse?
Flight? Shall this land indeed see Turnus fled?
Is death an ill so great? Ye Shades below,
Befriend me, since the Gods their grace withhold!
Naught of that last dishonour will I know,
But pass, a stainless spirit, to the dead,
Nor shame my glorious forefathers of old."
    Scarce said, when Saces through the carnage came,
Mounted on foaming steed, his visage scored

With arrow from the front; on Turnus' name
He cried aloud, and instant aid implored:
"Have pity, Turnus: none can save but thou!
Æneas thunders at the gates, with vow
To cast our towers and temples to the flame.
Ev'n now the fire is at the roofs. On thee
All eyes, all thoughts are bent; nor knows the king
With whom to mate his daughter, share his throne.
Nay, worse: the queen, thy trustiest champion,
Hath slain herself, from life's despair set free.
Messapus, brave Atinas—these alone
The fight sustain, and round them, in a ring,
Stark sword-points stand, like iron crop up-grown.
But thou—what boots it thus these wastes to ride?"
    Fixed in mute gaze stood Turnus, stupefied
By surging throng of thoughts. Within him burned
Deep shame, and madness with compunction blent,
And love by fury scourged, and conscious pride.
Then, when the shadows passed, and light returned,
To those far walls his glowing eyes he bent,
And gazed from chariot, where the city lay.
Lo! tongues of fire were soaring to the sky,
Clasping one lofty tower in pitiless play—
The tower himself had built, with stout beams walled,
Nor massy wheels it lacked, nor drawbridge high.
"Sister, delay not more; too strong is fate.
I go where heaven and fortune's curse have called.
'Tis fixed I meet Æneas; fixed, I bear
The bitterness of death, how deep soe'er.
Look thou! no craven fears henceforth have I:
But prithee first this frenzy let me sate."
    So saying, he lightly leapt to ground, and left
His weeping sister; then through glancing spears,
Where thickest raged the fight, a way he cleft:
As bounds a crag from some steep mountain's crown,
By windy gusts from its high station reft,
Or sapped by rain, or loosed by lapse of years;

Reckless through dizzy depths it plunges down,
Spurning the soil, while trees and herds and men
It whirls along its course: so Turnus then
Rushed through receding foes, and sought the town,
Where earth with blood was sodden, and a cloud
Of shrieking javelins hurtled through the air;
And signalled with his hand, and cried aloud:
"Rutulians, Latins, from this strife forbear!
'Tis mine to take what fortune shall award;
Mine to make just atonement in your place,
For broken truce, and quit me with the sword."
Back fell they all, and left the middle space.

But instant, at the sound of Turnus' name,
From those beleaguered heights Æneas came;
Aught that could stay his course he cast aside,
In joy exultant, with dread clash of steel;
As Athos great; as Eryx, towering high;
Or great as father Apennine, when reel
His tempest-shaken forests, and in pride
He lifts his snowy summit to the sky.
Then host by host they watched in rivalry,
And to that combat turned the eyes of all—
The guard that manned the bulwarks of the wall,
The foe whose batteries on its base were bent—
All doffed their armour. Deep amazed, the king
Saw warriors twain, in diverse regions bred,
Met, hand to hand, for war's arbitrament.
So they, in swift advance on open field,
First from afar their flying javelins fling,
Then close, with clang on clang of brazen shield:
Loud groans the earth, as blow on blow they shed,
And Chance and Courage mingle in fierce fight.
As when on Sila or Taburnus' height
Two bulls in shock of battle charge amain,
Matched front to front, their keepers gaze aghast;
Dumb stands the herd, the wondering heifers wait
Which lord henceforth o'er dale and drove shall reign;

They with fierce horns deal many a goring wound,
From neck and side the streaming blood flows fast,
And with their bellowing all the banks resound:
So did those champions charge infuriate;
Shields clash; the din through heights of heaven is rolled.
    Then did great Jove two equal scales uphold,
Whereon their rival destinies were laid,
Till one should sink foredoomed, to death down-weighed.
Lo, Turnus, leaping forth adventurously,
With strength upgathered, heaved aloft his blade,
And struck: from either camp arose a cry,
All eyes were strained. Then broke that faithless brand,
And left him in mid-blow discomfited.
No hope but flight; swifter he fled than wind,
Seeing strange sword-hilt in his helpless hand.
Fame says that, when his steeds were harnесséd,
Eager to mount his chariot for the fray,
His father's trusty sword he left behind,
And in his haste Metiscus' weapon brought,
His charioteer—the which might long suffice,
While scattered Trojans fled in disarray;
But when it crossed the steel that Vulcan wrought,
The mortal blade, splintered like brittle ice,
On the brown sand in glittering fragments lay.
Whereat through distant fields he fled distraught,
Now here, now there, his wavering circles wound;
Yet still his thronging foemen barred the way;
Here marshes wild, there ramparts ringed him round.
    Forthwith Æneas, though his speed was stayed
By arrow's earlier wound, remorseless, slow,
Still followed, step by step, the flying foe:
As when a stag, in river-valley found,
By hunter's crimson feather-screen dismayed,
Is tracked and close beset by baying hound,
Then, frighted, scours the banks again, again,
With thousand shifts; but still the deer-hound bold
Pursues the prey well-nigh within his hold,

And deems him held, and snaps his jaws in vain.
Then shout the hosts, and far o'er lake and land
Echoes the din, loud thundering through the skies;
While Turnus, flying, on each comrade cries
By name, and for his good sword makes demand;
Æneas, vowing death and vengeance stern
On whoso dare approach, sore terrifies
Their hearts that tremble for their city's sake;
Wounded, yet tireless still, and nigh at hand.
Five times they circle round, as oft return;
No sportive race they run, nor slight the prize,
For Turnus' very life-blood is at stake.

  It chanced anear that spot, in days by-gone,
Sacred to Faunus a wild olive grew,
Honoured when shipwrecked mariners thereon
Hung votive vesture and thank-offerings due.
This tree, unreverenced, had the Trojans felled,
That thus on open plain they might advance;
And there, by strength of stalwart arm impelled,
Fixed in the tough trunk stood Æneas' spear:
Bent o'er it, he would fain pluck forth the lance,
Wherewith his fleeter foeman to pursue
More close: then Turnus cried, all wild with fear:
"Have pity, Faunus! and may kind Earth's grasp
Loose not that shaft, since never did I wrong
Thy sacred tree which Trojan hands profane!"
Thus to the god he cried, nor cried in vain:
Albeit Æneas strove and struggled long,
No might of mortal hand could e'er unclasp
The grip of that stout bole. Then, 'mid the stress,
In garb of charioteer disguised anew
Juturna to her brother passed the sword;
And Venus, wroth at nymph's audaciousness,
Herself from its deep hold the spear-head drew.
So they, those rivals proud, with arms restored,
And hearts refreshed—one grasping trusty brand,
One with uplifted javelin towering tall—

Still front to front in breathless battle stand.
   To Juno then did heaven's great monarch speak,
As on the fight from fulvous cloud she gazed:
"What wouldst thou further, Queen? What end dost seek?
Thyself well know'st, nor knowing canst deny,
How fate hath willed Æneas to be raised
And dwell, a god, in mansions of the sky:
Why schem'st thou, then, in this chill cloud so long?
Meet was it that one born of heavenly blood
By wound of earthly shaft should suffer wrong;
And Turnus wield anew his missing brand?
For who, save thee, could nerve Juturna's hand,
Cheering the vanquished to fresh fortitude?
Cease now, though late, I pray thee, nor repine
Consumed in silent grief, nor fling me still
Reproachful words from those sweet lips of thine.
The crowning hour draws nigh. O'er land and brine
Thou'st chased thy foes; thou'st lit war's baleful fire,
Wrecked homes, and torn the bridegroom from the bride:
More I forbid thee do." So spake the Sire;
Whereto, with humble mien, Juno replied:
   "Because thy will, great Jove, to me was known,
I left the earth and Turnus to his fate;
Else had I sat not on this sky-tower lone,
Suffering whate'er befell—but girt with flame
Had stood i' the thick of battle, with fierce hate
Hounding the craven Trojans to the strife.
Juturna by my bidding (this I own)
Aid to her brother brought, nor would I blame
Deeds of ev'n greater daring for his life;
Yet bade I not bend bow or sharpen spear—
This swear I by the solemn Stygian tide,
That one dread oath whereof the gods have fear.
And now I yield, and quit the fight outworn.
This only boon, by no stern fate denied,
For Latium's sake I crave, and for the pride
Of Saturn's kin—that when the destined peace

(I grudge it not) with blissful marriage-morn
Well-stablished laws and lasting union brings,
Thou bid not then these folk, Italian-born,
To Trojan change their Latin name, nor cease
To keep their speech, their garb, without alloy:
Be Latium Latium still; let Alba's kings
Far down the years their glorious reign prolong;
Be Rome's proud sons with native valour strong:
Troy fallen, let naught recall the name of Troy."
    Then smiling spake the Lord of earth and heaven:
"Thou art Jove's sister; Saturn was thy sire:
Can such resentment swell within thine heart?
Nay, let this vain and fruitless wrath expire!
Freely thy wish I grant; my word is given.
Ne'er shall these tribes from ancient customs part;
Their name shall change not, though within their race
The gallant blood of Troy they shall embrace,
And in their worship Trojan rites infold;
Yet Latins all in language shall they be:
Thence shall arise a faithful folk and bold,
Duteous o'er aught that men and gods have seen,
And ever foremost in their praise of Thee."
Thereat was Juno's bitter grief consoled,
And from her cloudy height she passed serene.
    This done, a new design in Jove's mind springs,
Whereby to drive Juturna from the fight.
Twin plagues there are, as Furies known on earth,
Who with the dread Megæra, at one birth—
Girded with serpent coils and windy wings—
Sprang from the black womb of abysmal Night.
By Jove's high throne they sit with awful frown,
And scare men's souls in dark imaginings,
Whene'er the Almighty spreads disease and death,
Or guilty tribes with vengeance visiteth.
Of those fell sisters one He sendeth down
To cross Juturna's path with omen dread;
She, at his bidding, flew on stormy squall,

Like viewless arrow from strong bowstring sped,
Which, steeped by Parthian hand in venomous gall,
Parthian or Cretan, fraught with deadly doom,
Goes hurtling undetected through the gloom:
So passed Night's daughter earthward from the skies.
    There, when Troy's ranks and Turnus' troop she spies,
She shrinks to form of that small ominous bird
Which oft, on tombs and lonely roofs alit,
With bodeful cry at dead of night is heard;
Thus shaped, round Turnus' helm she flits and flies,
Hooting, and flaps her pennons 'gainst his shield.
Then strange benumbing fears his strength undo,
Bristles his hair with dread, his lips are sealed.
But when the Fury's strident wings she knew,
In passionate grief her locks Juturna tore,
And cried, as with her palms her breast she beat:
    "Ah, Turnus, how can sister help thee more?
What further sorrow waits me at the end?
No power is mine death's summons to defeat,
Or with yon grisly presence to contend.
Now must I quit the fight. Your terrors spare,
Ye wingéd fiends! Too well the strokes I know
Of your death-sounding pinions. Can I dare
The proud will of most gracious Jove to slight?
Is't thus my maiden love He would requite?
Why deigned He life eternal to bestow?
Why saved from death? Far gladlier would I share
My brother's lot, and seek the Shades below.
Immortal am I? Nay, bereft of thee,
Brother, all life is joyless. May the ground
Yawn deep, and send me, goddess though I be,
To dwell where broods the darkness of the grave!"
So cried the nymph, then o'er her temples wound
Her steel-grey cloak, and plunged beneath the wave.
    Onward Æneas pressed, with brandished spear
Huge, tree-like, and in savage mockery cried:
"Why now dost tarry, Turnus? Draw thou near!

BOOK XII 303

No foot-race fleet, but combat close is ours.
Transform thee as thou wilt—put forth thy powers
Of craft or courage—scale the sky above
On wings, or 'neath earth's deepest cavern hide."
But he, more grave: "Not thy wild words I fear,
Braggart! The gods I fear, and hostile Jove."
So saying, a stone he spied of monstrous girth,
Which on that soil had lain from ancient days,
Left as a landmark to divide the plain.
Its bulk scarce twelve picked warriors could up-raise,
Such folk as now are born of mother earth:
He with his poised hand flourished it amain,
And hurled it, towering high with gesture bold;
Yet, running, wist not of his own intent,
Nor whose the hand that massive boulder hurled:
Tottered his knees, his very blood ran cold;
Ay, ev'n the rock, through the empty welkin whirled,
Fell short, and missed its mark, with strength fore-spent.
As, when sick dreams our weary eyelids bind,
Eager on some vain quest we seem to run,
Then baffled in mid-effort faint and fall—
Tied is the tongue, unnerved our actions all;
And fain to cry, nor voice nor words we find—
So Turnus, where a way his valour won,
By that foul fiend was thwarted. Then his mind
Was vexed by veering fancies; now his glance
He cast on city walls and comrades dear;
Now halted, fearful of the impending spear;
How to retreat he knew not, nor advance,
Nor chariot saw, nor sister charioteer.
'Twas then Æneas poised the fateful lance,
Seeing where fortune beckoned, and with might
Far flung it. Ne'er did rock with crash so loud
From battle-engine on strong rampart smite,
Or din so deafening burst from thunder-cloud.
Swift on its whirlwind course the javelin goes,
Till, fraught with ruin irresistible,

Through corslet driven, and rim of seven-fold shield,
Deep in his thigh it lodges. To the field,
Sore stricken, on bended knee great Turnus fell.
Then from Rutulian ranks one cry arose,
And far o'er wood and wold its echo pealed.
He, with uplifted hand and suppliant eyes:
"For mine own life I plead not, nor repine;
Use thou thy fortune. Yet, if thought be thine,
Compassionate, for a father's agonies
(And thou, too, in such sire thyself hadst pride),
Let agéd Daunus die not all unblest,
But me, or if thou wilt, my corse restore.
Thou'st conquered, and the Italian host has seen
My downfall. Take Lavinia for thy bride.
Let hatred there have ending." Sworded, keen,
Stood he, with wavering eyes, and hand repressed;
And now those words had moved him more and more,
When, luckless, on the shoulders of his foe,
Glimmered the studded belt that well he knew,
From Pallas torn, the boy whom Turnus slew,
And on his arm the fatal trophy wore.
Deeply on that memorial of past woe
He gazed, then flamed with wrath that terrified:
"Shalt thou, bedecked in spoils of them I love,
'Scape me? 'Tis Pallas, Pallas, with this blow
Requites his murderer for that death he died."
Hot-handed in his breast the steel he drove:
Then chill grew Turnus' limbs; his spirit sighed,
And fled indignant to the Shades below.